BRICKING IT
The UK Housing Crisis and the Failure of Policy

Charlie Winstanley

First published in Great Britain in 2025 by

Policy Press, an imprint of
Bristol University Press
University of Bristol
1–9 Old Park Hill
Bristol
BS2 8BB
UK
t: +44 (0)117 374 6645
e: bup-info@bristol.ac.uk

Details of international sales and distribution partners are available at policy.bristoluniversitypress.co.uk

© Bristol University Press 2025

https://doi.org/10.51952/9781447377078

British Library Cataloguing in Publication Data
A catalogue record for this book is available from the British Library

ISBN 978-1-4473-7704-7 hardcover
ISBN 978-1-4473-7705-4 paperback
ISBN 978-1-4473-7706-1 ePub
ISBN 978-1-4473-7707-8 ePdf

The right of Charlie Winstanley to be identified as author of this work has been asserted by him in accordance with the Copyright, Designs and Patents Act 1988.

All rights reserved: no part of this publication may be reproduced, stored in a retrieval system, or transmitted in any form or by any means, electronic, mechanical, photocopying, recording, or otherwise without the prior permission of Bristol University Press.

Every reasonable effort has been made to obtain permission to reproduce copyrighted material. If, however, anyone knows of an oversight, please contact the publisher.

The statements and opinions contained within this publication are solely those of the author and not of the University of Bristol or Bristol University Press. The University of Bristol and Bristol University Press disclaim responsibility for any injury to persons or property resulting from any material published in this publication.

Bristol University Press and Policy Press work to counter discrimination on grounds of gender, race, disability, age and sexuality.

Cover design: Lyn Davies Design
Front cover image: Stocksy/Giada Canu

Contents

Acknowledgements	iv
Preface	v
Introduction	1

PART I Defining the housing crisis — 23

1	Housing supply and the shrinking stock	27
2	Affordability	35
3	Quality	42
4	Community and gentrification	56
Conclusion to Part I		58

PART II Why policy is failing — 59

5	Delivery	61
6	Regional and political iniquities in policy making	89
7	Existing stock condition	98
8	Homelessness	109
9	Delivering council and social housing	122
10	Homeownership and house price inflation	136
11	A failed growth model	143
Conclusion to Part II		164

PART III How do we fix it? — 167

12	Council and social housing	169
13	Controlling house price inflation	177
14	Regulate the private rented sector	185
15	Housing standards	190

Conclusion	196
Notes	199
References	214
Index	230

Acknowledgements

There are a great many people I must thank, without whom this book could not have been completed. First, my partner Khinezar, who has so patiently tolerated my solitary writing late into the evenings – as well as my two sons Daeza and Zudi who continue to be an endless source of joy and inspiration. I would also like to thank all of my interviewees for the book; Tim Heatley, Charlotte Norman, John Merry, Molly Bishop, Peter Openshaw, Yvonne McDermott, Ben Clay and Salford Mayor Paul Dennett. I would like to pay an additional thank you to Paul Dennett, whom I worked for as a political assistant for eight years, for providing me the opportunity to develop a knowledge and passion for the world of local government and housing policy. In a similar train, I would like to thank Liz Holland, Jackie McPhail and Tom Curran from the mayoral team, and a special thanks to Joanne Farell who contributed so much to the establishment of the council's housing development company Derive.

There are many more who I consulted in the process of writing this book – of whom I would like to particularly thank Steven Fyfe, Anne Morgan and Brendan Nevin – our conversations were hugely impactful in developing my analysis and structure. I would also like to thank Joel Cohen for his incredibly useful advice, Tristan Carlyon for his patient explanation of key pieces of research and Kate Wareing for her time and incredible work on the business case for social housing.

Lastly, I would like to dedicate this book to the memory of the late Councillor Paul Longshaw, a dedicated and passionate advocate for the cause of tackling homelessness and building council housing.

Preface

This book is the product of nearly a decade of work and thinking on housing policy, from the perspective of a Local Government Political Advisor to the City of Salford's elected Mayor, Paul Dennett. As Paul's advisor, I worked closely with him as a researcher, organiser and confidante while he held several political portfolios within the Greater Manchester Combined Authority, in particular his five-year stint as political lead for Planning, Housing and Homelessness. Through this time, I also worked closely with local government officers and civil servants at the coal face of delivering practical solutions for the housing crisis engulfing our country, dealing closely with the limitations of budgets, the imposition of politics and the absurdities of legislation in the attempt to deliver meaningful change for Greater Manchester's residents. The content of this book is borne largely from this experience, and the struggle of delivering practical policy solutions on housing for Salford and Greater Manchester residents. That, and the kindly imparted wisdom of some of my esteemed and dedicated colleagues, many of whom have worked for decades within the world of housing policy and delivery.

The main part of this book provides a fairly contemporary assessment of the present state of UK housing policy. Wherever possible, I have utilised the most up to date instances of government documentation, legislation, national datasets and political commentary to contextualise my historical assessments and predictions for the evolution of both the UK's housing crisis, and our policy response. Much of the material is very current. It's possible that by the time it has come to print, some parts will already be out of date. In any case, I believe that as a 'snapshot' of the UK's housing crisis today, and the state of housing policy, the book will continue to provide a useful insight into both the history behind and the practical limitations of housing policy.

The book is also fairly short – at least, much shorter than it could have been. Each section could easily have merited a book in itself. It is separated into four parts: the introduction provides a definition and historical clarification of the book's central thesis. Part I deals with the nature of our housing crisis, as we are experiencing it as a country today. Part II delves into the policy failings which sit beneath the crisis, taking a long view back encompassing much of the 20th century. The third and final part, rather optimistically, proposes a set of policy solutions. By the end, my hope is that the reader will have a decent and relatively thorough knowledge of the present housing policy landscape in the UK, its immediate antecedents and insight into our direction of travel.

Introduction

There is broad agreement across politics and policy-making circles that the UK today is in the midst of a housing crisis – but while it is strikingly clear that housing is becoming more and more of an issue in modern Britain, our present situation is still favourable on most metrics to most historical periods. In the past 70 years, house prices in the UK have risen on average, in real terms, by 365 per cent,[1] street homelessness has increased by 75 per cent since 2010,[2] and many of our large urban centres have become unaffordable to live in for anyone on an average British income. In 1955, the average house in the UK cost under £2,000, 4.5 times the average salary at around £48,000 in today's money. Today the average house costs over £282,000 – more than eight times the average UK resident's annual income.

But the 1950s benchmark was never representative of 'normal' in historical terms. In 1845, the average price of a house stood at 12 times average annual earnings for a British resident. Homeownership rates may be dropping now, but at roughly 62.5 per cent they are still higher than at any time since the early 1980s. Between 1939 and 1953 they stood at around 30 per cent – and prior to 1918, 25 per cent. As an alternative to homeownership, the proportion of private renters is increasing at a rapid rate, at around 19 per cent of residents. Yet as early as 1961, the private rental sector made up around 30 per cent of the housing market, nearly 60 per cent in 1939 and over 75 per cent in 1918. Today, rent makes up 32 per cent of an average UK renter's income, up from 14 per cent in the 1970s. But in the late 19th century, many UK residents could expect to pay as much as 50 per cent of their income in rent.[3] Today, we look at these trends and talk of housing crisis. For most of recorded history, what we call a crisis today has in fact been the norm.

For most modern observers, our perception of 'normality' in housing and its provision is in fact predicated in a very particular moment in time – specifically, the post-war settlement. For our purposes, in policy terms this period would be loosely defined as operating from the post-1945 reforms of the incoming Labour government through to the advent of the Thatcher government in 1979.

This is not to say that as a system the post-war period magically sprang into being in 1945 – rather, it was the product of multiple forces operating within British politics, legislation and housing policy over the course of more than a century. Equally, the effects of the post-war policy landscape did not disappear immediately overnight on the advent of the election of the Thatcher government in 1979 – rather, they have drifted away over time, throughout much of which the majority of the British public have continued to enjoy relatively affordable housing (albeit less so over the past 20 years).

However, what did exist during this period was a coherent set of complementary pieces of legislation, process and regulation, with several clearly defined aims, which provided a sustained period of affordability, continued improvements to tenure quality and near universal access to housing in the UK. Not coincidentally, during this time subsidised housing in the form of council housing was readily available, and the most acute housing crises such as homelessness and rough sleeping were reduced to historic lows (at the height of the economic crisis in 1975, Hansard records a Lords debate prompted by Lord Donald Soper's concerns that the numbers of families in temporary accommodation had peaked at 33,000 ... compared to 116,660 in 2023[4]). For most during this period, the story of housing was one of consistent, if piecemeal, improvement. Living conditions and the quality of homes were consistently getting better, access to housing – both rental and in homeownership – was widespread, and tenure was secure and long-term.

Through this book, we will look both at the origins of the British post-war housing system, its subsequent dissolution, and contemporarily address the current housing policy landscape and its failure over the course of several decades to address the questions of affordability, availability and quality for which it is designed.

The building blocks of the UK's post-war housing system
The Victorian reformers

Much of the tale of the UK's post-war housing period begins with the 19th century Victorian reformers, repulsed by the horrific conditions which had been created as a by-product of industrialisation, urbanisation and overcrowding – particularly in the UK's emerging industrial cities. The huge and rapid growth of these cities placed incredible strain on public infrastructure and housing stock, with almost total lack of planning and regulation leading to the creation of hellish scenes of squalor, poverty and disease.

Between 1700 and 1750, the population of Birmingham ballooned from around 5,000 to 23,688, growing further to 48,253 by 1778 and up to 296,000 by 1861. Though relatively famed for its well-constructed houses and clean water, in the mid-19th century contemporary historian W. Hutton still documented open sewers in Bordesley and Deritend, and areas such as Hagley Road where there 'were no drains, and the water closets discharged their contents into open ditches on each side of the road'. The city of Manchester perhaps saw the most intense contemporary documentation of conditions, which appalled contemporary writers, clinicians and social researchers. Between 1772 and 1851, the population of Manchester exploded from 25,000 to 455,000 – with entire families living in single rooms, packed on top of one another in damp and unstable rookeries, cellars and hovels. Writing of Manchester's neighbouring Salford in 1844, Friedrich Engels wrote of the 'courts or narrow lanes, so narrow that they remind me of the narrowest I have ever seen' and the squalid conditions he found therein:

> [B]etween Oldfield Road and Cross Lane, where a mass of courts and alleys are to be found in the worst possible state, vie[ing] with the dwellings of the Old Town in filth and overcrowding. In this district I found a man, apparently sixty years old, living in a cow stable. He had constructed a sort of chimney for his square pen, which had neither windows, floor nor ceiling, had obtained a bedstead and lived there, though the rain dripped through his rotten roof.[5]

Engels' findings were mirrored by other contemporary accounts. In 1842, Edwin Chadwick brought his 'Report on the Sanitary Condition of the Labouring Population and on the Means of its Improvement' to Parliament, filled with testimony from regional researchers who had taken to the slums of industrial Britain to document their findings. In Stockport, Dr William Raynor documented a series of buildings that,

> consist of two rows of houses with a street seven yards wide between them; each row consists of what are styled back and front houses–that is two houses placed back to back. There are no yards or outconveniences; the privies are in the centre of each row, about a yard wide; over them there is part of a sleeping-room; there is no ventilation in the bedrooms. ... In one of these houses there are nine persons belonging to one family, and the mother on the eve of her confinement. There are 44 houses in the two rows, and 22 cellars, all of the same size. The cellars are let off as separate dwellings; these are dark, damp, and very low, not more than six feet between the ceiling and floor. The street between the two rows is seven yards wide, in the centre of which is the common gutter, or more properly sink, into which all sorts of refuse is thrown; it is a foot in depth.[6]

And in 'the wynds of Edinburgh', Dr Arnott reported entering

> a dirty low passage like a house door, which led from the street through the first house to a square court immediately behind, which court, with the exception of a narrow path around it leading to another long passage through a second house, was occupied entirely as a dung receptacle of the most disgusting kind. Beyond this court the second passage led to a second square court, occupied in the same way by its dunghill; and from this court there was yet a third passage leading to a

third court, and third dungheap. There were no privies or drains there, and the dungheaps received all filth which the swarm of wretched inhabitants could give.[7]

Unsurprisingly, disease was rife within these appalling lodgings, with scarlet fever, typhus, smallpox and cholera ravaging particularly urban populations throughout the early period of industrialisation. Such was the depth of squalor that life expectancy in Britain's urban areas stalled entirely between 1820 and 1870, even dropping to pre-historic levels in cities like Manchester and Liverpool where a life expectancy of 25 years was recorded in 1841.[8] While there is active debate over the efficacy of urban life expectancy data across the period, a drop in life expectancy tracks with experience across other urbanising areas of Europe in this period with increases in mortality in urban areas of Sweden, Belgium, Prussia, Russia, the Netherlands and Italy.[9] This situation was all the more stark a reflection of the horrors of early urbanisation and industrialisation given that it occurred during a period of huge population growth spurred partly by improvements in medical practice and infant mortality.

It is no coincidence that William Blake penned his critique of industrialism and urbanism in 1808, decrying the encroachment of 'dark satanic mills' against England's verdant 'green and pleasant lands' in his anthemic hymn 'Jerusalem'. Nor is it a coincidence that the mid-19th century saw increasing social disquiet, with the French revolution of 1789, the revolutions of 1848 in France, Germany, Austria, Italy and across Eastern Europe and Scandinavia. The combined processes of early industrialisation and urbanisation had created veritable hellscapes which genuinely horrified contemporaries – a horror perhaps most lucidly reflected in the words of Alexis de Tocqueville, a French social critic who described his visit to Manchester in 1835 thus:

> On ground below the level of the river and overshadowed on every side by immense workshops, stretches marshy land which widely spaced muddy ditches can neither drain nor cleanse. Narrow, twisting roads lead down to it. They are lined with one-story houses whose ill-fitting planks and broken windows show them up, even from a distance, as the last refuge a man might find between poverty and death. None-the-less the wretched people reduced to living in them can still inspire jealousy of their fellow human beings. Below some of their miserable dwellings is a row of cellars to which a sunken corridor leads. Twelve to fifteen human beings are crowded pell-mell into each of these damp, repulsive holes.[10]

In response to the publication of E. Chadwick's report on 'The Sanitary Condition of the Labouring Population' in 1842, the Public Health Act of

1848 enacted many of his recommendations, including the establishment of the General Board of Health, provision for councils to raise local rates to establish local health boards, which would take control of sewers, water supply and street cleaning, and forced the establishment of local health boards in areas with particularly high death rates. Following the Great Stink (during which Parliament had to close due to the smell of putrefying sewage from the Thames), Joseph Bazalgette was appointed chief engineer of a gigantic sewer-building project in 1859, developing 1,300 miles of new sewers and pumping stations. The first steps towards planning regulations in construction were also introduced to tackle the country's warrens of hastily constructed slum housing. Prior to his election as prime minister in 1874, Benjamin Disraeli promised substantial reforms to public health and housing in a speech in Manchester in 1872: 'Pure air, pure water and the inspection of unhealthy houses. It is impossible to overrate the importance of these subjects. The first consideration of a Minister should be the health of the people.'[11]

A central focus of many such reforms were the profusion of 'courts' (back-to-back terraces) and rookeries, which featured so heavily in many of Britain's towns and cities. Courts, in particular, were often poorly designed and thrown up cheaply – sometimes with single skin brick walls and poor ventilation, sharing party walls on two to three of their four sides, leaving window space only towards the front. The first back-to-back courts appeared in Birmingham and Nottingham in the 1770s, Manchester and Liverpool in the 1780s, and the first appeared in Leeds in 1787.[12] Most of these early back-to-backs took advantage of the absence of planning regulations to construct dwellings without damp proof coursing, plumbing or sewage connections, also saving on the delivery of roads. These homes proved extremely economical for builders and industrialists, who at the time often built homes to house their workers, and subsequently proliferated across industrial cities.

The term 'rookery' developed in the late 18th century to describe impoverished neighbourhoods which had become enveloped in criminal activity, derived from the common 17th-century slang expression 'to rook' (to cheat or steal). Such neighbourhoods often developed in densely packed urban areas, such as St. Giles in Central London, with criminal activity thriving within densely packed populations packed into multi-storey buildings and courts, hidden within an unplanned maze of narrow streets and alleyways.

The 1875 Public Health Act required all new homes to be connected to sewage mains, the installation of damp proof courses in walls, the creation of local byelaws to ensure structural stability in new builds, the provision of 'air space' around buildings, provision of pavements and street lighting, and the prohibition of shoddy housing development. In the same year, the

Artisans' and Labourers' Dwellings Act gave local authorities powers to compulsorily purchase and redevelop slum areas and rehouse those who lived there, using a specialist loan facility (a further act in 1890 bolstered these provisions, and by 1904 80 towns had borrowed £4.5 million towards such clearances – the equivalent of around £458 million today). One slum which was demolished under these provisions was particularly notorious. 'The Old Nichol' slum in East London, located between Shoreditch and Spitalfields, was known colloquially as 'The Sweaters' Hell' due to the number of artisan workshops operated under sweated conditions. In 1883, a seminal 'penny pamphlet' written by Andrew Mearns was published describing the slum, which produced a huge public outcry, feeding the case for demolition:

> To get into them you have to penetrate courts reeking with poisonous and malodorous gases arising from accumulations of sewage and refuse scattered in all directions and often flowing beneath your feet; courts, many of them which the sun never penetrates, which are never visited by a breath of fresh air, and which rarely know the virtues of a drop of cleansing water. You have to ascend rotten staircases, which threaten to give way beneath every step, and which, in some places, have already broken down, leaving gaps that imperil the limbs and lives of the unwary. You have to grope your way along dark and filthy passages swarming with vermin.[13]

With harrowing frankness, Mearns documents the disease and misery which proliferated within the slum:

> In one cellar a sanitary inspector reports finding a father, mother, three children, and four pigs! In another room a missionary found a man ill with small-pox, his wife just recovering from her eighth confinement, and the children running about half naked and covered with dirt. Here are seven people living in one underground kitchen, and a little dead child lying in the same room. Elsewhere is a poor widow, her three children, and a child who had been dead thirteen days. Her husband, who was a cabman, had shortly before committed suicide.[14]

In 1893, the recently established London County Council was granted permission from the Home Secretary to demolish and rebuild a large area of the slum, beginning at Boundary Street. The Boundary Street scheme displaced 5,719 residents and demolished 730 dwellings – replacing them with 50ft wide tree-lined streets emanating from a central area named Arnold Circus. In total, 1,069 two- to three-roomed tenements were built to house 5,524 residents, including a laundry and 18 shops. The scheme was a great success, transforming the slum and setting new architectural standards for construction and design. The now Grade II listed buildings form 'The Boundary Estate' in Tower Hamlets, and comprise one of the first council housing schemes in the country, continuing to be largely council-owned to this day.

The public health and planning reforms of the late Victorian era formed the foundations on which later legislation, regulation and planning reforms would be built in the UK, particularly in relation to the developing role of municipalities as 'planners' and adjudicators on quality, design and demand, as well as proactive developers. Perhaps just as importantly, these reforms emerged from and embedded a cultural revulsion against the horrors of unplanned early urbanism, a cultural revulsion which would go on to inspire the development of significant layers of Britain's emerging housing system as well as the UK's cultural psyche.

The Garden City movement

Perhaps the clearest example of this rejection of unplanned urbanism in emergent British planning principles was the growth of the Garden City movement, which developed around a set of design principles which would go on to have a huge impact on the evolution of the planning system. The movement's leader, Ebenezer Howard, developed a series of principles for architectural planning and design which he published in 1898, emphasising spacious tree-lined avenues, parks and ready access to the countryside.

Howard himself was inspired by the burgeoning Arts and Crafts movement led by William Morris, which emphasised the importance of artifice and decoration, both for aesthetic purposes and also as a route to centring the role of the arts within manual professions and trades. Similarly, his vision for 'Garden Cities' was inspired by the late Victorian 'model villages', planned communities built by industrialists to house their workers in sanitary and pleasant conditions. Two contemporary model villages which particularly fed these ideas were Port Sunlight constructed in 1888 in the Wirral by the Lever Brothers, and Bourneville built by Cadbury's in Birmingham constructed in 1893. Both Port Sunlight and Bourneville were built considering the health and fitness of inhabitants, laid out to encourage walking, swimming and outdoor sports.

Howard's principles sought to combine what he perceived as the 'best' elements of urbanism – jobs, transport, infrastructure and culture with the health and therapeutic benefits of the countryside. His vision was for a new, reimagined urbanism centred around centrally planned cities, whose physical design would foster strong communities, a wide range of employment, good and beautiful design practices, green infrastructure and integrated transport systems. The first Garden City was Letchworth, in Hertfordshire which began construction in 1903. Following Letchworth came Hampstead Garden Suburb in 1907 and Welwyn Garden City in 1920.[15]

Howard's Garden City principles inspired many areas of the UK housing system – not least the centring of low-density detached and semi-detached housing with large gardens (a style which would come to define the UK's preference for housing development for years to come). One particular idea within the Garden City movement would emerge to have an enormous impact on Britain's emerging planning system, namely the green belt. Within Howard's designs, he envisioned networks of self-sufficient communities linked via multiple transport nodes, and surrounded by protected undeveloped green land which he referred to as the 'agricultural belt'. These 'belts' would serve the purpose of controlling unplanned urban sprawl, making impossible a repeat of the 19th century's densely populated population centres. In their original iteration, these agricultural belts were also to provide an essential function in the provision of employment, leisure and goods to residents of nearby towns, and a source of primary or secondary income to residents. Howard envisioned a blurred boundary between urban and agricultural labour, with residents of the towns able to buy up smallholdings and farm the land, creating a positive symbiosis between urban life and small-scale agriculture. To achieve this, his writings presumed the collective purchase of this land through the municipality and its lease to residents. In practice, these latter aspirations to integrate the urban and rural economies failed to be realised – but the agricultural belts, which were to become known as the 'green belt', survived.[16]

In 1909, the Housing and Town Planning Act was introduced and heavily inspired by the Garden City movement. Within the act, the building of 'back-to-back' housing was illegalised, and Garden City design principles and models were explicitly encouraged for use among local authorities in designing new estates.

The creation of a green belt around London was proposed by the Greater London Regional Planning Committee in 1935, powers which were further enhanced through the passage of the 1947 Town and Country Planning Act. In 1955, green belts were adopted nationally following a circular issued from the Ministry of Housing, encouraging all planning authorities to designate protected green land surrounding their towns and cities. Despite significant criticism, and particularly allegations that green belt designation is contributing to Britain's acute housing crisis by restricting developable land, green belt designations remain in place to this day, often unchanged from the boundaries selected in the 1950s.

In 1946, the New Towns Act was passed, building from Garden City principles, with a huge programme for slum clearances and overspill estates in a programme which ran on until 1970. The act internalised the Garden City movement's key aims to decentralise population centres, widen the geographic scope of economic opportunity and limit urban sprawl by providing 'overspill' estates outside of urban centres. In all, 32 new towns were created under the principles of the act.

Building societies

Building societies today form a curious segment of the today's banking system, particular to the UK and current and former Imperial possessions and Commonwealth countries. Established first as working-class 'self-help organisations', today these institutions are almost indistinguishable from any other high street bank.[17] Yet their origins lay in the radical co-operative and mutual aid principles of the early 18th-century working-class movement, and their establishment was arguably a forerunner for the foundation of consumers' co-operatives half a century later by the Rochdale pioneers.[18] Within the history of the development of Britain's post-war housing system, the role of building societies in financing the development of new housing, and also in establishing Britain's culture of owner-occupation, has been critical. As has the story of building societies and their relative domination of mortgage finance for most of the 20th century.

Early societies were building clubs, through which members pooled their resources to build each one a home. The order of homes to be built for each member was dictated by a lottery, and operated on a 'terminating' basis (that is, the society would shut down once every member had built their home). Each member was a shareholder of the society, and the society in turn owned all of the properties built until its termination – accruing rental payments from the members (in addition to their membership stipend) to spend towards the development of its planned homes. Shares also yielded interest (or dividends) to members. The earliest recorded incidence of a building society was 'The Birmingham Society' founded in 1781 at The Old Fountain Inn in Deritend. Its founding documents laid out the organisation's mission: 'each subscriber for three shares shall have one or more houses built of the value of 200 guineas and each subscriber of two shares shall have one or more houses value £70, and each subscriber of one share shall have a single house value £70'.[19]

In 1846, the first non-terminating building society was formed and between 1840 and 1870 the societies were transforming rapidly into loan and investment companies. In 1836, Parliament formally recognised the legal status of building societies with the Regulation of Benefit Building Societies Act. The Act recognised building societies under the Act for Friendly Societies (1793), under which terms they were granted tax exemptions but were restrained from seeking profit. The role of societies in providing mortgages for the acquisition of 'small freehold or leasehold property' for their members was also formally recognised – and further consolidated with the Building Societies Act of 1874.

In 1869, the Building Societies Protection Association was formed as a national industry body by James Higham, with a stated goal of 'watch(ing) the proceedings in Parliament in reference to Building Societies, and to protect and extend their interests, privileges and advantages'. By 1871, 2,000 societies existed with advances amounting to £16 million (around £1.6 billion today) and were the clear preference for investors, sometimes forced to punitively slash their interest payments to check the influx of new deposits.

In 1874, the sector experienced a huge shock following the liquidation of the 'Liberator', one of the largest existing building societies. The Liberator had collapsed in dramatic fashion following a 20-year case of fraud perpetrated by its founder and chairman Jabez Balfour. But by this stage, building societies had become huge financial figures within the banking landscape and in 1894 the Building Societies Act consolidated their position in the world of banking even further, creating new specifications around the legal terms of mortgage lending.

Despite this rapid institutionalisation, most building societies were still enmeshed within reforming Methodist, Quaker and other non-conformist Christian traditions. Effectively, a sector of banking had been created which had a specialised focus on providing lending instruments to working people, and which possessed a broad moral mission to improve the lot of the working poor. These cultural facets of building societies would prove transformative through various opportunities for expansion they received in the 20th century.

Following the stratospheric expansion of building societies and their domination of mortgage lending and construction investment, the sector was primed for its next serious expansion following the First World War and the interwar building boom. Post-war, incomes among the working population were at record highs and demand for new housing reached a new zenith. Combined with the policy of cheap money under Prime Minister Lloyd George (in which interest rates were cut to 2 per cent to promote post-war regeneration following the UK's removal of the Gold Standard), building societies were able to massively expand their mortgage lending practices, creating 'a new mass market for owner-occupation'.[20]

Prior to 1914, less than 10 per cent of Britain's housing stock had been owner-occupied, and less than 1 per cent municipally owned.[21] During the war, the introduction of rent controls in 1915 had caused a huge fall in private renting – and increasing numbers of council houses were emerging as its primary replacement. By 1939, owner-occupation had increased to around 32 per cent of the British public, and municipally owned housing to 10 per cent. Particularly throughout the 1930s, a huge proportion of these changes were due to new builds, and many of these new builds were built on cheap rural land away from urban centres. In 1934, the number of new privately built houses in the UK reached its historic record at 293,000, a figure which has never since been surpassed.

Introduction

Driving this private sector building frenzy were the newly liberalised terms of mortgages offered by the UK's building societies. Societies had emerged, following the war, as high-interest and low-risk savings vehicles – and as such had received large numbers of deposits.[22] The traditional investment destinations from the private rented sector had dried up due to fears regarding further rent controls, so building societies began to develop a residential market for mortgages, extending terms from 20 to as many as 30 years for the first time. Reduced deposits were enabled through the creation of a deposit insurance scheme, reducing standard deposits required from 25 per cent to 10 per cent of the total value of the mortgage. Deposits on loans to builders were reduced even further through the development of 'Builder's Pool Arrangements' by builders, securing risk against larger 'pools' of prospective properties and reducing deposit requirements to as little as 5 per cent of the mortgage value. For residential mortgages to home buyers, such changes were the difference between a £50 deposit and a £25 deposit. These changes meant that, for the first time in history, mortgages became cheaper on a weekly basis than rental payments.

In addition to these changes, building societies pursued an aggressive and sophisticated marketing strategy to sell the appeal of homeownership to working-class families. Printed press advertisements, roadside hoardings and estate brochures were produced to flood working-class communities with aspirational visions of their potential new homes. Other novel techniques were also deployed, such as the recruitment of new home buyers as advertising agents, providing commissions to purchases for forwarding new customers. The process of signing for a mortgage was also streamlined and simplified, in conjunction with developers. 'All in' offers for new housing, often via Builder's Pools, which incorporated the arranging of the mortgage and legal and admin fees, were all important in reducing the barriers to sale and broadening the appeal of the market. It was during the 1930s that the modern residential mortgage was truly born, popularised and established as a mechanism for a working-class person on an average income to access the housing ladder.

Between 1931 and 1938, building societies increased their mortgage lending from £90 million to £137 million – far outstripping either the absolute or relative growth in mortgage lending from competitor sectors.[23] The central role of building societies in providing mortgage and development finance was once again recognised by the Building Societies Act of 1939, creating a legal framework around the mortgage lending system and Builder's Pool arrangements to protect customers from abuse.[24] In the same year as the act, the Building Society Protection Association (now the Building Societies Association) introduced the Recommended Rate System, an agreed system of mortgage rates which could be afforded by all building societies. Through the Recommended Rate System, the Building Societies Association operated as a legal cartel, and building societies collectively limited the amounts of mortgage lending undertaken by the sector on an annual basis.[25] In the same year, the Exchange Controls Act restricted the convertibility of sterling to protect against a potential run on the pound on the eve of the Second World War, controls which were strengthened in 1947 following the end of the war to remain in place until 1979. These controls subjected official limits to the currency exposure of banks, their maturity mismatch exposure as well as their credit risk (the extent of their lending). Credit ceilings were also imposed by the Bank of England in response to a deteriorating external balance of payments.[26] The ceilings were used to restrict general lending, and were replaced by Competition and Credit Control in 1971, imposing Reserve Asset Ratios (as opposed to direct 'ceilings'). Further controls were placed on the sector with the introduction of the Supplementary Special Deposits Scheme in 1973, a series of direct controls on deposit-taking financial houses and banks which imposed penalties on institutions whose sterling deposits grew faster than a prescribed rate.

Thus, from the eve of the Second World War through to the removal of exchange controls in 1979, building societies operated in a tightly controlled banking environment where caps on lending and exposure reduced the risk of external competition from other banking sectors. During this time the sector achieved near monopoly status in the arena of residential mortgage lending – lending as much as 79 per cent of mortgages each year. Additionally, the 'mutual' and mission-driven mentality of the societies dampened potential profit-seeking impulses – as a disdainful Bank of England report from 1990 opines:

> Competition between societies was restricted through cartel arrangements; in particular, the Building Societies Association (BSA) recommended interest rates which all the larger societies followed. These were not adjusted frequently nor fully to changing conditions, so that rates were often below market clearing levels. As mutual institutions, societies tended not to maximise profits, but rather attempted to reconcile the conflicting demands of borrowers for low rates and savers for high rates by keeping rates fairly steady. ... An important and frequent consequence of this behaviour was the emergence of excess demand, with borrowers having to queue for mortgages.[27]

This confluence of events meant that access to mortgage credit through the post-war period was guarded by building societies, who rather than seek to profiteer on their monopoly instead opted to control their lending, restricting the amounts of potentially inflationary credit entering the housing system. As we will explore in later chapters of this book, the removal of credit controls in the 1980s saw the destruction of building societies' monopoly on mortgage lending, and opened the door for a huge swathe of credit to enter the housing market each year.

Rent controls

Rent controls were a staple feature of the UK's housing system for over half of the 20th century, measures which enormously influenced the nature of the UK's housing market and helped to define the post-war era of housing stability.

The impulse to control rents was a reaction against profiteering among landlords during the First World War, a period where demand for housing outstripped supply and new housing production was stalled. Profiteering was feeding into wider social unrest, fomented by the trade unions and wider labour movement. Perhaps the most notable event in this period was the rent strike by workers in Glasgow, which fed into parts of the 'Red Clydeside' disputes from 1915 to 1916. In response to increased demand for workers' homes near industry for the war, landlords had hiked rents by 25 per cent. In response, the Glasgow Women's Housing Association formed and led a series of mobilisations to prevent evictions and co-ordinated for a mass withholding of rent from September that year. Around 20,000 families participated in the strike, managing to overturn attempts by the city to charge striking tenants. The strike is widely seen to have precipitated the Increase of Rent and Mortgage Interest (War Restrictions) Act of 1915, which imposed a rent freeze at 1914 rent levels unless landlords could prove they had made improvements to their property.

The impact of rent control had a huge and immediate impact on landlords, owner-occupation increased by over 10 per cent during the course of the war – primarily due to the exit of landlords following the reforms.

While the specific terms of rent controls would vary, they remained firmly in place until the Housing Act in 1988 introduced the Assured Shorthold Tenancy. Between 1915 and 1919, privately let houses under a rateable value of £35 in London (£30 in Scotland and £26 elsewhere) were subject to a nationally set standard rent, provided security of tenure (protection from eviction) for tenants unless they explicitly broke the terms of their rental agreement, and protections against premiums or charges on the property. From 1920, these protections were expanded to all homes with a rateable value under £105 in London, £90 in Scotland and £78 elsewhere, incorporating the vast bulk of privately let homes. New build for private rent collapsed as a sector in construction, replaced increasingly by a mixture of homes for owner-occupation and municipal housing. Between 1918 and 1939, private rent as a proportion of the country's housing stock fell from 76 per cent of all households to under 58 per cent.[28]

Between 1925 and 1939, rent controls began to be phased out. However this process failed to revive new build private rent homes – and controls were reinforced again at the start of the Second World War. The sector continued to decline precipitously – falling to 50 per cent of tenures by 1953, 34 per cent by 1961 and ultimately an all time low of 9 per cent by 1992.

A major innovation was made to rent control with the imposition of the Rent Act 1965, which introduced long-term regulated tenancies alongside a more variable system of 'fair rents' assessed by a local authority rent officer. This legislation changed the emphasis of rent control from rigid national rents to a series of 'regulated rents' viewed more holistically on the basis of market conditions, property conditions, location and quality of a rented property (as ascertained by the rent officer). A network of governance was put in place around this new regulatory regime, with Rent Assessment Committees established to process objections and appeals. Furthermore, the act made it illegal to evict any tenant without a court order or to harass a tenant with the intention of persuading them to move.

Existing rent controls and tenancy protections were consolidated in the 1968 Rent Act and the Housing Act 1969 further guaranteed a conversion of all existing tenancies to new regulated tenancies through a grant system to upgrade and repair properties, establishing the new system. The Housing Act for the first time created the legal definition of a 'house in multiple occupation', as well as powers for local authorities to close or lay a compulsory purchase order against them. In the 1970s, rent freezes were imposed periodically on properties to reduce general inflation and tenancies across all private rented property were consolidated under the 1977 Rent Act.

Rent controls from 1915 played a gigantic role in redefining the UK's housing tenure mix, enabling the growth of homeownership and improving the condition of the UK's housing stock. As a general rule throughout the period of rent controls, the quality and condition of a property was deployed via an array of carrot and stick methods to control applications for rental increases – either via restrictions on rental levels without justification based on repairs, or through grant regimes (such as those introduced through the 1969 Housing Act). The private rented sector itself barely survived the process, as has been noted by many commentators on this period. Historian Peter Kemp believes that the sector was caught, for a long time, within a polarised political landscape through which neither of the main political parties saw good cause to fight its corner:

> Private renting has been a subject of considerable political controversy and polarised views. For much of the post-war period, the Labour Party has viewed private renting as a tenure which should be left to wither on the vine or, better still, be municipalised. The Conservatives have seen private renting as an inferior tenure to owner occupation,

believing that the latter should be expanded, even if this is at the cost of the profitability of the former.[29]

While many Western countries saw the imposition of some regulation and controls on private renting during the 20th century (and a corollary increase in owner-occupation) – in the UK these trends were substantially more marked. By the early 1980s, the UK had the lowest proportion of its housing stock turned to private renting of any country in Western Europe at around 10 per cent, comparing starkly with neighbouring countries like Norway (27 per cent), Germany (48 per cent) and Switzerland (63 per cent). Today the figure stands at 19 per cent, a proportion that is more in line with the European average of 22 per cent (it should be noted that the average European figures are substantially altered by the introduction of former Eastern bloc states, where rates of homeownership are substantially higher than the European average).

Homeownership in the UK, relatedly, rose to substantially higher levels than comparable countries within Western Europe, rising to 54 per cent by 1979[30] (and going on to peak at 70.9 per cent in 2003).[31] The connection between rent controls and homeownership is not unique to the UK or Western Europe: the huge 10 per cent spike in homeownership in the United States through the Second World War is often attributed to the imposition of rent controls between 1940 and 1945, and the legacy of the controls had a continued impact on increasing rates of homeownership and the relative decline of private renting even after their removal.[32]

Thus, rent controls throughout the 20th century facilitated the growth of British homeownership, controlling and regulating the quality and standard of private rented stock, protecting tenants and extending the lifetime of tenure as well as restraining the growth of rents. The culmination of these factors hugely help to define the parameters, particularly, of Britain's post-war housing system – equally their removal in 1980 has massively shaped the UK's housing landscape in the years since.

Municipal housing

As discussed in previous sections, one impact of Victorian public health and housing reforms had been the empowerment of local authorities, and the codification of their roles and responsibilities in ensuring adequate accommodation for their populations. From 1866, councils had been enabled to purchase sites for the building of homes under the Labouring Classes Dwelling Houses Act, and this role as a housing developer was further embedded by the passing of the Housing of the Working Classes Act in 1890, legislation that required councils to build back at least 50 per cent of new houses following slum clearances. The first municipally built houses in Europe were constructed by the then Conservative council in Liverpool, which in 1869 constructed St. Martin's Cottages following the designation of 5,000 cellar dwellings in the city as unfit for human habitation by the new Council Medical Officer of Health, Dr Duncan. One hundred and forty-six flats and maisonettes in two four-storey blocks were constructed on Ashfield Street in Vauxhall, and the building survived until 1977. The council continued in its pioneering work with the construction of a further 270 flats at Victoria Square in 1885. The first spate of municipal homes built under the 1890 Act were in London, beginning with the construction of 400 homes in Shoreditch on the corner of Nile Street and Provost Street, followed soon after by the development of the Boundary Estate in the current area of Tower Hamlets on the former site of the Old Nichol rookery.

Many histories of council housing begin with the Addison Act of 1919, where council housing was encouraged by the Liberal Prime Minister Lloyd George as a solution to post-war housing shortages – 'Homes fit for Heroes'. However 24,000 municipal housing units had already been constructed prior to 1919, by pioneering councils often in heavily industrialised cities. The Addison Act did, however, hugely accelerate this process – providing government subsidies for the building of 213,000 homes over the following three years.

In conjunction with the publication of the 1918 Tudor Walters Report, the new emphasis on council housing revolutionised not just trends in housing tenure, but also construction methods themselves. The Tudor Walters Committee, heavily influenced by the Garden Cities movement, developed a new series of recommendations for building design standards to '[p]rofoundly influence the general standard of housing in this country and to encourage the building of houses of such quality that they would remain above the acceptable minimum standards for at least sixty years' while considering it 'essential that each house should contain a minimum of three rooms on the ground floor ... and three bedrooms above, two of these capable of containing two beds. A larder and a bathroom are essential'.[33]

The report stipulated new space standards, as well as density limitations to ensure natural light penetration at all times of year. Semi-detached terraces were favoured, often built in cul-de-sacs to prevent through-traffic. District heating systems were proposed, as well as complete integration with public transport systems. The standards set the benchmark for construction of new builds for the next 90 years, rendering outdoor toilets and outhouses obsolete and defining the first generation of council homes.

In 1930, the Housing Act was passed, providing funding and also encouraging mass slum clearances. Between 1934 and 1939, the height of Britain's interwar building boom, local authorities contributed 25 per cent of all new housing units.[34]

But the true era of council housing was yet to come. From 1946, house-building exploded with social housing developers (councils being overwhelmingly predominant in this sector) constructing 71 per cent of the 3,186,403 new homes built by 1958. Of the entire number of 10,230,253 new homes built in the UK between 1946 and 1979, social developers built 5,561,720 (around 54 per cent).[35]

This period correlates with the fastest and most sustained period of housebuilding in the UK's history. The highest number of social homes built in any given year was in 1953, where social developers built 261,960 new dwellings – 80 per cent of the total for that year. The highest number of homes ever built in any given year was in 1968, with 425,830 new completions, 199,770 built by social developers (47 per cent). By 1981, 31.7 per cent of all British households lived in social rented accommodation (primarily council-owned), representing as much as 40 per cent of the population.[36]

In addition to rent controls, this huge social rented sector contributed to 'crowding out' private lettings, which by 1981 had fallen to 11 per cent of all household tenures.[37] Social rents were subsidised by the local authorities (and social landlords) which administered them. In 1979, the average council rent was £6.40 a week, around 6.3 per cent of the average weekly income.[38,39] At these rates, the private rented sector was simply unprofitable in most instances. In 1980, average social rents in local authority housing had increased to £7.70 per week – an increase to 6.9 per cent of an average weekly income. By contrast, private rents in the same year were £11.18, over 10 per cent of an average weekly income[40] (today, average rents in the private sector are £232 per week, 33.6 per cent of an average weekly income – by contrast, social rents are now around £111 per week, 16 per cent of an average weekly income[41]).

Council house building throughout this period often accompanied slum clearances, which had been sustained since the late 19th century and throughout the interwar years. From the mid-1950s in particular, slum clearances picked up pace. Almost a million slums were cleared between the 1950s and 1960s. A grand vision for the replacement of these dwellings had been set in motion since 1946 and the passing of the New Towns Act; the task of replacing slums lost through clearances combined with wider aspirations to decentralise the UK's population and, following the Barlow Commission in 1938, to redevelop and regenerate industrial areas of the North which had begun to fall behind since the start of the century. The New Towns movement was predicated in modernism and the principles of economic planning – and council house builders once again led a revolution in design principles through their integration en masse into the new towns and overspill estates which were constructed post-war – particularly the entrance of the controversial modernist architectural movement of Brutalism. Following the 1956 Housing Subsidy Act, which provided subsidy for councils to build, an additional subsidy was placed to encourage the development of high-rise developments which saw 4,500 high-rise tower blocks built by 1979.

As such, council houses contributed to the development of Britain's post-war housing system threefold: in the first instance, by enabling the increase in production of new homes to heretofore never seen levels, in the second by precipitating a revolution in design standards (particularly in the 1930s) which would see the back of many antiquated design principles, and third through the creation of a hugely subsidised section of the rental market, which contributed to the suppression of both the size of the private sector and private sector rents.

The Town and Country Planning Act

We have discussed the role of the Victorian public health reformers and the Garden City movement in creating the foundations of what would become the British planning system. A huge cultural backlash against the excesses of unregulated building in the 19th century had engendered a deep distrust of urban density, a huge outlet for which had been the development of the Garden City movement and its emphasis on space, light, green amenity and economic planning. These principles guided contemporary ideas of best practice in the development of the UK's nascent planning system, which would ultimately be consolidated in the Town and Country Planning Act of 1947.

Emerging from the latter half of the 18th century, the 1909 Housing and Town Planning Act had established several town planning principles, including space standards between houses, legal standards for the quality of homes and implored the use of 'Garden City principles'. In 1919, the act was followed by the Housing and Town Planning Act committing subsidies towards the construction of new 'Homes for Heroes' following the First World War, a huge boost to early council house building programmes.

As we have discussed, the 1920s and 1930s were a period of huge growth in private house-building, financed by the policy of 'cheap money' from the Bank of England, and innovative models of credit dispensation and mortgage lending from banks and building societies. Combined with a now embedded cultural reaction against the horrors of early industrial urbanism (as well as relatively cheap land) much of this private-sector-led building was occurring outside of urban centres in an unplanned and chaotic manner. To save on build costs, many developers were building out along arterial roads in 'ribbon developments' to avoid having to provide new infrastructure such as roads and utility connections. While the 1930s is widely considered to be a positive period for design and build quality, not all of these new private developments lived up to these standards – generally falling short of the new space standards imposed on municipally driven development. Equally, many experimented with new rapid methods of construction, piece-work, untrained workmen and poor quality materials – an issue which set off a national conversation about 'Jerry-building'.[42] Traffic also became a major concern, with roads unable to cope with increased passage and the recent introduction of the motor car to a mass market contributing to a huge spike in road deaths,[43] and concerns were also raised that the layout of ribbon developments along roads further prevented the development of community. Likenesses between ribbon developments and the slums which had been replaced in the previous century were raised, particularly in regards to the often poor connections to utilities such as water and sewerage systems. In the words of Lord Elton during a parliamentary debate in 1935: 'His Majesty's Government, side by side with their unprecedented drive against slums, were in fact promoting the creation of new slums which, equally inevitably and at an equally formidable cost, some future generation will have to destroy.'[44]

In 1926, the Council for the Preservation of Rural England was established in response to concerns about urban sprawl, and particularly towards the end of the 1930s concerns were increasingly raised that a portion of the new development was built in the wrong places, surplus to demand, and feeding a speculative property bubble in the industry. Such concerns greatly inspired the passing of the Town Planning Act in 1925, which included in its scope 'the general object of controlling the development of the land comprised in the area to which the scheme applies, of securing proper sanitary conditions, amenity and convenience … and generally protecting existing amenities whether in urban or rural portions of the area'.[45]

In 1932, the first Town and Country Planning Act was enacted – mandating the clearance of huge numbers of slums, and provisioning for the building of 700,000 new council homes. These initiatives were certainly successful, with around 1.1 million council homes built in the interwar period – but the system was still weak and unable to provide for some of the more strategic concerns of planners and economists for the country's future. Particularly, the issue of vast dereliction within industrial communities in the North of England and the Midlands. Increasingly, there was a sense that the housing sector should form part of a wider effort for economic planning and industrial regeneration. The Barlow Commission was established in 1938 and produced its findings in 1940. Chief among these findings were recommendations for the decentralisation of industrial communities away from congested urban centres and the establishment of an 'industrial location board' to plan for the geo-spatial development of industrial sectors strategically. In response to the report, the Ministry of Works and Planning was established, and the report heavily influenced the development of the New Towns Act in 1946.

The public policy convergence around the importance of planning wasn't restricted to housing and economic policy: equally, the 1942 Beveridge Report into social insurance, which would go on to form the principles behind the creation of the welfare state and the National Health Service, named 'want', 'squalor' and 'idleness' among its five 'giant' obstacles to post-war reconstruction. In particular, 'squalor', according to Beveridge, 'arises mainly through haphazard distribution of industry and population'. For Beveridge, the 'four stones' to slay the giant of squalor were the planned use of land, planned transport systems, well-trained architects, and increased efficiency in the building industry.[46]

As such, when the 1947 Town and Country Planning Act was introduced, it was not a standalone document but an integrated element of a much broader conversation, and vision, for economic planning. The act brought in several weighty measures, most of which still form the basis of the UK's planning system today. Most significantly, the act nationalised rights to all land, requiring planning permission prior to development of any kind. Local authorities were hugely empowered in this process, tasked with the duties of the new and powerful planning authorities, with powers for compulsory purchase, redevelopment and preservation of cultural, historic and environmental amenities. The original act also brought in a charge against all developments against the difference in land value created pre- and post-planning permission, as a mechanism for financing local authority activities and preventing speculation on planning permissions.

Although land value capture proved to be tricky – reducing private development to extremely low levels for over a decade – the essential functions of the 1947 Act remain in place today.

The UK's post-war housing system, defined

Taken as a totality, it can therefore be gleaned that through the various strands which made up the post-war housing system within the UK a set of clear and consistent policy directives converged around several key themes.

Number one was the control and standardisation of building standards and design, a deep commitment to planning and an integrated vision for the functions of economic policy, public health and social policy, and urban planning. Central to this was a de-urbanising mission, the destruction of poor quality housing from previous eras, a distrust of spontaneous development and an emphasis on the preservation of the landscape by gatekeeping access to developable land. Taken as a whole, the result of these measures led to vast improvements in the quality of the British housing stock and infrastructure – albeit a few hard-learned lessons in the applicability of some modernist assumptions in building and public realm design. The industrial planning and the redistribution of industrial populations away from industrial centres was successful in ensuring a more equitable pattern of growth across the UK, and a taste for low-density housing mirrored the aspirations of the majority of the British public through this time. As such, the period also boasted a level of satisfaction with the home and built environment which had heretofore not been experienced among the general population.

Next was a series of features which cumulatively prevented speculation, profiteering and the commodification of homes. Rent controls inhibited the profitability of private rented homes, a huge stock of publicly owned housing and capital controls at a national level preventing the financialisation of land and property. Through this combination of features, the value of homes as assets was reduced to a negligible quantity, preventing its use as a financial instrument either as a financial investment or as a rental property. A by-product of these features was a sustained period of affordability, historically unprecedented, which carried forward beyond 1979 and on until the millennium.

Lastly, these factors came together to deliver huge numbers of residential properties, partly due to the emphasis on planning housing delivery around social need, and a contributory factor in the sustained affordability of housing costs in this period. The sheer quantity and availability of accommodation through this period, at a standard which met or exceeded contemporary expectations, has not been matched in any historical epoch – possibly in all of human history.

They say the past is a different country. For many contemporary readers, it can be hard to imagine how different this country's housing system was not all that long ago. This book does not seek to argue that the post-war UK housing system was perfect; far from it. In the following chapters we will discuss in detail the competing questions and issues facing our housing system today, some of which bear direct relevance to decisions made in this period. The book does, however, argue strongly that the post-war housing period proved that some of the seemingly irreconcilable issues which define our present housing crisis are, in fact, solvable. The real question is, as a society, are we truly committed to solving it?

PART I

Defining the housing crisis

What defines a housing crisis?

While political leaders across the spectrum acknowledge that the UK is facing a housing crisis, the precise nature of this crisis is often poorly understood or oversimplified. Much public commentary around the crisis is reactive; the costs of rents and mortgages are increasing, there is a rise in homelessness and homeownership is becoming more difficult. But the solutions to these issues rarely touch upon the underlying causes, and the crisis is rarely addressed in the round – experienced instead as a series of intractable individual policies and questions of resource scarcity. But defining the housing crisis, and placing it within its historical context, is essential in developing effective mitigations and solutions.

At its core, the crisis can be broken down into three fundamental pillars: availability, affordability and quality. Each of these interwoven issues contributes to the growing instability in Britain's housing market, affecting millions of residents nationwide. The UK's current crisis is the result of decades of shifting economic policies, changing demographic patterns and legislative reforms that have shaped the housing landscape.

A crisis of availability

The housing crisis is on one major level a crisis of availability of accommodation to those that would wish to use it, and particularly those for whom alternatives are not an option. The availability crisis in the UK's housing system draws from several spheres; partly, it is a matter of general housing supply and the number of housing units failing to keep change with the combined impact of population growth and changing usage patterns. The UK's population has grown significantly over the course of the century, and while the average number of dwellings per capita is only marginally lower than at its peak today, other changes in usage have realised a real-terms constriction in supply. These changes include the decreasing size of UK households, the rise in single-occupant households particularly among the elderly, and different cultural expectations for space standards which have arisen.

The availability question is also a crisis of the lack of particular accommodation types. There is a shortage of adapted accommodation for those with disabilities and mobility issues, as well as a shortage of suitable 'move on' accommodation for particular service areas (particularly social care, homelessness prevention, and asylum seeker and refugee accommodation). We also have a shortage of residential care facilities for the elderly, and those in need of chronic medical supervision. The lack of social rented accommodation also creates a huge crisis, with 1.1 million families currently on waiting lists for council and social housing often waiting decades.

In short, many of the obstacles facing the UK's housing system are represented as an inadequate supply of and access to specific accommodation types in the areas that they are needed.

A crisis of affordability

In recent decades, housing costs have risen far beyond wage growth. In the 1970s, an average home cost four times the median salary; today, it costs more than eight times. Rental costs have similarly spiralled, consuming over 30 per cent of the average tenant's income, compared to 14 per cent in the 1970s. For millions of people, the dream of homeownership has become unattainable, while renters face a relentless squeeze on their budgets.

For much of the post-war period, the relative cost of housing was reduced to historically low sums across much of the British population. This was achieved through a mixture of direct price controls, increased supply of affordable accommodation (particularly council housing and social housing with regulated rents) and increased general supply of housing per capita. It also occurred within a context of severe capital controls regulating the expansion of housing investment which were in place up to the mid-1980s, as well as planning policy which sought to decentralise and redistribute housing supply across the country as opposed to stacking investment upon investment within urban cores.

Housing costs that make up a large proportion of our incomes are, however, nothing new in historical terms: the era of housing affordability (which appears to be ending now) was in many sense an aberration from the norm. Particularly since the millennium, the combined impact of the removal of counter-balances to the market development of housing have begun to have a wider impact on house-price affordability, feeding a cycle of increased costs (observed not just in the UK, but across much of the developed world).

In the absence of the effective reintroduction of such counter-measures, housing cost inflation – particularly relative to incomes – presently appears 'baked in' to our expectations for the future.

A crisis of quality and security

Even when housing is available and technically affordable, it can often be unsuitable and of substandard quality. Across the UK, four million homes are classified as endangering the health of their occupants due to disrepair, dampness or poor insulation. Meanwhile, insecure tenancy agreements in the private rented sector leave many renters in a state of permanent uncertainty, vulnerable to sudden rent increases or eviction with minimal notice.

Britain has the oldest housing stock in the entire world, with substantial numbers of properties built in the 19th and early 20th centuries. These houses are often poorly insulated, lacking in modern facilities and prone to damp and cold. Previously, and throughout much of the 20th century, huge sums of money were invested in constantly upgrading the UK's housing stock, initially via slum clearances and latterly through incentives for the renovation and retrofit of old properties. The last such programme to operate at scale, 'Pathfinder' or Housing Market Renewal, was wound up in 2011 and since then no subsequent scheme has effectively tackled the need for the consistent upkeep and upgrading of poor quality housing.

Adding to this, changing patterns of dwelling usage are contributing to worsening conditions within particular sectors. Within the private rented sector, increasing designations of homes of multiple occupancy and increasingly transient populations of renters on short-term leases are rapidly speeding up the decline in condition of some of Britain's housing stock. Equally, decline in real-terms grant for housing associations and councils owning and managing council and social housing has contributed to maintenance issues within the sector, contributing to the mass sell-off of properties and shocking conditions such as those responsible for the death of Awaab Ishak in Rochdale.

While the quality of general housing for the UK population remains good by historical standards, the country lags behind other comparative nations and in many particular areas of the housing market there are increasing signs of regression.

Why this matters

The housing crisis is not just an abstract policy failure; it is a daily reality affecting individuals, families and entire communities. It influences economic mobility, health outcomes and social cohesion. The inability to secure stable, affordable housing has ripple effects across society, from increased homelessness to mental health struggles, from declining birth rates to widening regional inequalities.

This book aims to dissect the roots of the housing crisis, expose the policy failures that have exacerbated it and propose tangible solutions. In Part I, we will explore the symptoms of the crisis as they manifest today – examining the data, lived experiences and structural weaknesses that define the UK's broken housing market. By the end of this section, readers will have a comprehensive understanding of why this crisis exists and how it impacts different segments of society.

In the subsequent parts, we will delve deeper into the historical and political factors that shaped our current housing system before outlining pragmatic solutions for the future. Housing is more than just bricks and mortar – it is the foundation of economic security, social stability and personal dignity. Addressing this crisis is not just an economic necessity but a moral imperative.

1

Housing supply and the shrinking stock

As noted in the introduction to Part I, inadequate housing supply is an integral element of the UK's present crisis though the question is more complicated than simply a matter of dwelling units per capita. The supply problem in housing is as much an issue of inadequate supply of particular types of housing in particular areas, or in response to particular problems, as it is an issue with the overall number of houses available for use. This chapter will break down the various aggravating factors behind the UK's housing supply crisis, providing an overview of some of the prevailing debates among policy makers, academics and industry.

Changing household composition and distribution of housing

Since 2001 at least, it is clear that the number of dwellings per head of population has increased at a marginally slower rate than population growth. The UK had an estimated 21 million dwellings in 2001, with a population of almost 59 million (ONS) – around 2.8 homes per person. In 2022, the number of dwellings had grown only by around four million to 25 million – while the population had risen by eight million to 67.5 million (ONS) – around 2.7 homes per person.[1]

At the same time, the average size of a UK household has consistently fallen since the early 20th century, meaning that the same number of dwellings must be stretched farther to accommodate more people. In 1911, the mean household size in England and Wales was roughly 4.75 people, which by 1961 had fallen to 3.1.[2] In 1996, an average UK household consisted of 2.42 people – in 2022, that number had fallen to 2.36.[3] The most recent English Housing Survey for 2022–2023 estimates that the number of lone households has also increased in recent years – with female lone households representing 18 per cent of all households (up from 15 per cent in 2019–2020) and lone male households representing 16 per cent (up from 13 per cent).[4] According to the 'Bedroom Standard' (a formal measurement under which households with two or more 'guest' or 'spare' bedrooms are considered 'under-occupied') in 2021, it was estimated that under-occupied homes account for 68.8 per cent of all dwellings in England (Census, 2021).

Overcrowding in particular sections of the housing market is still acute. Approximately 4.4 per cent of households in the UK are overcrowded (roughly 1.2 million) with the bulk of those in the social rented sector and private rented sector (PRS) (Census, 2021). Although there has been a small drop in overcrowding across all tenures since 2021, overcrowding in both rented sectors has been steadily increasing since the mid-1990s, from 5.1 per cent to 8.1 per cent in the social rented sector between 1996 and 2022, and from 3.2 per cent to 5.3 per cent in the PRS during the same period.[5]

The UK is a particularly regionally uneven country, and housing availability reflects this, with huge differences in the number of available units in different areas, as well as their cost. In general, outside of London where values tend to be the highest, the South East and other desirable rural areas contain areas with the largest divergence between earnings and house prices, alongside pockets of high value urban conurbations such as Birmingham and Manchester. Smaller urban areas, particularly concentrated in the country's former industrial heartlands, are where values are most constrained.

Economic insecurity and lack of affordability is also contributing significantly to the migration of populations and the breakup of communities. 'Gentrification' is the term often used in built-urban areas to describe the inability of individuals to afford the increased house prices and rents being experienced in areas they have lived for a long time, and their replacement by young professionals or buy-to-let landlords. 'Gentrification' is a regionally specific issue – faced primarily by those living in urban cores or highly desirable areas such as national parks or the Home Counties. But a parallel issue of migration is felt in many regions of the UK, in which declining employment prospects combined with more modest increases in rents and house prices feeds an exodus of particularly young people from their homes in search of better prospects elsewhere.

In general, it is clear that the UK's available housing supply has not been increasing in line with either population growth, income level or modern trends and expectations for living. While this problem is most acute in urban centres, equally its effects are felt in almost every corner of the UK.

The most important plank of the solution to our housing crisis must be increasing the delivery of new housing. Yet, in addition to the need for more housing we must also consider the distribution of our existing housing stock, questions of under-occupancy and changing family types and sizes. As the manner in which we use homes continues to evolve, our social demographics change and increased life expectancy drives increased lone occupancy, these new demands on our existing housing stock will continue to drive a disjuncture between our needs and expectations, and the reality.

Numbers of empty properties

In recent years, significant attention has been paid to the number of 'empty homes' within the British housing market, and emphasis has been placed on increasing the efficiency of our housing stock in addition to (or as opposed to) focusing primarily on increasing numbers of housing units.

Since 2012 and the allocation of £156 million to the 'Empty Homes Programme' (and an additional £50 million allocated to the 'Clusters of Empty Homes Programme'), empty or unoccupied homes have been a recognised feature of the government's approach to dealing with the housing crisis. Yet the numbers of empty homes continue to grow. In 2023, the Liberal Democrat Party claimed that England has 'more than twice as many long-term empty homes this Christmas as there are children living in temporary accommodation'[6] – arguing that the 261,189 homes in England classed as 'long-term vacant' (empty for six months or more) could be more effectively utilised to house the country's homeless. At any given time, as many as 676,304 homes in England are classed as vacant, a more than 200 per cent increase from the 'all time low' of 203,596 in 2015.[7] Furthermore, as of 2021, there are as many as 1.6 million unoccupied dwellings in England and Wales, 6.1 per cent of dwellings in England and 8.2 per cent of dwellings in Wales, respectively.[8] In 2024, a London School of Economics paper written by Charlotte Rogers and Ian Gough argued that through the utilisation of progressive property and land taxes and the regulation of second homes, the housing crisis could be solved without any increase in the numbers of new homes for private sale or rent,[9] and many other commentators increasingly argue that the number of empty homes within the UK's housing stock is a major – if not the major – contributory factor in Britain's rapidly increasing housing crisis.

But the thesis of a housing crisis caused primarily by unnecessarily vacant properties does not go unchallenged. Writing for *The Critic*, Kristian Niemitz notes that Organisation for Economic Co-operation and Development (OECD) research estimates that Britain has among the lowest vacant housing stock of any European Union (EU) nation, and below the OECD average, while experiencing a significantly more acute housing crisis in comparison to equivalent EU nations.[10] By contrast, across the EU, only 8 per cent of the population spend more than 40 per cent of their incomes on housing costs – whereas in the UK, this is over 20 per cent at 11.3 million. The figure of 11.3 million is notably 'millions more than in many European countries with similar or larger populations, including 2.8 million people more than in Turkey (2020 population 83.1 million)'.[11] England also has far fewer homes per capita than the OECD average, at 434 homes per thousand (as opposed to an OECD average of 487, or 590 in France, 587 in Italy and 547 in Norway).[12] Contrary to the idea that the UK should seek to reduce its number of vacancies, with respect to these figures, the Home Builders Federation notes that 'vacant dwellings are a sign of a functioning housing market', allowing for flexibility to changes in demand for different types of housing.[13] Indeed, it seems unlikely that vacant dwellings alone can account for the severity of the UK's housing crisis relative to other equivalent nations.

Regardless, the trend towards increasing numbers of vacant or unoccupied properties is clearly troubling – and in particular areas of the country clearly having a serious effect on the general housing supply, particularly in tourist destinations where short-term rentals and second homes have ballooned in recent years. Writing in 2023, Neil Gutteridge of the *Telegraph* estimates that the number of second homes in England had increased by 170,000 since 2010,[14] and the Office for National Statistics calculates that as of 2021 Census data, over one in ten UK homes are being used as 'holiday homes' in some areas of England and Wales.[15]

However, the conclusion sometimes drawn from this issue, that policy makers should look to dispossess homeowners of their properties, presents significant ethical and political challenges. Equally, the argument that homes could be used more efficiently does not dilute the underlying need for a higher supply of properties into the British housing market. Increasing numbers of unoccupied or vacant properties are an exacerbatory symptom, rather than a cause, of the fundamental questions facing the UK's dysfunctional housing market – and while measures to increase the efficiency of our usage of existing homes is welcome, in and of itself it is an unrealistic approach to resolving the supply issue.

Nowhere to 'move on'

Britain is currently suffering from an acute shortage in specialist accommodation types, which are creating blockages in the housing system and support services more generally (particularly in healthcare). Specialist accommodation in social and old age care, intermediate healthcare and accessibility all play an oversized role in maintaining the most 'efficient' use of our existing housing stock, particularly through their role in providing individuals an option to 'move on' from unsuitable accommodation they are already inhabiting.

For instance, suitable 'move on' accommodation is critical in the rehabilitation of individuals transitioning from street homelessness, particularly the provision of accommodation which is safe, secure and provides access to private space. However social services and councils repeatedly report huge shortages in such accommodation. Homelessness charity Centrepoint identifies[16] several key blockages for services in delivering 'move on' accommodation to the young people it supports, including:

- a critical lack of social housing;
- high rents and upfront costs;
- a shortage of affordable shared accommodation in the PRS;
- private landlords' mortgage and insurance conditions;
- lower benefit rates for young people;
- PRS landlords' reluctance to let to tenants receiving benefits; and
- a lack of security and quality control within the PRS.

Resulting from a mixture of these factors, Centrepoint estimate that between 2010 and 2023 the number of supported accommodation bed spaces in the UK has reduced by one-fifth, with a current shortfall of nearly 30,000. Further, it reports that in 2016/2017, 30 per cent of individuals ready to move on from temporary accommodation projects were unable to due to a shortage of affordable housing.

Traditionally, social and council housing was the primary route through which homeless individuals were rehabilitated back into the housing market. Social and council housing is especially suited to this role, given the long-term assured tenancies and wrap-around services which are often provided alongside residence in these properties – not to mention the reduced rental rates expected by landlords.

But with almost 1.3 million households on local authority waiting lists for social homes in the UK today,[17] and an estimated annual net loss of 24,000 social homes each and every year since 1991,[18] the prospects for gaining a social tenancy for many individuals looking to move out of temporary accommodation is slim and getting slimmer.

The alternative, for the most part, is subsidised accommodation in the PRS. However finding suitable 'move on' accommodation in the PRS is often fraught with difficulty. Many private landlords are unwilling to accept tenants from temporary or supported accommodation, those in receipt of benefits or those they perceive to be at risk of a sudden loss of income.

In the worst cases, unsuitable 'move on' accommodation can be actively dangerous for vulnerable individuals. Temporary accommodation is often targeted by organised crime for access to its tenants for exploitation, recruitment and even trafficking and kidnapping. Many of these children are trafficked into criminal activities such as drug dealing, smuggling and prostitution.[19] At one hotel used for temporary accommodation for asylum seekers in Essex, police reported 48 missing children in August 2021 alone. The government's last available estimates from 2015 suggest that 651,000 supportive housing units were operating in Britain at any one time – costing £4.12 billion in Housing Benefit payments annually,[20] providing additional opportunities for criminal gangs. In 2022, the *Guardian* reported that criminal gangs were making in excess of £6 million a year from Housing Benefit payments to 'exempt accommodation', properties set up to temporarily house vulnerable adults 'such as prison-leavers, recovering addicts and those fleeing domestic violence' by buying up properties and setting them up as supported accommodation.[21] Given the wider issues of accessibility, affordability and supply of PRS properties, the PRS continues to be a poor fit for the bulk of individuals looking to move on from temporary accommodation.

This chronic shortage of 'move on' accommodation exacerbates the under-utilisation of British housing stock, contributing to bed-blocking in the healthcare system and creating a huge public cost to the Exchequer in finding alternatives to the PRS.

Shortage of adapted/accessible homes

Within the UK, an estimated four million homes 'endanger the health of the people who live there', with over 50 per cent of these homes lived in by someone over the age of 55.[22] However, with only 9 per cent of current housing stock deemed 'accessible',[23] suitable options for individuals looking to either downsize or 'rightsize' their property are severely limited.

This is both an issue for the elderly and impaired who are resident in their existing unadapted or inaccessible properties, but few options for downsizing or rightsizing means fewer opportunities to free up larger properties which could house families or house-shares. In 2019, 176,000 households requiring adaptations said that they wished to move to get somewhere more suitable for their needs, with tenants in the PRS most likely to wish to move. Yet in many cases, the appropriate options are not available to facilitate this.

Homes within the social rented sector are significantly more likely to require accessibility improvements than those in the PRS, reflecting the different socio-economic, demographic and health conditions of residents. Housing association tenants are also more likely to report a required adaptation than private rented counterparts, the willingness to report required adaptations reflecting differing expectations of service from the landlord (8 per cent of those living in unsuitably unadapted accommodation stated that their landlord wouldn't pay for the adaptations even if requested). Living with uncatered needs for adaptations can be a taxing experience. In 2016, Aspire published a report on the experiences of those requiring residential adaptations to their homes, reporting that as many as 86 per cent of patients discharged from hospital with spinal cord injuries move back into homes which are unsuitably adapted to their needs, forcing them to live on the ground floor and struggling to take care of their basic needs.[24]

The result of this shortage is an overly brittle housing market for adapted and accessible homes, which feeds an inefficient use of existing housing stock and contributes to a wider experience of housing shortage. Increasing the supply of suitable accessible accommodation could be one of the most effective ways to increase the efficient use of Britain's housing stock, as well as providing necessary and even cost-saving assets to reduce the suffering of those with chronic illnesses, injuries and disabilities.

Shortage of care facilities and supported accommodation

With Britain's ageing population, demand for care facilities is growing exponentially yet provision continues to freefall. This does not merely have an impact upon the housing market and the ability of residents to downsize, but also on the National Health Service and health services who face an unprecedented bed-blocking crisis, preventing them from treating a backlog of 5.6 million patients, almost 10 per cent of all those requiring treatment in England. At present, AgeUK estimates that 1.6 million people aged 65+ are not receiving the care and support they need with 'essential living activities'.[25] The King's Fund estimates that only 43 per cent of people who request support receive some kind of service.[26]

Between 2015 and 2020, the UK has seen a net loss of 775 care homes and a net loss of 9,894 bed spaces. The closures were not linked to quality of care – of those homes that closed in 2020, almost half had a rating of 'Good' from the Care Quality Commission. Of those homes that closed in the public sector, 88 per cent were rated Good.[27] Between 2020 and 2022, a further 1,600 care home beds have been lost following the COVID-19 pandemic, with a further net loss of 134 homes.

There is a general consensus that Britain's care system is in crisis – and a central tenet of this crisis is a lack of capacity, particularly in residential care facilities, to absorb the ever-increasing demands on the sector.

This loss to capacity in the care sector creates huge blockages within the housing system, as with the shortage of adapted and accessible properties, in removing options for individuals who may have otherwise found more appropriate care and accommodation for their needs. Closing the gap between demand and supply will also be a crucial component in opening access to a substantial stock of housing.

Access to social housing

Social and council housing has turned from being an available option for an average UK renter, to being a highly sought-after rarity. In 1979, up to 42 per cent of the British population were resident in council or social housing.[28] By contrast, today that figure is 16 per cent.[29]

Evidence of demand and appetite for increased social and council accommodation is overwhelming. YouGov polling in 2023 suggested that voters of all political parties favour building more council housing, including 52 per cent of Conservative voters.[30] Nationally, 1.16 million households are currently on local authority waiting lists for housing, however the National Housing Federation estimates that this figure could be as high as 1.6 million households, or 4.2 million people.[31,32] There is also significant evidence to suggest that many current residents in the PRS aspire to move into social or council housing. Salford University's study in 2024, 'Precarious Lives', detailing the lived experiences of those in the PRS, found that at least half of their sample of PRS residents hoped to access social housing – though felt that they wouldn't be able to obtain it.

None of this should be surprising, particularly in relation to those currently living in the PRS. Social and council housing consistently outperforms the PRS in housing quality, customer service and price – on average £37 a week cheaper than a PRS alternative. Tenancies in the social rented sector are generally set at five-year intervals, as opposed to rolling annual or biannual contracts in the PRS.

However, the number of social and council houses available continues to diminish, and the stock continues to age. According to evidence submitted to government by the Northern Housing Consortium, 73 per cent of local authority housing within the social sector was built between 1945 and 1980, as well as 47 per cent of housing association homes.[33] In the same report, the Northern Housing Consortium notes that just 11 per cent of local authority housing stock has been built since 1980, and only 38 per cent of housing association homes.

The National Housing Federation believes that 90,000 new local authority or social homes should be built each and every year to keep pace with demand: in 2022, only 6,554 were actually built.

The continued atrophy of the nation's social and council housing stock is a huge contributor to the lack of availability of housing for millions of Britain's residents, and a major contributor to our inability to provide the quantity and quality of the homes that people expect.

2

Affordability

Since the post-war era, Britons have experienced a major shift in their expectations of the proportion of income they should expect to pay for their accommodation. At the turn of the 20th century, an average Briton could expect to pay out around 50 per cent of their income in rent.[1] By the late 1960s, this figure had fallen as low as 9 per cent.[2] Today, measures of housing affordability tend to estimate approximately 30 per cent of income on housing costs as the 'affordability threshold' for an average person or household before housing costs become a major driver of poverty and deprivation. With rents making up an average of 34 per cent of a UK renter's income today (and as high as 39.8 per cent in London[3]), affordability is clearly becoming a key problem in today's housing market.[4]

While affordability of accommodation by pre-war standards remains normal in the UK, it is clear that in the past three decades living expenses across all tenures have increased substantially as a proportion of incomes, and this trend is anticipated to continue. In this chapter, we will interrogate the different aspects of affordability and the main drivers behind the worsening relationship of incomes to housing costs for UK residents.

Homeownership

A huge element of our contemporary discussion on the housing crisis relates to the ability of our next generation to access the housing ladder. Homeownership remains by far and away the central housing aspiration for most British people, and is widely seen as the most desirable housing situation. As such, a central pillar of the housing crisis as it is experienced by Britons is in the rising relative cost of purchasing a home. This problem is extremely pertinent to today's public perceptions on the crisis, especially considering the increased importance homeownership has in contemporary UK society as a nest-egg investment and retirement fund.

In recent years, the expectation of an affordable first home has all but vanished for millions of British people – with the Office for National Statistics (ONS) estimating that in 2021, average house prices were equivalent to 9.1 times the average annual earnings of a British resident (concerningly the trend is markedly upward – the ONS survey also states that the previous year, 2020, saw average house prices only 7.9 times average annual earnings[5]). According to Schroders' analysis of Bank of England data, we must travel back to the 1880s before we find an equivalent divergence between average earnings and house prices.[6] By way of historical contrast, between 1960 to around 2006–2007 house prices in the UK floated between four and six times annual average earnings.[7] On average today, 27 per cent of a tenant's salary is spent on rent – this rises to almost 40 per cent in London – compared to a national average of 17 per cent of a homeowner's salary spent on their mortgage. According to the Institute for Fiscal Studies, in 1977 the percentage of household income spent on 'housing' (not broken down to rent versus mortgage payments) was merely 14 per cent,[8] and according to written evidence from UK Women's Budget Group, in 1980, the average working-age family renting privately spent only 12 per cent of its income on housing.[9]

It may be obvious to note that such a disjuncture between average earnings and prices is having a disproportionate impact on lower-income households. According to the Equality Trust, in the UK the majority of households have incomes below the median average for the country – £34,300 per annum as of 2022.[10] In that same year, the bottom 20 per cent of British households had an average disposable income of only £12,798 – compared with £69,126 for the top 20 per cent. For those in lower income brackets, the disparity between average earnings and prices has an even more acute impact on the relative affordability of a home – making homeownership all but impossible outside of the lowest value areas of the country.

As with the availability of housing, differences in regional affordability of housing vary widely across the UK. In London, the affordability crisis is most acute: average London properties cost more than 11 times the average London wage. Outside of the capital, properties in the South East and South West are also many multiple times an annual average income. In the Midlands this falls to 6.5 times, in the North West, Yorkshire and Wales it sits between 5.5 and 6 times annual earnings and in Scotland 4.7 times.[11]

Within these figures are huge variations. In Burnley, Lancashire, lower quartile house prices are still on average only 3.3 times the lower quartile median average earnings in the area – contrasted against Kensington and Chelsea in London, where that figure is 24.4 times.[12] For those taking out a mortgage, these figures average at an average payment of £174 per week – £244 a week in London and £163 outside. These figures have been consistently increasing – up £40 a week in London and £25 a week outside.

But despite varying levels of price, what is common between regions is the dysfunctionality of the housing market. In areas of the country with less demand, returns on investment in these properties is likely to be less than in high value areas. Homes are harder to sell on and therefore contain more risk. Furthermore, areas with the lowest house prices tend to be areas with broader economic problems; low rates of employment, high rates of deprivation, fewer employment opportunities and less access to mortgage finance. As such, areas with relatively lower incomes often correlate with lower house prices – meaning the benefits of greater affordability by national standards are not necessarily felt by local populations.

With homeownership becoming less viable, the housing market has developed a self-fulfilling prophecy through which demand for renting further accentuates runaway prices. In the UK, the private rented sector (PRS) has more than doubled in size between the year 2000 and 2021, from around two million households to 4.7 million.[13] While the PRS sector is in direct competition with prospective homeowners for the purchase of housing, an inflationary dynamic is baked into the cycle where those who view homes as investments are able to leverage greater levels of investment into purchasing properties, driving more and more prospective homeowners from the market, increasing the demand for renting and thus increasing the capacity of the PRS to invest.

Interest rate rises

Since the Russian invasion of Ukraine in February 2022, the British economy has been reacting to an inflationary shock which has seen inflation rise as high as 11.1 per cent. In response, the Bank of England has attempted to curb inflation through increasing interest rates, up to 5.25 per cent by April 2024. Between 2022 and 2023, mortgage defaults shot up by almost 29 per cent.[14] This squeeze on lending has, however, not correlated with similar falls in house prices, which declined by only 1.8 per cent in 2023.[15] The result is a marginal increase in affordability of homeownership since the recent peak in house prices during the COVID-19 pandemic, though at the cost of increasing the cost of mortgages for the average household, up by an average of 61 per cent between December 2021 and December 2022 alone (with the number of defaults increasing well into 2024 and anticipated to rise further[16,17]). Although interest rate rises may act to slow house price growth, they do so primarily by increasing the relative cost of housing against average incomes, worsening the crisis of affordability for many residents, particularly those with mortgages or renting mortgaged properties.

Overall, the trends for homeownership show little sign of change without a serious policy intervention by government, with the tricky and potentially contradictory function of both lowering the cost of borrowing while continuing to reign in house price inflation. The only method through which to do so successfully will be through substantially increasing supply.

Private renting

In the UK, the ratio of rent relative to income has remained relatively stable in comparison to house prices – but in the past decade has started to markedly increase. In the UK, rents make up on average 32 per cent of a renter's annual income[18] – up to nearly 42 per cent in London. By the ONS's own definition of affordability – where the cost of rent does not exceed 30 per cent of earnings – this makes the average UK rent unaffordable in most regions of the country.

The ONS estimates that UK rental prices have increased by 13.2 per cent since January 2015 (Census, 2021) – with the bulk of that growth felt in England and Northern Ireland. According to Hamptons, rents are set to be 25 per cent higher in 2026 than they were at the end of 2022 – as against a 5.5 per cent growth in house prices during the same period.[19] Interest rate hikes by the Bank of England, intended to curb inflation, have counter-intuitively contributed to inflationary rents. According to Aneisha Beveridge of Hamptons:

> There's a strong argument that the Bank of England's quest to quash inflation by successive base rate hikes has hit the rental sector harder than any other part of the housing market. Homeowners have been squeezed by increase in mortgage repayments. But landlords' ability to absorb higher rates is more limited because many rely on interest-only mortgages. When the interest-rate doubles, so do their repayments.[20]

As private rents continue to make up an increasing share of the UK's housing market, at roughly 20 per cent today, these increases are impacting an increasingly substantial subset of the UK population – particularly those of working age. According to the English Housing Survey, the most common age group of private renters is 25–34, accounting for 32 per cent of the total. Only 5 per cent of private renters are aged 65 to 74, and only 3 per cent are 75 or over. Private renters are the most likely of any residential demographic to be in work (73 per cent) – as opposed to owner-occupiers (52 per cent) or social renters (38 per cent).

Despite this high rate of employment, the PRS now contains the largest group in poverty of any tenure type in the UK – with PRS being described by the Joseph Rowntree Foundation as the 'new home of poverty' in 2016. Nationally as many as 26 per cent of PRS households claim Housing Benefit,[21] up from 20 per cent in 2019.[22] On average, their claim is significantly higher than in the social rented sector – at £128 per week against £85 per week (for private renters, this is up from an average of £113 per week in 2019).

This effect is having a huge bearing on the lives of young working people, from their ability to save to their mental health and their ability to start a family. The US-based real-estate company 'Zillow' published analysis in 2018 which found a clear inverse correlation between the speed at which house prices increase as against the falling birth rate.[23] The study found that every 10 per cent increase in housing costs translated to a 1.5 per cent drop in fertility for 25–29-year-old women. The impact of high house prices on fertility has to be disaggregated between renters and homeowners: for many homeowners, high house prices correspond to an increase in birth rates. However, according to estimates from the Royal Economic Society, for renters every 10 per cent increase in rent leads to a decline in fertility of 4.9 per cent.[24]

In a 2018 study[25] conducted through a partnership between Salford Council and Salford University, the research paper 'Precarious Lives' documented 'lived experiences in the Private Rented Sector' in areas of Salford and found that a combination of insecurity of tenure, changing tenures (particularly in favour of houses of multiple occupancy), poor housing conditions, rising rents, welfare reform and wage stagnation formed a perfect storm of financial insecurity for tenants in the PRS.

In respect to their financial positions, residents identified fees and deposits, rental increases and increased competition for accommodation as the primary issues which created an affordability barrier. Fees of between £70 and £300 to agents, sometimes charged in addition to the landlord's deposit (usually set at 4–6 weeks rent) meant charges of between £1,200 to £3,000 simply to move into a new property. Contract renewal fees – sometimes to be signed every six months – were also added, with one resident indicating they paid a renewal fee of £90 every three months.

All but one of the respondents interviewed indicated that they were struggling financially, including from professional households on two decent incomes. Most respondents mentioned that they were 'unable to put much, if anything, into savings' and in one instance an interviewee was 'spending her savings as her pension was insufficient to cover all her household expenditure'.

In 2021, 25 per cent of private renters reported finding it either 'fairly or very difficult' to afford their rent in response to the English Housing Survey, which on average was £201 per week (twice that of the social rented sector, at £103 per week). Over two-thirds – 69 per cent – of private renters in the lower two income quintiles spent 30 per cent or more of their income on rent, representing £1.2 million PRS households, and 8 per cent of private renters reported to the English Housing Survey in 2021 that they had been in rent arrears over the past year.

Given that the PRS is by far and away the fastest growing section of our housing market, these trends are deeply concerning and point to rapidly increasing problems with affordability within the sector over the coming years.

Homelessness and rough sleeping

Accompanied by over a decade of income stagnation, and huge cost of living pressures caused by recent bouts of inflation, the UK has also seen an epidemic of homelessness which has visibly scarred the streets of most British cities – particularly since 2010.

From 2010 onwards, the number of recorded 'rough sleepers' on Britain's streets expanded exponentially, in a visible crisis which touched deeply upon the public consciousness – homelessness charity Crisis estimates that between 2010 and 2018, the number of 'rough sleepers' alone has risen by 165 per cent.[26] While rough sleeping numbers are crude estimates, the government believes that numbers of rough sleepers rose by over 250 per cent from 1,770 to 4,750 between 2010 and 2018, before falling back to 2,440.[27] However, since 2022 numbers have risen again by almost a third to 3,898.[28] The use of Section 21 'No Fault' evictions (evictions in which no fault has been committed by the tenant to justify the eviction) have hugely increased since 2010, and particularly within the private sector,[29] and in many years are the single biggest cause of rough sleeping.

Rough sleeping is, however, only the most visible element of the nation's current homelessness crisis. Since 2017, the Homelessness Reduction Act has passed statutory duties on to local councils to find accommodation for anyone registering themselves as homeless within 56 days. One of the central mechanisms through which these statutory duties has been enacted is through the use of 'temporary accommodation', often private accommodation procured by the local authority on a temporary basis to house vulnerable individuals.

These dwellings are often unsuitable and unsafe for those placed there – comprising of anything from B&Bs to church halls and refuges – lacking in facilities such as kitchens and private bathrooms, often undertaken at great expense to the councils responsible for provisioning them. According to Shelter, the annual bill for temporary accommodation is £1.7 billion in England alone, up from £986 million in 2017.[30]

And for those not forced onto the streets through Section 21 notices or rising rents, for many the condition of their rented property is incredibly poor. According to the English Homes Survey, in 2022 around 23 per cent of PRS homes failed to meet the decent homes standard, as did 10 per cent of social rented homes (and 14 per cent of owner-occupier homes).[31] PRS remained the only tenure type not to see a fall in non-decency from the previous survey in 2019. Among the reasons for non-decency is overcrowding, caused in part through the explosion in numbers of homes of multiple occupancy, which the government estimates represent almost 25 per cent of all PRS homes. Britain is currently struggling to upgrade its existing housing stock – with improvements in energy efficiency and insulation too slow.

The Local Government Association believes that there has been a 430 per cent increase in the use of temporary accommodation by councils since 2010 with 10,510 households across the country currently being put up in B&Bs,

and over 95,000 people living in temporary accommodation of all kinds across the country.[32] The National Housing Federation states that as of 2022/2023, 105,750 households in total are now using temporary accommodation, including 138,930 children charting a 62 per cent increase in spending on temporary accommodation over the past five years. The number of children living in temporary accommodation is anticipated to increase to 130,000 by 2030, the equivalent of six children in every school in England. According to government data, in 2021 over £1 billion was spent on homeless services of one form or another in England.[33] By 2022/2023, English councils *alone* spent £1.74 billion on temporary accommodation *specifically*, 9 per cent of their budgets. The *Financial Times* believes that 'Britain is the world's worse on homelessness', with a 2024 article from John Burn-Murdoch arguing that including temporary accommodation, Britain has 'by far the highest rate of homelessness in the developed world'.[34]

Between August to December 2018, Jennifer Williams of the *Manchester Evening News* chronicled the 'Dickensian conditions' of 'Manchester's grim private guesthouses', in which children live amidst flea infestations, drug abuse and prostitution in a network of B&B accommodation procured as an emergency measure by the local council. Figures from Greater Manchester show that 3,881 households are currently being held in temporary accommodation across the conurbation – 2,537 of them in the city of Manchester itself. Conditions in temporary accommodation have not improved in this time, leading to fears of a generation of families with children losing their most developmentally important years.

Britain's homelessness crisis continues to grow at an alarming rate – as does its cost to the taxpayer. The true extent of our homelessness crisis has been concealed by the vast expansion of temporary accommodation, at inordinate expense to local authorities. But this situation cannot continue. With many councils declaring bankruptcy, neither the funding model nor the model of temporary accommodation itself can stand the strain. The true costs of the lost generations of families and children who have spent many of their formative years in these highly unsuitable, and often unsanitary and unsafe, environments will only be truly revealed over the coming decades.

3

Quality

Quality of housing has been a major measure of social success in the UK since the Victorian era, when the first proper regulatory standards around housing design and spacing were devised and slums systematically demolished to make way for more appropriate new designs. In 1875, the Public Health Act allowed councils to ban 'back-to-back' housing, terraces without gardens which were built directly against each other and often over several storeys.

This act was one of several moves by the Victorians to tighten up legislation around housing quality and begin to improve the quality of housing stock, primarily on the basis of public health and tackling squalor. After the Victorians, the recognition of the importance of housing quality to environmental health and wellbeing continued to be codified into the British governmental system. In 1919, the Ministry of Health Act established the Ministry of Health, incorporating planning and housing. During the Second World War, the Beveridge Report set out squalor as among the five 'giants' to be eradicated from society and post-war, in 1951, the Ministry of Health was merged with the Ministry of Local Government and Planning.

Some of the outcomes of these changes included the huge expansion of council housing throughout the 1920s and 1930s, houses built to the highest specification with good space standards and modern amenities – as well as slum clearances and the creation of many new towns such as Milton Keynes. Although many of the stylistic preferences of the era, particularly an appetite for Brutalist architecture and highly problematic road planning, have not aged well – this era saw the greatest improvements in general housing standards in the UK's history, and was carried through to the 1980s, at which point the reforms most responsible for these changes were reversed. The Housing Act of 1980 introduced the Right to Buy, and almost overnight cut rates of council house building to negligible levels. Space standards for new builds, last set in 1961, were also scrapped – allowing properties to become smaller. Building control functions were watered down then privatised, beginning with the Building Act of 1984 which introduced the category of non-mandatory 'guidance' on the safety of building materials, followed by the privatisation of building control through the establishment of the Construction Industry Council. In 1988, Health was formerly removed from its position alongside Housing in government through the creation of the Department for Health and Social Care – ending a partnership which had lasted over half a century.

Throughout most of the post-war era, the intrinsic connection between housing and public health had driven a social mission in housing, with regular slum clearances, renovations and adaptations to properties – after which little systemic attention was paid to improving the state of the country's housing stock. While various schemes such as Housing Market Renewal were revived under the New Labour government from 1997, they were connected primarily to renovation and delivered in the context of an approach to urban renewal or 'regeneration', and significantly smaller in scale than the pre- and post-war interventions which had so drastically improved the general housing stock condition throughout much of the 20th century. The quality of the UK's housing stock has noticeably begun to lag behind that of other comparative nations, and this divide is becoming more and more acute. In this chapter, we will explore the various issues of housing quality faced within the UK's housing market, as well as the historic significance of the new direction of travel we have taken since the 1980s.

Existing stock and tenancy types

Britain has the oldest housing stock in Europe – a legacy of the early industrial revolution, when following a population explosion millions of homes were constructed in new urban centres to house the migrating working-class populations who manned the new factories. Significant numbers of the homes built during this era still survive. Twenty per cent of British dwellings were built before 1919, many of which consist of Victorian Britain's iconic brick terraces which still form huge swathes of the country's housing stock in cities and towns.

Slum clearances, improvements in safety standards and building regulations as well as periodic investment into retrofit and upgrading housing condition has removed and replaced many of the worst pre-war properties from the housing market – and in general, the story of British housing conditions has been one of gradual but consistent improvement since the late Victorian era.

However, the quality of Britain's housing stock still significantly lags behind that of other developed nations on a number of metrics. On energy efficiency, Britain's homes are the least efficient in Europe, with 13.2 per cent of households living in 'fuel poverty'.[1] Seventeen per cent of Britain's homes are considered to be 'non-decent', with the poorest stock condition in the rapidly growing private rented sector (PRS) (EHS, 2022–2023).[2] In respect of issues such as damp and mould, poor housing quality in the UK is estimated to cost health services £1.4 billion a year[3] – and according to the Centre for Ageing Better, an estimated ten million people in England live at risk due to their home failing to meet basic standards.[4]

Much of the national discourse around this issue relates to the quality of social and council housing stock. In December 2020, the tragic case of Awaab Ishak showed up the perilously dangerous housing conditions which are still far too common an occurrence within the social housing sector. Two-year-old Awaab died from respiratory complications following extensive exposure to damp and mould. The two-year-old's death triggered a national conversation in 2021 following revelations that persistent reports of damp and mould had been made by Ishak's parents to the housing provider, Rochdale Borough Housing for at least three years prior to his death.

ITV journalist Daniel Hewitt has also chronicled the extensive pattern of poor conditions across many social and council housing estates in repeated investigative reports for ITV news, in addition to a documentary, *Surviving Squalor: Britain's Housing Shame*, which was broadcast in September 2021. The documentary chronicled dozens of cases not just of damp, but serious structural defects which went unaddressed in housing association and council properties the length and breadth of the country.

But despite the national media focus, this is far from being an issue which is specific to the social and council housing sector. The best data we have on the UK's housing market comes from the English Housing Survey, a government survey of housing standards which is updated each year. The survey splits tenure into three categories: owner-occupation, PRS and social rent. Of all different tenures, the social rented sector contains the most consistent standards of 'decency' – with only 10 per cent failing to meet the decent homes standard. This rises to 14 per cent for owner-occupied homes and 23 per cent for PRS. The social rented sector is also more energy efficient, with 66 per cent of dwellings in Energy Efficiency Rating bands A–C – for both PRS and owner-occupied, this figure is 42 per cent.[5]

The PRS is understandably the sector of the market most resistant to change; unlike social housing, consistent improvements are not able to be made by councils or housing associations to add accessibility improvements or repairs – and unlike in the homeownership sector, landlords responsible for these improvements do not have a vested interest in this kind of investment when they are not living in the property themselves. PRS was the only tenure type not to register an improvement in its decency rating between the 2019 and 2022 English Housing Surveys.

Other trends within the PRS sector are hastening these problems. The expansion of houses of multiple occupancy is seeing an increase in overcrowding – with associated wear and tear to properties. At present, approximately 1.1 million households in the UK are overcrowded,[6] an issue which has corollary issues for the upkeep of properties. Tenants on short-term tenancies have less investment in their home, and no incentive to invest in repairs or improvements themselves. Research from Octane Capital shows there are around 500,000 houses of multiple occupancy in Britain – reflecting huge growth which in turn is driving down stock condition.

In 2018, two years prior to the death of Awaab Ishak, Salford Council published a paper documenting the lived experiences of Salford residents in the PRS which chronicled horrendous conditions which were tolerated by PRS tenants.

The paper documented evidence of private renters paying significant sums for single-room bedsits, with inadequate amenities. Damp and cold were the most common problems referenced by residents – as well as waiting long periods for essential repairs, which were often shoddily completed.

One couple described their experience of damp weakening the structure of their daughter's bedroom wall:

> When we first moved in the roof leaked and that was leaking for about a year before [the landlord] fixed it. The little girl's room, the wall fell off … when [the landlord] eventually got it fixed, they literally just told them to slap some plaster in the holes, and now when it's raining you can just see it getting wet again.[7]

Other residents spoke of serious problems with accessibility. One resident, 'Lutfah', described a harrowing experience following her birth of a baby with serious health complications, for whom she had to leave work to become a full-time carer. The report documents Lutfah's tragic story.

> While Lutfah loved the flat itself, its position proved problematic. It was a top floor flat and the lift tended to break once or twice a month; on one occasion Lutfah could not leave the flat for four days because she could not get the special buggy and life-support equipment for her baby down the stairs. When she complained to the property management, they simply responded that she should not have taken a flat on the top floor. Meanwhile her support worker was trying to find her appropriate social housing and mediating with the property management company.
>
> After a year and a half of trying to find a more appropriate flat, Lutfah's child died. This meant not only tragedy and grief for her as a mother, but the beginning of a financial crisis as it triggered an immediate end to the living allowance given to her for taking care of her child.[8]

In 2021, the Building Research Establishment reported that poor housing costs the UK's healthcare system as much as £1.4 billion annually.[9] Furthermore, the paper states that these costs are the first year treatment costs only, excluding longer-term considerations such as loss of employee productivity, educational attainment and mental health.

In all, the quality of many PRS homes, and additionally the quality of service provided to PRS tenants, should leave us in no doubt that each and every year, significant numbers of tenants in both the social and PRS tenancies are being subjected to unhealthy, unsanitary and unsuitable conditions – many of these will be children. The impact of this poor stock both in related economic costs, and social costs, is huge.

New builds

In the UK, more than half of home buyers of new-build homes report 'major problems' with unfinished fittings, construction and faults with utilities according to Shelter.[10] The Home Builders Federation and National House Building Council carry out annual customer satisfaction surveys and have found that 99 per cent of new-build homeowners report at least one defect once their property is complete,[11] and on average, a new-build property in the UK comes with 157 defects according to industry specialists BuildScan.[12]

The BBC has reported new-build owner complaints including 'substandard ceilings to badly-fitted fire doors, missing insulation and condensation issues' – and the Homeowners Alliance report that only two-thirds of new-build homeowners report they are satisfied with their developer's response to resolve defects with their home.[13]

Further to this, around 5.2 million properties in the UK are currently at risk of flooding according to the Environment Agency – many of these are new-build properties built on flood plains, with 5,000 such homes approved for development in 2021 alone.[14] The poor quality of many of the UK's new-build homes has, in recent years, been picked up as a political priority. Defending previous accusations that volume house builders operated a 'cartel', in 2022 Secretary for Levelling Up, Housing and Communities Michael Gove stated that 'it's also been the case that some volume house builders have been producing homes that are shoddy and low quality'.[15]

Poor quality materials and practices play a significant role in creating these problems, as do lax planning regulations and huge pressure on planners to agree to new development following the introduction of the previous government's targets for building 300,000 new houses per year. Large-volume house-building could also be contributing to these issues, with staff on site under pressure to finish large jobs.

The lack of character in new builds has also been criticised, with identikit designs regularly used by the large-volume house-builders who today build over 88 per cent of all new homes in the UK. This has been framed through the conversations on 'beauty' by government, who have promised successive failed attempts to introduce new legislation to supersede the existing Town and Country Planning Act and address 'beauty standards' in design – yet it is unclear as to what measures are feasible to improve this situation within the present construction industry. Since 2021, the National Model Design Guide has been introduced as a framework through which local authorities designate 'provably popular design' in their local plans – however the problem with identikit designs is embedded more into the scale of volume house-building, and economic pressures exerting downwards pressure on the quality of materials.

The declining quality of new builds is a huge and growing issue within the British housing market, storing up huge economic costs in the medium-term future in repairs and replacements of shoddily developed properties. As the problem develops, serious long-term measures for reform of the construction industry and its approach to design will be needed.

Conversions

The issue of the conversion of unsuitable properties into residential units under permitted development rights has been subject to scrutiny in recent years, with allegations that many such conversions – particularly from office use to residential – are creating tomorrow's slums.

Through permitted development, additions or adaptations to a building need not be taken through the scrutiny of the planning process provided they fulfil certain stipulations or are deemed to be within the bounds of certain requirements. This effectively means no regulatory oversight of such developments. In recent years (particularly since 2013), government has been expanding the criteria for development which falls under the permitted development category in order to facilitate growth in housing, in particularly loosening criteria on 'converting' commercial office space from one type of development to another.

The London Labour Assembly published a report in 2019 detailing the issue of such conversions, condemning moves by government to 'speed up' the planning system through the expansion of permitted development rights. The report found that 59 per cent of London's permitted development homes are smaller than the national minimum space standard, that only 0.4 per cent of such conversions have been defined as 'affordable', and that through these conversions London has missed out on an estimated 5,504 affordable homes based on the thresholds set in Greater London's Local Plan document.[16]

The report states that '[s]uch units often have few and small windows, no outdoor space, no storage space, and no play space outdoors' and that '[t]his brings significant health and social costs, and harms children's educational development'.

Although such developments have had a particular impact within London, permitted development has had an impact across the country. Cross-party local government advocacy group the Local Government Association estimates that through bypassing affordable housing requirements, such office to residential conversions have meant a loss of 18,000 affordable homes since 2015 – from a total of 73,575 conversions.[17] In 2019, a BBC investigation highlighted living conditions experienced by children living in Terminus House in Harlow, Essex, where entire families were placed by housing services into tiny 'studio flats' where children had to 'eat, drink and sleep in their beds'.[18] The Raynsford Review of Planning highlighted in the same year that permitted development conversions of office blocks were resulting in homes being delivered 'on isolated industrial estates that lack basic social services and amenities' such as schools and doctor's surgeries, causing many homeless families including lone mothers with young children being accommodated on polluted industrial sites many miles from their homes and communities.[19]

In 2021, attempts were made by several Central London Boroughs to restrict the use of permitted development but were blocked by government ministers.[20] Government policy continues to see the use of permitted development as a tool to expedite the delivery of homes.

With such shocking breaches of standards and quality among converted business to residential properties, it's no surprise many commentators are labelling these homes the slums of the future. The continued use of permitted development rights to create these units is a crucial factor in the present crisis of quality facing the UK's housing market.

Fire safety and building regulations

Following the disastrous blaze at Grenfell Tower on 14 June 2017, a rare national spotlight was shone on Britain's building regulatory framework, through the apparent absence of quality control and transparency which appeared to be in place following the tragic loss of 72 lives in the fire.

Early on into the investigation around Grenfell, Aluminium Composite Material (ACM) cladding was identified as the primary culprit of the fire – as it combusted at high speed around the exterior of the building, allowing it to climb through the structure, trapping residents inside. The panels contained a layer of polyethylene plastic held between thin aluminium skins – a material which has been compared to 'solid petrol' by experts in the construction industry.[21] Despite previous tests showing that an unacceptable level of fire risk from the product following particular methods of installation (installed with rivets the product reached a Euroclass rating of B, installed in cassette formation the product was so dangerous as to be considered unclassifiable), the manufacturer Arconic had advertised its product on the UK market with the highest fire safety rating (0) based upon a far more fire retardant version of the product manufactured and sold separately in the United States. The British Board of Agrément (BBA) certified the product for UK markets based upon this grading and the Euroclass B grading for its installation via riveting. Hundreds of thousands of square metres of the product was sold across the UK based on this certification – without public clarity on the dangers of its installation in cassette formation.

Further tests in 2013 saw even the riveted grade of the product downgraded to Euroclass C grade, leading Arconic to recategorise the product as an 'E' in February 2014 – however the early BBA certificate was provided by Arconic sales reps to the team refurbishing Grenfell Tower in April that year.

However, it was not simply the ACM cladding which was found to have contributed to the fire at Grenfell. Celotex RS5000 boards made from the highly combustible 'polyisocyanurate' (which releases cyanide gas when burnt) were also used as the primary insulation on the building. These boards had been approved for use as part of large-scale whole system testing which assessed its use as part of a more complex system of products – not as an individual product. However, following its certification through these whole system tests it was subsequently marketed as a fire safe product in its own right.

Additionally, an extremely popular form of insulation, Kingspan's 'K15', was also used on part of the facade of Grenfell Tower. This was a material which had been granted a BBA certificate in 2008 despite failing tests in 2007 which internal Kingspan documents described as a 'raging inferno' where the insulation was 'burning on its own steam' after the flame had been extinguished. The material gained further certification from Local Authority Building Control in 2009 confirming the product to be of 'limited combustibility'. When asked by a colleague through internal emails how the certification had been obtained, one Kingspan manager explained that 'we [Kingspan] threw every bit of fire test data we could at him, we probably blocked his server' and added that they 'didn't even have to get any real ale down him!'[22]

Siderise cavity barriers were also used within Grenfell following its own bespoke test, and subsequently marketed for use in large cavity spaces for which it had never been trialled. Aluglaze window panels were utilised to fill gaps between the windows in Grenfell, composing a thin aluminium sheet converted in polystyrene insulation boards.

Taken together, the extent of unsuitable materials used within the construction of Grenfell – including widely available and marketed materials used across the country – created clarity on the fact that the UK's regulatory system was failing entirely to protect UK residents from unsafe materials and fire safe systems being installed on British buildings.

Wider tests conducted on the flammability of available cladding materials further confirmed this view, when samples of materials taken from buildings up and down the country came back with a 100 per cent failure rate in 2017.[23]

Total failure of system testing was a clear sign that regulators did not even fully understand what they were testing for; following this methods were revised, and 'full system testing' of materials (which tested combustibility not simply of the materials themselves, but of the manner in which they had been installed) was implemented after the Association of British Insurers damned the British regulatory system as 'broken'.[24]

Following the publication of Dame Judith Hackitt's review into fire safety, it has become clear that following years of privatisation, the UK's building regulatory system has become vague, untransparent and lacking in accountability. With different certification bodies competing for custom from manufacturers, a privatised system of building control competing for custom from developers, and no need for an 'on site' verification of the fire safety or otherwise of a development by any specially trained individual, quality control has declined.

Additionally, the UK's labyrinthine 'guidance' documents for the use of materials and fire safe systems is so ambiguous, and often contradictory, that bureaucratic loopholes are rife in distinguishing safe from unsafe systems.

The process of deregulation and privatisation within the UK planning system since the 1980s has, thus, created an entirely unsuitable and ineffective method of planning control. Such a process has now been in place for over 30 years, meaning that millions of buildings have been constructed under an incredibly lax system of regulation which has not effectively been preventing unsafe materials or practices from being used in British construction.

Following the Hackitt Review, government reforms have focused on creating stringent design codes for buildings over ten storeys, but at heart, the complex interdependency within the British building regulatory system between mandatory building regulations and non-mandatory 'Approved Documents' is still in force, as is the privatised building control function which has seen a race to the bottom in standards on signing off finished designs. A system of 'Dutyholders' and 'Accountable Persons' has been introduced since October 2023, which aims to replicate the personal accountability of key persons through the course of a build, which would once have been recognised as a function of a clerk of works. However, this new system is significantly more complicated than the system pre-privatisation. Ultimately, perhaps the most damning account of the post-Hackitt reforms is that they only apply to high-rises: the system for buildings with seven storeys or less remains unchanged.

Salford's Kafkaesque cladding odyssey

While the government has been negotiating its reforms to building regulation post-Grenfell, local authorities, housing associations and high-rise owners and leaseholders up and down the country have been tasked with retroactively removing and replacing materials which are now deemed unsafe. The process of doing so, and the difficulties faced, have illuminated further the dysfunctional nature of both our building regulatory system, the lack of clear lines of accountability and the interplay with national legislation and Whitehall. Following the disaster, councils across the country engaged in a mad scramble to find the cash and resources to strip their dangerously clad blocks. While writing this book, I conducted interviews with Salford Mayor Paul Dennett in relation to his role as Chair of the High Rise and Building Safety Taskforce at Greater Manchester, as well as Deputy Mayor and councillor John Merry in relation to his management of the removal and replacement of cladding in Salford. Salford provides an interesting case study in the task of removing and replacing dangerous cladding – particularly due to the nature of the Private Finance Initiative (PFI) under which most of those blocks were run. None of the PFI blocks in Salford have yet had their works completed – along with a further 70 high-rise buildings across Greater Manchester. Mayor Dennett recalls his initial response to the tragedy at Grenfell.

> We quickly audited the high-rise buildings in the city and we did discover we have non compliant material on those buildings. Originally it was aluminium composite material (ACM). And our city council, as far as I understand, were the first in the country to say, we want to remove and replace this non compliant building material, and it was specifically present on the Pendleton PFI.

Councillor Merry also remembers the early rush to identify and strip the ACM-cladded blocks: 'The first approach was that we were prepared to lend the money to the PFI from council coffers in order to make sure that this happened. So we gave a commitment to actually sort out the money. We had the special council meeting to actually approve it.'

Salford Council convened a special council meeting to approve an emergency loan to rip the cladding from the blocks. But soon after the motion had passed to provide the finance, the payment was blocked by the Treasury. Councillor Merry continues:

> There wasn't a party divide on it. Everybody was absolutely committed to doing it, but then we had to get the approval of DCLG [Department for Communities and Local Government] to do it, and this is where the problem started. First they said, 'Oh, well, people on holiday, it's going to be a while before we can approve the release of this money'. And then they were umming and ahhing about it, not sure whether they wanted to go ahead with it or not, and said they had to get Treasury approval. The Treasury turned it down on the grounds that it was a private sector initiative and they weren't going to find the cash.

Both Mayor Dennett and Councillor Merry suspect that a desire to return the PFI's 'credits' to the Treasury, realising a budget saving, were driving the decision to block the loan. Dennett speculates:

> Was this about trying to get off the hook on PFI credits? Don't know, but certainly that is a question that I have in the back of my head. And, you know, they even,

I think, suggested this idea of crashing the PFI, doing away with it, dispensing it, and that obviously would get them off the hook on the PFI credits that they're putting in to do the work.

Councillor Merry agrees:

When we asked, 'What should we do?' the suggestion was that we should make the private finance initiative bankrupt and take the blocks into public ownership. I think that the Treasury had their eye on the fact that the credits that they'd given for the PFI wouldn't have to be spent.

According to Councillor Merry, the prospect of liquidating the PFI was never practical:

We'd have had to liquidate the company, and that would have caused a major issue. They [the Treasury] would have weaselled out of the fact that they would have had to contribute. We'd have had to find it from our own resources, with the possibility of a grant for both the tenants and the widespread aspiration for the area.

[The PFI] might well have resisted that too. I felt that they would have been entitled to compensation, and the whole thing, I think, would have taken years of litigation to unravel.

Salford, among others, continued to lobby for a funding solution for the Pendleton blocks. The efforts yielded some results – but sadly not for Salford's blocks. Dennett recalls:

The Treasury, reluctantly after a lot of lobbying and influencing, came forward with the building safety fund (BSF), which today is a very complex and elaborate scheme. But the bottom line is, they came forward with the BSF for social housing. Despite this being social housing, our PFI was still not eligible to actually apply for the BSF money.

And it gets worse, because we then knew when we were looking at this across the city, across Greater Manchester, a lot of private buildings also have non-compliant material on it. And the developers, their supply chains, the freeholders all of these people didn't want to take responsibility for this issue. And you know, government was trying to get them to take responsibility.

So then we're in the space of this is dragging on. It's taking time. People are now living in buildings where they've had joint inspections of the Fire and Rescue Service. The evacuation procedure has changed. They've got waking watches on site, so people literally walking the buildings, 24/7, to ensure safety. Some of them are moving to have fire alarms installed, a whole host of activity going on to ensure we don't end up basically en masse decanting all of these people from these buildings. Because if that happened, there would be a crisis, because all of those people would turn up to the city council's door.

Dennett, along with Mayor Burnham and Sadiq Khan, continued to lobby alongside civic organisations such as Manchester Cladiators, a group of residents affected by the cladding scandal. Dennett continues:

> Some of the situations they [residents] were facing were very personal. Their health and wellbeing was being hugely impacted, their properties were deemed worthless, they couldn't sell them, they couldn't remortgage. They felt trapped in something they devoted their lives to acquiring.
>
> I remember myself and Mayor Burnham and many MPs, I think it was just before one of the budgets, or the autumn statement, going down to London and having a big event outside Westminster. Sadiq Khan turned up, and we were basically lobbying Westminster and Whitehall to say enough is enough. The building safety fund is not adequate. We've got people who are living in homes which literally are valueless. They don't know where to turn. It's impacting their health and wellbeing. And you, central government, given that the building regulations were not fit for purpose, need to come forward with support for these people. Because it's not right that leaseholders, residents, tenants, innocent people, ultimately, in all of this, should have to foot the bill for utter incompetence.
>
> We won the campaign because government then announced that they would make money available for private housing. And the reason why that's quite interesting is because the PFI in Salford still couldn't apply.

Still trapped without recourse to funding, the PFI was forced to seek credit from the stock market. Councillor Merry recalls:

> [The PFI] decided, very sensibly in my view, they'd come up with the cash themselves, which they raised on the Irish stock exchange. I remember being advised that I needed to guard my public comments carefully, as my remarks were market-sensitive on the Irish stock market – a slightly bizarre experience.

But access to finance wasn't the only barrier:

> Now, what we then had to do is to find a suitable alternative to put on the blocks, and that took a hell of a long time, because the one thing we were clear about was there was no point in putting something on that was going to be inflammable or even flame retardant. You know, we had to get it right this time.
>
> So we had various materials which we then had to fire test. And the only place we could do an effective fire test was Dubai. So they took the materials after Dubai in order to test whether they were suitable. I remember being told we've done the test and they've not worked, we can't go with that particular material, so we had to continually look for an alternative to put on the blocks. Eventually we found it, but it's taken an awful long time in order to find it,

and then, unfortunately, you're in a bit of a queue, because everybody else is looking at the same material and wanting the same material for their blocks as well.

Once work finally began on the blocks, it was clear that far more would be required than simply re-cladding. Councillor Merry continues:

> I was chair of Gold [the council Committee leading on removal and replacement of cladding] and we spent an awful lot of time discussing why there was slowness in terms of the progress being made, because in some cases, there was issues around subcontractors not doing the work, but also there was all the work that required to be done internally in the blocks as well.
>
> When we started to remove the cladding, we discovered that the work that had been done to attach it to the side of the flats hadn't been do- I need to be careful, because there's litigation still going on. But it appeared to be a very sort of casual way in which it had been done. So we had to, as we took the cladding off, take photographs of how the actual ties that were involved in fixing the cladding to the side had been put in place. And again, that took a long time.

Today, works are still being undertaken on the flats. Mayor Dennett expresses his frustration with the Treasury for not enabling it to progress faster:

> So here we are, seven years plus on from Grenfell and those high rise blocks that were not compliant have still not had all the works done to remove and replace the non-compliant cladding. That is scandalous. We were the first council in the country to go public on saying we've got ACM on our buildings. We want it off, and we want to ensure the safety of those tenants and residents. So the question becomes, well, if you were the first mover, why seven years plus on hasn't it been done? And I think that's a genuinely legitimate question to ask. And the bottom line in all of this is, we've been stopped by the Treasury.

For both Mayor Dennett and Councillor Merry, the experience of removing and replacing cladding from the tower blocks in Salford presents more significant concerns about the UK's housing and regulatory system. Councillor Merry considers that the experience has transformed his perspective on the use of PFI:

> The whole point of the PFI structure is that somebody else assumes the risk because it's coming off the [Treasury's] balance sheet. The Council does not assume the risk, and we're willing to pay a little bit more, was the theory in order to minimise the risk, and in fact, we were ending up with the risk.
>
> I've become very doubtful about PFI as a solution, and therefore I want to try and move away from that, if possible.

For Mayor Dennett, Grenfell unearths more troubling concerns regarding the state of the UK's regulatory regime:

> Back in the day, we used to have something called a clerk of works that would be on site, observing the work being done and gradually work through in a very structured, thematic way, the different pieces of work to sign things off when buildings were being built. That stopped a long time ago, certainly way before I became the Mayor. And again, I think we've paid the price. We've increasingly involved the market in that regulatory environment, with people signing off whether or not a building is safe.

Dennett has further concerns regarding the feasibility of future work, which will be required under the new post-Hackitt regulatory environment:

> There's still this requirement for approved inspectors, which can be provided by the market. So an individual working for themselves, trained, certificated, there's only a scarce supply of these people who can actually sign these buildings off. So the economic consequences of all of this are quite significant. I don't think we've ended up with necessarily a less complex regulatory environment. We've probably ended up with a more complex regulatory environment within which the market still has quite a significant role to play, and that worries me. Because you know, what we've seen today post-Grenfell, is all of this complexity is about people limiting their liabilities. And you know, it operates under the veneer of 'risk management'.
>
> [Under the new system] you have to look at this through the lens of just buildings over time and renovations and just work that is done to buildings that potentially could compromise some of the issues that shouldn't be compromised and should always be upheld, which points to a real weakness in the regulatory system (which has been exacerbated by, you know, 14 years of austerity). It [austerity] has meant a huge de-skilling of the public sector, and it's also meant that people are no longer trained through higher education, further education, to be in the labour market doing this work. So to be able to tackle all of this will require us to also properly embrace the skills and works deficit that we're facing around how we deliver all of this work moving forward, especially in a new regulatory environment that, in and of itself, creates its own skills challenges.

4

Community and gentrification

In many areas of the country, the housing crisis is also experienced through pressures on long-standing communities, particularly in areas where high affordability pressure creates 'gentrification' (the pricing out of residents and their children from the areas they have lived in throughout most of their lives). Within the UK, these pressures have to date been felt most acutely in the Greater London and Greater Manchester conurbation areas, both areas which are widely celebrated within the development sector as prime examples of successful urban regeneration from post-industrial decline. However, increasingly, in many urban areas pockets of gentrification are occurring and gentrification is also emerging as an issue in rural areas, particularly those seen as tourist destinations with a high demand for holiday properties and short-term rentals.

Any rapid changes to the social and economic composition of an area can create tensions for communities – particularly in the context of residents being 'priced out' of housing and amenities. Such impacts are directly counterposed to many strategic intentions of both national and local government housing policies; yet at the same time are exacerbated by the approaches taken to house-building and community regeneration pursued by experts and policy makers. Creating areas of 'high value' is a central ambition of many local and national planners, driving investment into new and old building stock, which increases housing numbers, housing quality and improves the public realm and social amenity. Yet, in doing so, an affordability crisis is created in many areas which has a deleterious impact on long-standing residents, their ability to access and enjoy the areas in which they have lived their lives, and the ability of their children to continue living in those areas as well. The inability of many areas which have succeeded in achieving growth in the number of housing units to square this growth with increased affordability and availability of housing as a commodity for long-standing local residents is a stark reminder of the complexity of the housing crisis faced by the country. This issue is accelerated further in instances where international finance and investment begins to view accelerating property and house prices as a source of safe investments – creating demand for 'luxury' products which are never intended for first-time buyers or domestic residents. The building of 'luxury flats' is a hot political issue in many British cities, particularly so in Greater Manchester and Greater London – as significant numbers of new units delivered are sold offshore before even being completed.

The desirability of areas of high value also leads to another unintended consequence – tourism and the increasing prevalence of 'party pads' and short-term rental units used by visitors, often creating tension with long-standing residents. The impact of 'Airbnb' properties on local housing markets not just in urban centres but also in the countryside, particularly small villages, is increasingly cited as a problem which is driving up localised inflation of house prices and preventing their use by residential occupants in favour of short-term visitors. This issue has already resulted in localised instances of restrictions on Airbnb lets in certain areas of the country, such as a limitation on the length of rentals in London to 90 days without an official change of use for the property, and a required licence for all short-term lets in Scotland.

Conversely – as certain areas of our economy are becoming more and more densely populated – other areas of the country are seeing very little in the way of development and housing and property price growth at a significantly slower pace – with high streets struggling for custom and few local employment opportunities. Our societal strategies for house-building in over-heated housing markets where returns are highest is inextricably linked to our national economic model, which is overwhelmingly focused on tertiary and service sector industries usually clustered around large urban centres and metropolises. By this model, development, employment and populations cluster around geographically specific centres of growth in which land and property become part of the investable proposition of an area – taking on the function of assets rather than homes.

New units, more units, are of course necessary – but the types of units, where they are located and who they are built for is also of key concern. The fact that significant sections of our house-building and real-estate industry appear to be contributing to a problem of house price inflation, the disruption of communities and damaging local economies – rather than solving it – is a stark indicator of the deeply complex nature of our housing crisis today.

Conclusion to Part I

The UK has both failed to build enough homes, and the right types of homes in the right places to keep pace with changing use and needs. The use of our housing stock is relatively inefficient as a result, creating huge bottlenecks in provision and contributing to uneven economic growth and development in different areas of the country. With house prices rising at twice the rate of wages over the past two decades, homeownership is increasingly unattainable – and renters increasingly face extreme cost burdens with median rents now over 30 per cent of income (compared with 14 per cent in the 1970s).

In numbers, it's clear that house-building rates have fallen well below the historically high levels witnessed from the post-war period until the late 1970s. Specifically, what has been lost from the delivery has been a ready supply of social and council housing – the absence of which, over time, has massively contributed to crises in other service areas adjacent to housing and the housing crisis. Concurrently, the UK has engaged in models for housing growth which, even at their most successful, prove to actively aggravate and intensify the underlying problems of availability, affordability and quality of housing which primarily make up our housing crisis through inflating values, worsening affordability and displacing communities.

The results are there for all to see. Homelessness and rough sleeping has exploded onto the streets of the UK in the past 15 years, as has the visible degradation of the street scene across many areas of the UK. Areas with large numbers of houses of multiple occupancy look increasingly run down, and the private rented sector in particular is failing to maintain a rate of improvement in standards seen in other sectors. Other less immediately visible questions of quality and quality control have also been made apparent in recent years, particularly the illumination of our failed building control system since the disaster at Grenfell Tower.

What is clear is that the UK's housing crisis is systemic, and not isolated to one or two areas of failed policy. The symptoms of this crisis – shortage of available homes, unaffordability, poor quality and the displacement of communities – are interconnected failures and deeply rooted within the policy decisions taken nationally.

PART II

Why policy is failing

It is very easy to be overwhelmed by the levels of dysfunction in the UK's policy and legislative landscape towards housing. The UK's housing crisis is not merely the result of short-term political dysfunction – it is the culmination of decades of policy missteps, ideological shifts and an erosion of the post-war housing settlement which still provides our general benchmark for 'normality'.

At the heart of this failure lies a lack of appreciation for the innovative policy solutions employed in that era which generated such a period of relative availability, affordability and increasing quality of housing. Between 1945 and the late 1970s, housing policy was guided by an integrated national vision connecting economic growth, public health and planning. Prior to this period, housing had never been affordable for most, nor good quality (with different conceptions of 'availability' in different historical epochs). For the first time, the average person on an average income could reliably and feasibly attain a house which met the contemporary standards in quality and decency, leading to a long-term and sustained increase in owner-occupation and the near historic obsolescence of age-old problems such as homelessness and rough sleeping. The kernel of this success was a system that prioritised large-scale social housing construction, state intervention to assure affordability, strict regulations enforcing housing quality and the construction of huge numbers of housing units, and one which restricted the availability of inflationary investments and credit. In effect, the chaos of a market-driven housing market was abolished through a connected chain of regulation, intervention and direct governmental control resulting in such a prolonged period of stability and improvement that the expectations developed during that period have remained so constant ever since.

Over the past 40 years, successive governments have not only failed to maintain the foundational principles that once ensured this phenomenon of widespread housing availability, affordability and sustainable improvements to quality of our housing stock – they have made a virtue of dispensing with these principles in and of themselves. As a result, we have witnessed policy inertia, market distortions and a chronic inability to address structural flaws.

Despite the growing acknowledgement that the system is broken, modern housing policy remains reactive, piecemeal and often counterproductive. The UK has cycled through 17 housing ministers in the last 15 years, with each administration introducing new initiatives that fail to meaningfully address the root causes of the crisis. Policies are often designed to stimulate demand rather than supply, leading to inflated house prices, a worsening affordability gap and an over-reliance on private developers who prioritise profit over need. They emphasise profit-making over delivery of homes – attempting to resolve housing shortages via indirect market incentives rather than focusing on resolving issues like homelessness directly through building and guaranteeing provision. To a great extent, they fail to appreciate the question of quality as a whole – privatising responsibility for the condition of housing stock to owner-occupiers and private landlords and dispensing of their strategic obligations.

This section will critically examine how government policies have failed on two key fronts:

- Misdiagnosing the real drivers of the housing crisis, leading to ineffective and contradictory policy interventions.
- Failing to achieve even their own stated policy goals, often exacerbating rather than alleviating the very problems they set out to solve.

Through this analysis, we will expose the policy decisions that have led us to this point, from the dismantling of social housing to the unchecked expansion of financial speculation in property markets. By the end the reader should, however, be in possession of a fairly comprehensive knowledge of the UK's present housing policy environment and the ways in which our policies are failing and even worsening present trends.

5

Delivery

In the UK, the delivery of new homes has been outpaced by the need for new housing units consistently for many decades. In the 29 years between 1951 and 1980, the UK saw a total of 8,263,000 new homes built. After factoring in the number of homes demolished through slum clearances and other losses, this amounted to a net increase of nearly six million additional dwellings. In the 29 years from 1981 to 2010, Office for National Statistics figures show that only 5,806,000 homes were built – a reduction in delivery of almost 2.5 million.

Something has happened to housing delivery in the UK which has significantly suppressed our delivery of new units for over 30 years. Between 1949 and 1979, housing completions averaged 327,000 a year. In 1968, the UK built over 350,000 homes – the highest number in history. From 1980 to 2018, the average number of completions was only 195,000 per year (ONS).

On the accession of David Cameron's Conservative government in 2010, a target was set to deliver 300,000 homes a year – increased from the Labour government's previous target of 240,000. This figure would equate to 8.7 million homes over a 29-year period up to 2040 – but the target has never been met. Between 2011 and the start of 2020, there were only 1,587,050 completions – 58 per cent of the target of 2,700,000. On these trends, over the 29-year period between 2011 and 2040 we could expect to see only 5,046,000 new homes completed – indicating that house-building continues to slow as policy levers are utilised to make it grow. Indeed, Bloomberg has recently reported that despite the continued growth of house prices, the UK's construction output is projected to continue to fall.[1]

In this chapter we will explore the UK's chronic housing delivery problem, why it is we are able to build so many fewer homes than in the past, and the failures of public policy to recognise or ameliorate the issue.

The planning system

Since 2010, the primary obstacle government has identified in terms of housing delivery has been planning authorities and their role in 'slowing down' development. This issue was central to the thinking behind many of the reforms to the planning system brought forward in the National Planning Policy Framework (NPPF) document in 2012, which introduced several reforms designed to streamline the process and place initiative in the hands of developers, as opposed to planning committees. The UK's planning system has long been pointed to by developers as a central reason for the under-delivery of homes, with industry campaigning bodies such as the House Builders Federation citing administrative costs for obtaining planning permission, as well as lengthy delays caused by under-resourced teams in planning authorities.[2]

This emphasis on reform of the planning system has also been taken up by Labour, with Labour leader Keir Starmer promising to 'bulldoze through' the planning system and 'get Britain building again'. At the 2022 Labour annual conference, Starmer stated in his address that a Labour government would 'fight the blockers' to build 1.5 million new homes and, since coming to office in 2024, Labour have majored on reforms to the NPPF and new powers to Combined Authorities to release land.

Since the Town and Country Planning Act was passed by the Labour government in 1947, the British planning system has remained broadly unchanged in its core structure. Under the act, all development proposals require planning permission from the relevant local authority, with subsequent rights to appeal decisions if a proposal is refused. The act also required local authorities to provide strategic planning documents for their areas – 'Local Plans' or 'Unitary Development Plans' – to designate the types of development allowable in different areas (such as property type, standards and materials and designs) (Town and Country Planning Act, 1947). Members of the public, councillors and prospective developers must be consulted through the planning committee process under these rules – with the public also able to make appeals against or in favour of proposals being brought forward.

In the original act, Section 52 agreements (planning obligation agreements) allowed local authorities to impose terms on the development such as contributions towards local infrastructure such as schools, transport nodes and affordable housing provision. A key reform in 1990 replaced Section 52 agreements with Section 106 agreements, allowed for more intricate and bespoke arrangements between planners and developers than those enabled through planning conditions in the Local Plan (Town and Country Planning Act, 1990).

Critics of the Town and Country Planning Act state that the requirement for individual planning permissions for every development reduces the certainty for builders, minimising their ability to buy land without planning permission for development and subsequently suppressing their output. Additionally, the mechanisms of democratic consultation and deliberation over plans is seen to add a layer of uncertainty and risk. Many cite the unique nature of the UK's planning system and its distinction from more commonly used 'zoning systems', where land is zoned with a series of accepted design codes, within which the development of new builds is assumed without specific permissions.

The green belt

Sitting alongside the UK's planning system is the 'green belt', a zoning designation in force around many of the UK's towns and cities designed to inhibit the development of previously undeveloped, agricultural or wild land. The creation of 'green belts' was enabled by the 1947 Town and Country Planning Act, as local authorities were able to create such designations within their Local Plans for development. The purpose of these designations was to constrain urban sprawl, both to conserve nature and wildlife but also to control the physical size of the UK's cities and concurrent strains on transport infrastructure.

When first introduced, green belt designations also sat alongside the development of 'new towns', a deliberate process of depopulating urban centres into planned developments and overspill estates such as Milton Keynes outside of London, Skelmersdale in Merseyside and Wythenshawe in Manchester. As such, the immediate effect of constraining the supply of land around the borders of cities was not immediately felt within the construction industry, and on prices. Green belts proved incredibly popular, both as havens for wildlife but also as perceived protection against overdevelopment within urban communities, and as a source of valuable amenity contributing to the desirability of neighbourhoods. Since their introduction, attempts to change the designation of green belt have regularly been met with stiff opposition – as such, the original green belt designations have become 'sticky', with few politicians or planners prepared to undergo the public opprobrium of their alteration or removal. The existence of the green belt has led, in many urban centres, to the building up of 'brownfield' sites or 'previously developed land'. This course has come to be referred to as 'brownfield first', a planning principle that available brownfield land should be exhausted before any encroachment on green belt is to be considered.

In recent years, however, green belt designations have begun to be identified by campaigners as a source of house-price inflation, restricting access to new developable land and suppressing the supply of new homes. In addition to restricting access to new sites, the alternative 'brownfield' sites are often contaminated with chemicals and pollution from their previous use (often in an industrial capacity) requiring costly remediation exercises. A 2023 report on behalf of Business LDN reflected this sentiment, stating that 'London's green belt was created to stop the city's physical growth when its population was falling', criticising many of the green belt designations as 'poor quality and inaccessible sites which serve no civic or environmental purpose'.[3] These criticisms have found a hearing within government, and since 2012 numerous mechanisms have been introduced or attempted to weaken green belt designation, particularly since the introduction of the 2012 NPPF.

The National Planning Policy Framework

Having identified the planning system as the central obstacle to development and delivery, government reforms have so far sought to mitigate the power of councils and the public at the planning stage of the process. One of the central thrusts of the 2012 NPPF reforms was a 'presumption in favour of sustainable development', which in effect reversed the relationship of planning authorities and developers within the planning process. Whereas previously it had been the onus of a developer to prove to a planning authority that its development was appropriate for the Local Plan of an area, with this reform it became the onus of a planning authority to prove that a proposal *was not* suitable, if it were to successfully reject it.

Another impact of this reform was to downgrade the status of green belt and brownfield first policies previously employed by local authority planning areas, which were able to prioritise the delivery of non-green-belt sites. Although it is still possible for local authorities to provide Local Plans which designate and protect green spaces, the burden of proof required to defend these designations at planning committees has substantially increased.

And a third impact was to significantly undermine the strength of planning authorities in negotiating Section 106 deals with developers. 'Sustainable development', as it is defined in the NPPF, refers primarily to the commercial sustainability of a development project. The presumption in favour of sustainable development in the NPPF also stipulates that should Section 106 contributions themselves damage the profitability of a given development (by convention, this is commonly assumed to allow for a profit margin of 20 per cent on any given scheme) that such contributions are not enforceable. In large areas of the country where values are low and margins tight, this change has effectively stripped local authorities of the right to demand such contributions towards the costs of upgrading infrastructure (such as providing new school places and doctor's surgeries, road improvements or contributions to affordable housing) that development can incur.

The NPPF further requires councils to provide a '5 year forward land supply', that is, provide a list of sites which will sustain a government-defined calculation for an area's housing need five years into the future. In addition to this, the concept of an 'objectively assessed housing need' has been introduced through which government use a methodology to calculate the housing need for a given area, for which a local planning authority must – by law – cater for.

Thus, with significantly truncated powers, and an obligation to provide a long-term forward supply of sites ready for development, government anticipated that planning authorities would no longer provide an obstacle to getting development off the ground.

Additional proposed reforms in the government's 2020 Planning White Paper threatened to further remove the powers of both communities and local authorities from the planning system, creating a 'zoning' process within which developments which conformed to a series of design codes signed off in Whitehall would not require planning permission. Under these proposals, the only participation both local authorities and the public would play in the planning process would be through periodically participating in consultations on strategic plan documents which, once set, would operate on the basis of assumed planning approval for all developments within zoned areas which conformed to the design codes and overarching rules set by Westminster.

Although Gove's announcement of the Regeneration and Levelling Up White Paper in February 2022 backtracked on many of these proposals – the reforms in the 2020 Planning White Paper were revealing in their intentions, and abided by the prevailing logic of government policy in regards to planning and development for the past decade. This assumption has been continued by the current Labour Government, with Prime Minister Starmer committing to renewed housing targets, release of green belt land and a new Planning and Infrastructure Bill which will 'back the builders not the blockers', reducing the delegation of decisions to council officers.

Evidence: the planning system

However, evidence suggests that the problem with the UK's sluggish delivery is more complex than local authorities slowing or blocking development through their planning powers. In February 2020, the Local Government Association produced research suggesting that more than a million homes which had been granted planning permission in the preceding decade had not been built – with the number of planning permissions doubling in the period from 2012/2013 to 2020 and councils approving nine in ten applications.[4]

Local Government Association housing spokesperson, Councillor David Richard, said of the report: 'The planning system is not a barrier to house building. The number of homes granted planning permission has far outpaced the number of homes being built. No one can live in a planning permission, or a half built house where work on site has begun but not been completed.' Further, he noted:

> Councils need powers to tackle our housing backlog and step in where a site with planning permission lies dormant and house building has stalled. If we are to solve our housing shortage, councils need to be able to get building again and resume their role as major builders of affordable homes.[5]

The evidence that developers themselves are holding back on developing sites is now well established. In 2018, the government published the Letwin Review on 'how to close the significant gap between housing completions and the amount of land allocated or permissioned' – and among its findings was a conscious decision on behalf of developers not to build beyond the 'absorption rate', that is, the rate at which the market can 'absorb' new builds without pushing down house prices.[6]

This is not simply an issue of willpower. The thinking behind limiting construction to below the absorption rate is hard-wired into the business models of most volume developers. When planning for the construction of homes, developers will begin with a notion of a Gross Development Value (GDV) for a site, which incorporates the three parts of (1) the cost of land, (2) the cost of construction and (3) the anticipated profit. To balance out increasing costs of (1) land and (2) construction, developers generally attempt to control the price of their finished units by moderating their supply of homes as and when the market in that area is able to sustain a preconceived price.

Tim Heatley, founder and chief executive officer of the ethical volume developer Capital and Centric, discussed with me the rationale behind staggering the build out of sites during the writing of this book:

> They'll [developers] buy land in advance. They'll get plan permissions in place, and they'll forecast. ... Therefore, they'll have a forecast of what rate they want to sell them [the houses]. And that's based on two things; how quickly they can build them and how quickly they can sell them.
>
> What they like to do is literally build a handful, sell a handful, build and keep rolling on, because they realise that if they compete against themselves, if they start to build, you know, 50 at a time, and people got a choice of which particular plot they want, they've not really done themselves any favours. They're not recycling the cash quick enough, so they are incentivised not to build too quick.
>
> And if they accelerate construction a lot, the costs go through the roof, because all of a sudden, everything's happening much more quickly. They've got much more people on site that they're double-doing things. And so they've found that, even if you've got excess demand, and they can sell more houses, they'll often churn along, because they go, 'we can increase our output, but our costs will go through the roof – so we're we're just gonna keep nibbling away at it'. And that is a problem, because it doesn't ever affect the house values of the existing stock enough to change the game. (Interview with the author)

The Letwin Review findings have since been bolstered by an investigation from the Competition and Markets Authority in 2024, which found that 'speculative Private Development', refusing to build beyond the 'absorption rate', is contributing significantly to the UK's undersupply of homes.[7]

Given that 'affordability' is one of the primary concerns in relation to the price of housing, it should be shocking to policy makers that volume developers, as the primary vehicles we rely upon to build our way out of our present crisis, consciously refuse to take steps which would address this issue. With the top ten construction firms in the UK responsible for over 50 per cent of Britain's housing supply,[8] this matter is nothing short of catastrophic for any government intending to control house price inflation through increasing the supply of new homes.

Where evidence does point to the planning system as an obstacle to development, often it is focused on the lack of resource present in planning authorities, particularly since austerity. In the Competition and Markets Authority's 2024 investigation, lack of resource and staffing within planning departments was found to contribute to delays in permissions, creating a backlog of development and upfront costs for developers. This is, however, quite different from a fundamental question around the efficacy of the structure of the UK's planning system.

In short, as opposed to a potentially disruptive wholesale reform of the UK's planning infrastructure, evidence suggests that better resourcing would go a long way to delivering against the identified bottlenecks. Meanwhile, the real culprit of our under-delivery of homes lies elsewhere, in our overdependence on a small number of volume developers with no financial interest in solving the housing crisis.

Evidence: the green belt

Most professional and expert opinion is presently convening around the idea that reform of the UK's current green belt boundaries is a necessary prerequisite of achieving the country's housing targets. According to government data from October 2022, 8.7 per cent of the UK's land is brownfield, with 54 per cent of all new homes built from 2021/2022 on brownfield sites.[9] Based on statistics from 2019, the National Housing Federation estimates that across 25,500 available hectares of brownfield land, supply was sufficient to deliver up to one million net additional homes.[10]

The paper notes several obstacles to the buildout of these sites. Of the total available brownfield supply, only 12 per cent is in public ownership, 61.8 per cent not in public ownership, and the remaining 22.6 per cent with ownership unrecorded. Lack of access to this restricted supply of land impedes the ability of government or public authorities from mandating the development of these sites for the purposes of housing, and also in mandating the types of housing which would be developed.

Additionally, the paper notes that while 53.2 per cent of these sites have already been granted planning permission, 42.6 per cent of them are not permissioned, or have data unrecorded. Given the premium on land currently driving up housing costs, there is no doubt that current green-belt designations are limiting the supply of land and contributing to increased house prices.

However, the green belt does possess many valuable features which should be preserved. Both from an ecological and a town planning perspective, the case that the discipline of the green belt has prevented urban sprawl as well as preserving areas of natural beauty and wildlife is compelling. Green-belt restrictions have encouraged planners and builders to build up, rather than out – engendering the beginnings of a cultural shift in British housing consumption habits away from post-war semi-detached houses with gardens, towards mid-density apartment living and tenements which are in many ways more suited to urban development.

In any case, the green belt remains too popular to have been subject to significant reforms from government. Since the publication of the 2012 NPPF, mandated release of green belt to meet 'objectively assessed housing need' targets in Local Plans has been the subject of fierce contestation and debate, culminating under the previous government with new guidance issued by government in 2022 that release of green belt is 'not required' if 'building on green belt land [is] the only way of meeting housing need' – in other words, the release of greenbelt is not mandated to achieve objectively assessed housing need targets. Rather, government have opted to revise their 'objectively' assessed need methodology to skew more housing numbers towards large urban conurbations, and away from rural areas in which green-belt release would be required at scale (measures which have been partially reversed by the incoming Labour government in 2024). In late 2021, following the disastrous defeat for the Conservatives in the Chesham and Amersham by-election to the Liberal Democrats in a result widely attributed to local anger against development on green belt, the objectively assessed housing need figures were revised with a 35 per cent uplift given to urban centres – requiring those areas to discover thousands of additional plots overnight.

What is required in the case of green-belt redevelopment is a measured approach to releasing particular tracts of green-belt land which either lack alternative amenity as farmland or public access. Such an approach has yet to be trialled, though as of April 2024 Labour has committed to a policy of releasing low-value 'grey belt' sites from the Green Belt, with Deputy Prime Minister Angela Raynor announcing updates to the National Planning Policy Framework producing five 'golden rules' under which proposed developments may conform, which would favour their release. These rules require community benefits and mitigation for loss of green space. Such measures may well provide a politically sustainable answer to the removal of specific sites from the green belt, though at the time of writing their success is yet to be measured in tangible outcomes.[11]

Planning reform failure

The failure of government's planning reforms to spur new development is a symptom of a broader misdiagnosis of the core questions which sit behind the UK's inadequate supply of new homes. Prior to 2012, the Town and Country Planning Act had been in force with far more stringent terms throughout the entire latter half of the 20th century. Between 1949 and 1979, housing completions average at 327,000 a year. In 1968, this country built over 4250,000 homes – the highest number in history – with the Town and Country Planning Act firmly in place. Interestingly, the beginning of the decline in the delivery of housing units in the UK did not coincide with any great strengthening of the UK's planning and regulatory regime, but with the advent of the Conservative government in 1979. From 1980 to 2018, the average number of completions was only 195,000 per year, down annually by 163,500 from the previous few decades (ONS).

So what did allow for the continuous reduction in house prices and high levels of delivery through most of the 20th century, which doesn't apply today?

Planning restrictions

The interwar years, from the 1920s through to the start of the Second World War in 1939, saw one of the largest construction booms in Britain of recent times. During this period, house-building reached a peak of nearly 350,000 completions per year by the mid-1930s, before plummeting during the war. Between 1919 and 1939, Britain increased its number of dwellings by 50 per cent, from eight million to 12 million.

Local authorities provided significant numbers of units during this period of housing growth too – making up nearly all completions between 1920 and 1923 and roughly a third of completions between 1924 and 1932. Since the Housing and Town Planning Act in 1909, local authorities had the power to deliver council housing and many took up their new powers with gusto. Only 1 per cent of households were council-rented accommodation in 1914, but by 1939 this figure had increased to 14 per cent – and throughout much of the 1930s such completions amounted to roughly 50,000 units each year, delivering 100,000 new units in 1939. In the interwar years, a total of 1.1 million council homes were built.

However, during the most rapid period of building between 1934 and 1939 the vast bulk of homes were delivered by small private developers, and much of it on greenfield land in what are now considered to be the 'suburbs' of Britain's cities. Prior to the Town and Country Planning Act, there was very little restriction on building on greenfield land and, as such, the price of land was extremely low. During the 1930s, cities such as London and Birmingham doubled their footprint. This period saw the revival of the 'Garden City' ideal, fuelled by the rise of personal car use, designed in what is now the classic 'Tudorbethan' style favoured by the Arts and Crafts movement.

In this period, the average size of a dwelling also reduced to around 100 square metres – and cheap construction costs were driven by Lloyd George's 'cheap money policy' (close to zero rates of interest and expansionary monetary policy from the Treasury).[12] As such, 85 per cent of houses built in the 1930s cost less than £750 – the equivalent of around £37,000 today. Terraced houses in London in the mid-1930s sold for an average of around £395 – with average earnings at £165 a year.

Despite generally being of good quality (following design standards which in many ways exceed modern standards) the unplanned nature of this approach created large communities with limited access to green space, and overcrowded or poorly designed infrastructure. Particularly in London, private sector housing sprawled along arterial roads in 'ribbon developments', creating traffic problems and pollution. Widespread industrial dereliction in large areas of the North and the Midlands also continued untreated – as housing and regeneration investment was unevenly distributed across the country (this issue was documented by the 1940 Barlow Commission, which commented on the regional distribution of the industrial population and the 1941 Scott Committee findings on rural land use). The lack of planning in production was also featured strongly in the 1942 Beveridge Report on health and the delivery of the welfare state and delivering on the desire to achieve social equity and reduce poverty in the post-war period. Many of these failings precipitated the expanded planning powers included in the 1947 Town and Country Planning Act, and the increased role of planners and strategic state investment involved in post-war construction.

The loss of local authorities as developers

Between 1949 and 1979, homes built by local authorities amounted for almost half of all new-build completions – and in many individual years exceeded completions by the private sector. Between 1946 and 1957, of the 2.5 million new houses and flats built, 75 per cent were owned by local authorities. During the late 1960s, a combination of private and council house-building combined reached a historic peak of over 400,000 completions a year (ONS).

Through the New Towns Committee established in 1945, 22 new towns were founded between 1946 and 1972 using powers granted in the New Towns Act 1946. Despite such a large number of local authority built and owned homes, rates of homeownership vastly increased through this period, from 26 per cent in 1945 to 49 per cent by 1970. In total, around five million homes were built either by or on behalf of local authorities in the first 75 years of the 20th century – the great bulk of which were constructed from 1946 onwards – and as much as 40 per cent of the UK's population resided in council houses by the late 1970s.[13]

But between 1979 and the mid-1990s, this number reduced to only a few thousand completions per year – and by the late 1990s and 2000s, it reduced again to the lower hundreds. In 2004, local authority building reached its nadir at only 130 homes. This trend continues until this day, where despite recent upticks in council house builds, the number of completions fails to increase beyond a few thousand per year.

However, in this time the number of private sector or housing association completions barely rose at all to cover the shortfall. In effect, almost half of the construction market fell away from 1979 onwards – and was never replaced. The collapse of councils and local authorities as developers is undoubtedly the largest single contributor to the UK's incapacity to deliver homes at the scale it has historically done.

Costs of construction

From the cost of acquiring land, the cost of labour and the rapidly increasing cost of materials, the overall costs of construction are increasing steadily, which is playing a significant role in stifling new construction. In the UK, construction costs are relatively very high in comparison to other nations, with construction intelligence firm Arcadis International's 'Construction Costs 2024' paper finding London the most expensive city in the world to build, with Bristol, Manchester, Birmingham, Glasgow, Edinburgh and Cardiff all in the top 20 (more than any other single country).[14] On top of prevailing trends within the market, this situation is quickly worsening. Social housing provider and housing developer Network Homes announced in a 2019 report that its average build cost alone for a new home was £285,000, 9.6 times the average UK income of £29,559 in that same year.[15,16] With costs for construction reaching unaffordable highs, it begs the question how new builds can be expected to deliver affordable products without subsidy. The root of the UK's inflated costs of construction has several causes.

Materials

In 2022, the cost of raw materials in the UK had increased by 19.8 per cent on the previous year according to the Building Cost Information Service (BCIS) Materials Cost Index.[17]

Throughout the COVID-19 pandemic, these costs had already increased five-fold to a 40-year high according to the Office for National Statistics. The director of BCIS, James Fiske, estimates that these increases have increased the cost of building a three-bed semi-detached house by 14 per cent – or £7,300.[18]

Since the Russian invasion of Ukraine, material costs have been impacted further with both Russia and Ukraine critical suppliers of metals, raw materials, chemicals and machinery. Ukraine is one of the world's leading producers of uranium, titanium, manganese, iron and mercury ore – and has the third largest shale gas reserve in Europe. As is well known, Russia historically supplies 40 per cent of European gas and 30 per cent of its oil – which are being curtailed by responsive sanctions.[19]

Neal Morris of the construction specialist legal firm Pinsent Masons has noted the increased inability of firms to pass on increased costs to consumers, documenting the recent insolvency of independent construction contractor MIDAS which left £20 million in unsecured debt following insolvency in January 2022: 'Midas is a very good example of how passing the extra cost down to supply chain customers no longer works as the vast majority of contracts are not short-term contracts.'[20] These increased costs of construction have had a huge knock-on effect within the housing market, contributing massively to the cancellation of new developments and the increasing cost price of finished homes.

Finance

Another by-product of Russia's invasion of the Ukraine has been a tightening of the availability of cheap finance. To combat fears of runaway inflation, central banks have globally raised interest rates and investors are concerned about the unpredictability and sustainability of projects and companies within the new environment. Both of these factors mean fewer sources of available finance, and less favourable terms on the finance which is available.

Increased borrowing costs both increase the cost of new builds for buyers, and simultaneously suppress demand for mortgages. The impacts of these changes were felt immediately by the construction industry, which saw the sharpest plummet in housing completions since the 2009 crash during the credit crunch only a month after the Bank of England raised interest rates to 4.5 per cent in May 2023. This proceeded from several years of falling housing completions, beginning in the COVID-19 pandemic and continuing from the introduction of the first interest rate rise by the Bank of England in December 2021.

The rate of inflation is beginning to show signs of slowing as of early 2024, yet remains at a stubborn 3.1 per cent at the beginning of March. The new material price increases are now baked into supply chains and unlikely to fall – and will remain an ongoing barrier to producing affordable housing for many years.

Skills shortage

Perhaps more concerning than the increasing cost of materials in the construction sector is the increasingly apparent lack of labour. According to the Office for National Statistics, there are nearly a quarter of a million fewer workers in the construction sector in 2022 than there were in 2019. The Construction Leadership Council has also warned that 'diminishing labour supply is now of greater concern than product availability in most construction sectors'.[21] The Construction Industry Training Board estimates that an additional 216,800 new workers will be required by 2025, with major projects like HS2 as well as housing creating a surge in demand.[22]

These concerns have been echoed by BCIS consultant Joe Martin, who has predicted:

> The pressure on materials prices and availability is expected to continue at least until the end of 2022. Labour shortages are expected to evolve as the significant driver for overall construction cost increases next year and the construction sector would need to compete [with other sectors] for [these workers].[23]

'The Great Resignation' – a phenomenon associated with the large number of working-age people who have voluntarily retired or resigned from their posts throughout the COVID-19 pandemic, has had a substantial effect on this process over the last few years. However, as early as 2016, chronic concerns about poor workforce planning in the UK construction sector were raised by industry specialist Mark Farmer in his review 'Modernise or Die', an overview of the British construction industry.

Among other factors, Farmer identified a lack of 'vertical integration' as key to the workforce planning issues which have plagued the British industry for decades. Whereas in countries like Germany, developers would usually 'vertically integrate' their business, employing construction staff in-house, providing long-term training pipelines and sometimes even managing and letting the properties they build at the end of the process, in Britain the construction system is often fragmented into a series of contractors, all responsible for a small constituent part of a development with no long-term strategic approach to future skills development or training. From an article written for *Construction Management* in 2021 by Farmer, the result of this system was an industry which was 'over-reliant on migrants, including EU nationals, and a perennial problem of failing to attract young talent'.[24] Farmer further noted that '[d]eclining resource resiliency, an increasing inelastic labour pool and a structural decline in competence, skills and learning exacerbated by the favoured models of employment and training the industry had moved towards in order to be flexible had created a self-fulfilling prophecy of declining productivity and capability'.

In Farmer's 2016 review, he bemoaned the use of 'self-employed' labour, short-term contracts and outsourced agency labour, noting: 'The recent advent of employment intermediaries or umbrella companies has further cascaded reluctance to directly employ labour down the supply chain and increased the distance between employment and the top tier transaction interface and between the end client and industry.'[25]

Following Britain's exit from the European Union, the long-term failure to plan and train new recruits to construction skills and training means that this historic dependency on migrant labour has created a particularly acute crisis in labour supply, and a chronic concern over declining competency and skills.

Without serious measures to combat the skills shortage, this key cost of construction is only likely to increase and our capacity to deliver new homes dwindle.

Structure of UK construction industries

We have already mentioned the Farmer Review findings on the lack of vertical integration in British construction in relation to workforce planning. But the impact of a lack of workforce planning has broader implications on the productivity of UK construction than simply a failure to strategically plan its workforce.

In Farmer's opinion, this fragmented system has created a situation in which productivity gains are generally sought by sweating labour on individual projects, or tailoring bespoke solutions to site by site issues, rather than investing in long-term strategic measures such as modern methods of construction, off-site manufacturing and new printing technology.

It also means the creation of a wasteful bureaucracy, in which energy and resources are spent managing contracts as opposed to directly delivering on projects. In Farmer's own words:

> The lack of integration across the supply chain, manifested in a wide-scale use of sub-contracting and tiered transactional interfaces is commonplace. This has created significant non value add costs in the supply chain through multiple on-costing, downward and often inappropriate risk transfer. This leads to an industry that tends to be cost focused rather than value focused.

He further adds:

> A natural consequence of fragmentation is that those tiers of the industry closest to clients or indeed forming parts of clients' organisation themselves have effectively become process managers for a wider cascaded supply chain rather than having direct delivery control by employing their own workforce.
>
> In this regard, the terms 'housebuilder' and 'contractor' are now potentially misnomers as the physical delivery is largely done by others.[26]

This fragmentation in the delivery arm of the UK construction sector is commonplace and easy to see. In 2018, the *Financial Times* reported from the construction site of the 'Can of Ham' – a colloquially nicknamed £135 million 24-storey development in London city centre. On the site, 41 subcontractors were responsible for the employment of over 400 workers, hired on a weekly if not hourly basis. The article comments on the outsourcing culture of the UK, noting that large contractors 'focus almost exclusively on winning and managing contracts, before outsourcing the rest of the work to the Small and Medium-sized Enterprises (SMEs) that make up 86 per cent of the UK's construction workforce'.[27] Noble Francis of the Construction Products Association is quoted, claiming that the small profit margins of contractors mean that they 'focus on pushing risk and cost-cutting down on to subcontractors'. Francis argued further that this was the model undertaken by Carillion, the now bust large contractor which was found to be willing to win contracts sometimes at even negative margins, then squeezing the supply chain, renegotiating contracts and extending the terms of payment.

The Institute of Civil Engineers claims that this 'highly transactional' model – involving lawyers and consultants at every stage – is central to the relatively high cost of construction in the UK, 'promot[ing] adversarial behaviours and the poor allocation of project risks'.[28]

The fragmentation of structures, lack of accountability and multiple intermediaries doesn't only have a financial cost. The construction sector is one of the worst offenders in the non-payment of wages to labourers, often linked to the 'self-employed' status of labourers as subcontracted support.[29] In some cases, these cases can boil over quite spectacularly. In 2018, workers on Regent Road in Manchester and Salford downed tools and blocked one of the main arterial routes into the city centre with their vehicles following an alleged £300,000 non-payment from their contractor.[30] In 2019, a viral online video appeared to show an aggrieved labourer destroying his work on the frontage of a Travelodge with a digger following his allegation that he had several hundred pounds in unpaid wages.[31]

In all, the wasteful structure of the UK's outsourced construction industry adds significant costs to production – even outside of recent supply shocks and price inflation. The UK's particular model of outsourcing and contracting is unique in the developed world, embedding bureaucratic administration costs throughout the supply chain and removing strategic oversight and accountability for the delivery of projects. No wonder that the UK's construction industry consistently fails to deliver to cost, on time or with decent quality.

The commercial development model

During the writing of this book I conducted an interview with Tim Heatley, the founder and chief executive officer of the volume developer Capital and Centric – an ethical developer with a series of social value principles underpinning its developments. I asked him what rules the company followed in regards to their developments:

> Lots of restoration and conversion of historic and important buildings, everything we do is super energy efficient, everything has to be exemplary architecture that's democratically accessible (so public spaces, public realm and so on). If we develop homes, those homes are either sold to owner-occupiers or they are rented out as a good landlord. And two-thirds of all the homes that we develop are affordable in terms of judicial assessments of affordability (which takes an average income of an area and assesses the value of property and rents).
>
> We do workspace where there's high levels of unemployment and deprivation and worklessness, so they're some of the key factors that we have. And we spend about three million pounds a week on regeneration, and that grows every single year.

The company is also in the process of becoming a 'Registered Provider' (a provider of homes at social rents under the Regulator of Social Housing). I also asked Tim the reasons behind this ethical framework:

> You know, partly because of mine and my co-founder's background in terms of us understanding the challenges around social inclusive development and the issues that society has, especially in urban areas, which is where we focus and develop. So that's one thing. But also, equally, it's not bad for business. If you want to get on, especially in Manchester, then you have to be seen to be wanting to improve not just your own life, but the lives of others. I genuinely believe that the public in Manchester help people who want to help others. So there's a sound business sense to it as well. I think that's important, because I never want to appear to be holier than thou.

I asked Heatley how Capital and Centric's differing emphasis distinguishes it from other large developers:

> A lot of what we build at day one hasn't made any money. If you look at the total cost and the total value, often it's not made money, sometimes made a paper loss, but we retain it and look after it and rent it out and improve it over time and become a neighbour to that neighbourhood. And we've noticed that over time areas improve if you spend the right effort and time and money on a place, they improve. And as therefore, vacancy levels improve, or voids decrease, and over time, rent will improve, and the whole ecosystem starts to improve. So that's how we've made a lot of stuff that people have said, 'You're mad', 'It'll never work', 'It's impossible', 'It doesn't make money'. That's how I've made them work, by taking a long-term view of value creation and being a patient investor in an area.

They [other developers] want a profit immediately upon completion. Sometimes they want the profit prior to completion. So what they want to do is forward, sell or off plan to abstract investors who could be anywhere in the world who will never see that building or development of that apartment. So they're very short-termist in terms of their view. They're looking to make money there and then and they're not really thinking about growing a business over a longer period of time.

Unfortunately, that's how the banks like to finance things as well. It's short term. They're not looking for long-term value creation. So in a way, it's not necessarily just about the developer. It's the necessity from the funding system being structured in such a way that they have to de-risk and create immediate profit.

The other thing that they're probably thinking is the profit margin they're looking to get is about 20 per cent margin on the total cost. So if they're going to spend £10,000, they're looking to make £2,000 profit, and often there'll be lots of different bits of capital involved in that. There'll be an investor, who could be a corporation, venture capital, private equity, or it could be high net worth, or a collaboration of high net worth individuals. They'll want their share of the money. And then there's a bank. They want their share of the profit. And there'll often be a mezzanine finance bank as well, who loan the big risk money on top of it all. So the developer has to pay all those people. That's why the profit margins have been chunky. Profit margins that they need to spread around all the people that have financed the project.

Heatley believes that Capital and Centric's 'patient' model allows them to build where other developers can't, providing more affordable accommodation as a result:

I mean, one of the big things is not selling them, because then you crystallise the loss. If you rent them, then you've got a chance that if you kick the can down the road you can reduce that loss and erode it over time, you taper it off.

If you're going to sell it, then almost all of a sudden you absolutely are crystallising the fact that those affordable houses can only sell for less than the cost you put there. That's the first thing. And the second thing is us taking a reduced profit. But as you said, it's a view in the round. We can't always do it for nothing, because we will go bust. And that's no good to anybody. So there has to be some areas that we can make a return and so they're the key factor.

I think you can see one of the benefits is that so much of what we develop is already in an affordable location. So for example, Farnworth, in terms of Greater Manchester is one of the cheapest places to own a home in all Greater Manchester. So in a way, it already is a more affordable proposition.

Heatley believes that the standard model for commercial development incentivises profiteering at the expense of both build cost and affordability, but believes that many such construction companies are bound by their financial model. He believes Capital and Centric's privately funded model allows the company to think more strategically, and develop further 'vertical integration' of its functions:

> We didn't want to involve shareholders or funds or banks, because they would steer us away from that long-term view of value creation, but they're also short service. And so as time goes by, we're able to do that. We've become more vertically integrated, whereby we can add the different end to end bits.

Heatley cites concerns, however, that in many instances vertical integration of volume developers fails to feed down into greater quality or value for customers, and is instead contributing towards suppressing the ability of small and medium-sized developers to grow:

> They have construction in-house so they can invest in training, they can invest in long-term workforce, they'll even buy brick kilns and other things. But what they seem to have done in integrating vertically, is just allow each profit centre to make a profit. So rather than say, 'Oh, that's great. Now we can make bricks ourselves – we'll be able to reduce the cost of houses' they've said, 'No, that just allows us make more profit now because we own the brick company'. And that's how commerce works.
>
> But if you look at the profit per house for a major house builder, it's huge, huge profit per house. And they're the dominant in their market as well. They dominate so much of the residential market because they're very hard to compete with. They've driven their construction costs right down, which means that it's hard for a 'Dad and lad' house-building kind of business to compete with them, because it costs 'Dad and lad' a lot more to build stuff.

In Heatley's view, this crowding out of small and medium-sized developers is leaving the UK government exposed to a reliance on a small number of organisations:

> I think in the past it was 80 per cent of house-building was done by those guys [SMEs] but it's flipped the other way around. So there's a lot of skills that got lost with all that as well. So it means that the government becomes very aligned upon a very small number of organisations to deliver houses and affordable houses as a result.

For Heatley, the delivery of affordable housing does more than simply provide new homes; it also disciplines the private rented sector to improve the quality of its stock:

> If you can deliver affordable housing, you can motivate people to leave their existing poor quality housing behind, move into affordable housing, and then the landlord is forced to deliver higher quality homes. So I think there's a bit of a gap

there in people's analysis of affordable housing in terms of how important it is. It's not just about building affordable housing. It actually creates movement and improves the quality of all housing as a result, because landlords end up being forced to improve what they've got.

However, despite a commitment to affordable homes, Heatley believes that significant government intervention will still be required to deliver what is needed at scale. We began with a rough calculation of the build costs on an average sized UK home, with a footprint of 67.8 metres squared:

So if you put in £1,750 per square metre, that must be £118,000. Plus your roads and infrastructure, and that's just construction costs. So you've got finance costs, you know, you've got professional services costs, and you've got marketing costs, interest costs, all your stuff on top. Which is why you soon get up to a couple £100,000 (£200,000) by the time you've worked all that out. Then you've gotta add the landing on top, and the developer's profit – so that's £240,000. Plus the land – so let's say 20–30 grand the plot – you're up to £260,000, £270,000 before you've even started.

With such high costs of construction, Heatley believes that a large-scale government programme of building must be prepared and financed if we are to achieve our targets, akin to the 1940s:

We've got to have a collaborative effort. Because if you work in industry, you realise there is an issue. Developers have got to play their part, and we are absolutely a part of the solution. ... We need to be honest about it and collectively accept the amount of money that's needed to go into it, and realise it's going to be a good big government programme to make it happen. That'll be great for the industry as well, because we're going to need our development skills to deliver opportunity for everybody, a bit like it was in the 1940s, and lots of businesses are really on the market. We're gonna need to see something like that.

Land

Access to land for development in certain parts of the UK has become a hotly contested space in recent years, as prices continue to rise. Despite rising costs of construction, and a struggling market, both the price of houses and land for development continues to increase.

While 'developers' are often seen as the face of many unaffordable developments, it is landowners who often take the largest relative profits from the value from a development through the initial sale price. Typically, land makes up around 67 per cent of a residential property's value in the

UK – and the Office for National Statistics believes that £6.3 trillion – or three-fifths – of the UK's total net financial value of £10.7 trillion is land.

When approaching a site for development, developers calculate a GDV based on three inputs: (1) the cost to acquire the land; (2) the cost of developing the land; and (3) the profit made on top of costs. Thus, in a state of competition for scarce land, the cost to acquire the land is raised, raising the entire GDV of a site without any direct benefit to the developer.

Typically, in a context of high competition for sites (such as present market conditions in many areas of the country), the winning 'bid' on a site for development will be one which pushes for a combination of the highest price for their units, the highest number of units (density) and the lowest cost of construction possible. With land scarcity, therefore, also comes a squeeze on affordability as well as a push for more density and poorer quality materials and reduced labour costs.

Government has seized on land value as a core element of rising construction costs and has attempted to free up more land supply to bring it down, primarily through two mechanisms: reforms to the planning system and the privatisation of public land. We will explore both of these policy mechanisms in what follows.

Changes to the planning system

We have discussed the primary impetus of the NPPF earlier in this chapter, reforms which have implemented a 'presumption in favour of sustainable development' into the planning system and required local authority areas to introduce a five-year forward supply of sites for developers to choose from.

These reforms have, undoubtedly, increased the availability of greenfield sites for development in particular – and have spurred local authorities with old plans to renew them to identify the new sites. However, in many cases the land provided is still insufficient to overcome the general cost increases associated with procuring land, while in many instances reaching and often overstepping the boundaries of local political acceptability from affected communities.

Since introducing the new requirements, across the country localised campaigns have raged against local spatial plans which have included many valued greenfield sites. Conservative Home Counties heartlands, in particular, have been beset with disputes with their residents infuriated by the inclusion of these sites in local spatial planning documents. Local planning disputes have been credited with many local political successes for both Green and Liberal Democrat candidates in Home Counties areas, including the huge by-election upset in Chesham and Amersham which saw a gigantic 25 per cent swing to the Liberal Democrat candidate, Sarah Green, in June 2021. Following the election, Liberal Democrat leader Ed Davey noted in reference to the now scrapped 2021 Planning White Paper: 'Above all here, actually, was the proposed planning reforms which will give so much power to developers and take away from communities and not result in the affordable housing people need.'[32] In that document, put forward by then housing secretary Robert Jenrick, it was proposed that 'development zones' in which planning permission was assumed (following a tick-box criteria on quality and design codes set in Whitehall) were to replace the current system of planning permissions from local authorities.

Due in part to these protests, the Conservative government's commitment to increasing the supply of land via planning reform has been limited and inconsistent. In December 2020, government revised its formula for the 'Standard Method' of allocating housing numbers to local authorities, reducing the numbers of new homes required in many areas of the country (particularly in rural areas) while applying a 35 per cent uplift in numbers to the 20 largest cities and urban centres in England – reallocating the political burden of development away from painful political protests from among the core Conservative-voting constituencies. Though no methodology for these changes was provided, mathematically the changes balanced the housing targets nationally at the 300,000 a year target government had set previously.

And in May 2022 Michael Gove announced that the 2021 White Paper plans were to be scrapped as part of the Regeneration and Levelling Up Bill 2022.

In short, increasing access to land via changes to the planning system have proven too controversial for the government to pursue. The new Labour Government has opted to recommit to the government's 300,000 a year target for new homes – reintroducing mandatory house-building targets for local authorities and redistributing these targets for a more equitable regional spread. The new government may find itself under less pressure from the Home Counties, but the commitment to targets is still to be politically tested over the course of the present Parliament.

Privatising public land

The second strand of government policy towards increased access to land has been the sell-off of public assets, which has been ongoing for decades but sped up significantly since 2010.

As documented in *The New Enclosure* by Brett Christopher, over two million hectares of public land (equivalent to 10 per cent of the land mass of Britain) has been sold to private interests since 1979 – leaving another two million hectares within public ownership, roughly valued at £420 billion.[33]

But since 2010 and the start of public sector austerity, land sales have been consciously used by government both to supplement the supply of land for housing and also plug the gaps in public sector financing.

In 2013, government launched the 'One Public Estate' programme – a strategic approach to combining and then selling public sector land to create space for housing and commercial space and launched with a budget of £31 million. In 2017, the project was co-opted into the Ministry for Housing, Communities and Local Government's 'Land Release Fund' – specifically designed to deliver new homes.[34]

The same approach is taken across government departments. In the 2022/2023 strategy document for Homes England (formerly the Homes and Communities Agency) a key stated objective is 'unlocking land' by 'releas[ing] surplus public sector land for housing', as well as recommitting to

> Continue disposing of our surplus public sector land holdings under the government's Public Sector Land programme 2015–20.
> Drive forward the delivery of public sector land by working with other government departments, including through land transfers and partnership working.
> Unlock public and private land, with capacity for up to 27,000 homes, by funding on-site infrastructure and land remediation on small sites through our Small Sites Fund.[35]

National Health Service (NHS) Property Services, a wholly-owned state entity established to manage and run the NHS's property estate in 2013, also had as part of its core shareholder aims to '[m]ake operational savings of at least £57 million by the end of 2015–16' and '[r]elease land sufficient to allow the building of at least 991 new homes by the end of 2014–15, in support of the government's priority to create 100,000 new homes'.[36]

As of the end of 2017, 295 NHS properties had been sold through NHS Property Services totalling £203.3 million.[37]

And Network Rail, in 2019, were forced to relinquish their railway arches to finance their capital infrastructure programme.[38]

In 2019, an investigation by the Bureau of Investigative Journalism and HuffPost UK found 12,000 public spaces sold by councils to private hands since 2014, including anything from metropolitan libraries to small patches of scrubland. These sales achieved £9.1 billion of capital receipts for councils, much of which was found to have paid for cost-cutting and redundancy payments since April 2016.[39]

And in 2019, the *Guardian* reported that over half the land in the country is now owned by under 25,000 individuals – many of them foreign nationals or entities. In total, government claims to have sold 25 per cent of the public estate since 2010.[40]

But despite significant amounts of land made available for development, the price of land continues to climb. Furthermore, valuable plots of land sold by public sector bodies to finance their capital expenditure or service budget deficits amount to a loss in public sector assets of billions, in an entirely unsustainable fire-sale of properties which could otherwise be put to practical use at significantly lower cost. The sale of public land, as opposed to its development, is a huge missed opportunity to provide a substantial contribution to the UK's housing supply at reduced cost.

The financialisation of land

In his book, *Why Can't You Afford a Home?*, Josh Ryan-Collins argues that a significant part of government's error has been in failing to recognise the unique characteristics of land as a commodity: 'Two of the key ingredients of contemporary capitalist societies, private home ownership and a lightly regulated commercial banking system, are not mutually compatible.'[41] Collins argues that land is unlike many commodities, in that it is 'immobile, irreproducible and appreciates in value over time'. When this key feature of land is considered, it becomes clear that supply alone is not the only issue feeding into the constant inflation of land prices. A significant part of land's inflationary rise is the fundamental inability of land supply to keep pace with the ever-increasing amounts of investment directed into land and housing as a commodity.

Research from King's College London in 2018 estimated that between 2003 and 2015, overseas investment alone had directly added up to an additional 19 per cent onto UK house prices.[42]

The UK's financial system, along with that of other countries in the West, underwent significant structural transformations in the 1970s and 1980s. Prior to this period, banking was segmented into areas of speciality – with commercial banks, investment banks, life assurance, fund management and housing finance all operated by institutions focused on their particular areas of financing. While clearing banks provided services for domestic commercial partners, and investment banks provided finance for international interests, house-building capital was provided primarily through building societies – demarcations in roles which were enforced through exchange controls and lending constraints.

The first of these lending constraints was lifted in 1971, with Competition and Credit Control deregulation and the abandonment of the 'Corset controls' which saw the British state lose most of its direct controls on credit creation, instead relying on interest-rate manipulation to govern lending. The impact of these reforms heavily impacted small clearing banks operating within the UK, with access to international capital project financing opportunities.

The second was the removal of exchange controls in 1979, a move which again increased global financial competition from overseas banks impacting on domestic clearing banks. In the early 1980s, those banks began to diversify into the mortgage market, breaking apart the lending cartel which had restricted price growth and rationed the quantity of lending between building societies.[43] The last act of significant deregulation came in 1986, with the deregulation of the London Stock Exchange, enabling international mergers and takeovers, opening up London's market to international banks (an event known within banking as the 'Big Bang'). Following this change, the old separations within banking began to merge – particularly the distinction between traditional bank lending and securities (such as mortgages).

Ryan-Collins argues that the adoption of mortgage-lending by Western banks was driven by the popularity of homeownership in the post-Second World War period, effectively replacing corporate lending as the primary function of a bank's business.

He notes that business lending equated to around 40 per cent of gross domestic product in most advanced economies during the early 1980s, with mortgage lending at 25 per cent. However by the 2008 financial crash, mortgage lending had grown to 75 per cent of gross domestic product.[44] This in effect amounts to billions of pounds of inflationary investment into land and property which cannot be matched by increased availability of land. Collins argues that this huge infusion of cash is the largest single institutional cause behind the ever-inflating price of land – as an asset-price inflation spiral which has now been embedded into the fundamental principles of most advanced economies.

It is partly due to the nature of land as a commodity and its ever-increasing value that speculation on land and property is also rife. The term 'land banking' is a loaded phrase within the industry – referring to the practice of acquiring developable plots without progressing their development, while the asset appreciates in value. The industry debate over land banking centres primarily on whether or not this activity is a conscious, cynical ploy by landowning entities to extract maximum profits from their land sales as opposed to a normal function of the property market and development. However, either way, it is well known that developers will control the introduction of new homes and developments to the market, as and when they can be built without surpassing the 'absorption rate' at which those new homes would drag down house prices – regardless of the numbers of planning permissions granted (in 2020, the Local Government Association reported that over one million homes with planning permission granted since 2009 are still not yet being built. These findings are corroborated by numerous other surveys, including a Grant Thornton report from 2019 finding that only 46 per cent of new homes given planning permission in London are ever built out).[45]

Such figures account for sites with planning permission – but in addition to this, 'strategic land banking' is the process of acquiring land without planning permission and gaining from the land-value uplift acquired through the planning process. Planning permission for residential can uplift agricultural land from an average of £21,000 per hectare to £1.95 million per hectare, according to UK parliamentary reports.[46] These kinds of numbers provide a huge incentive for developers or strategic land-bankers to scope out and purchase land holdings which may potentially be suitable for development in the future. And behind these numbers are huge numbers of potentially developable sites – either now or in the future – being traded upon as commodities, further building up their speculative value.

Having successfully integrated and, as a result, vastly expanded the role of financial services in the UK's economy we are now at the head of a debt-driven cycle of permanent inflation across not just housing, but all tradable assets. Bank-issued mortgage finance driving demand for homeownership is financing developers who build their homes, themselves often servicing debt to the self-same bank which was issued to purchase inflated land which had been invested in as a speculative commodity by an investor.

As was also proven by the political response to the 2008 crash, this new integrated banking system has become so integral a feature of our economic and political reality that it is in fact 'too big to fail'. With tendrils across every conceivable area of our economy and society, and no available mechanisms to discipline a sector which is assured of gigantic bailouts in event of any catastrophic losses, for the foreseeable future this spiral will continue unabated as a huge source of house price and housing cost inflation.

The failure of government to recognise the financialisation of land as a significant contributory stream to our housing crisis is a huge factor in the unsuitability and lack of direction within our contemporary policy discussion on the housing crisis. Present policy discourse fails almost entirely to recognise the scale or the severity of the contribution of finance to the question of ever-increasing costs within the land and property market, and thus housing. This lack of attention can only be attributed either to an unwillingness or inability to comprehend the underlying causes of the situation we presently face, as arguably the single biggest contributor to the runaway prices we see in this sector.

Government investment, subsidy and spending

But it is not just banks pumping money into the housing system, in turn increasing the speculative price of developable land. Government housing subsidies, particularly Help to Buy and Housing Benefit, pump billions of pounds more into the privately owned and buy-to-let housing markets each and every year. In addition to this, government spending on infrastructure – particularly transport infrastructure – also hugely impacts residential and commercial land values. One UK parliamentary report on land value uplift reports that:

> The Greater London Authority (GLA) and Transport for London (TFL) highlighted a study by real estate advisors, GVA, which found

that development dependent on the new Elizabeth line would create a potential value uplift of £13 billion in residential values and £215 million in commercial values by 2026. Julian Ware, from TFL, told us that methodology prepared by KPMG and Savills estimated that eight prospective transport projects in London, including Crossrail 2 and the Bakerloo line extension, could generate a land value uplift of £87 billion, although 65% of this would be realised in the existing residential market.[47]

It has partly been in response to this that in the last decade, a conversation about 'land value capture' has gained prominence within government, particularly in relation to aspects of the state and local government 'capturing' some of the added land value embedded into the system through their investments.

At present, several disparate mechanisms capture elements of value from development and investment – Section 106 planning obligations, the Community Infrastructure Levy, Capital Gains Tax, Stamp Duty Land Tax, Business Rates, Corporation Tax and Council Tax. However, none of these are designed to target land value uplift and fail to benefit from the full value of land value uplift created by state investments. In dialogue with the parliamentary committee on Land Value Capture, the Centre for Progressive Capitalism commented that:

> The Committee in its deliberations around land value capture should seek to understand why it is that the current land market enables a handful of private individuals and investors to earn £9.3bn of monopoly profits each year due to the productive work of others and local authorities changing land use.[48]

Within the latest draft of planning reforms in the Regeneration and Levelling Up White Paper 2022, it has been proposed that a universal Community Infrastructure Levy replace Section 106 agreements guaranteeing a higher and more consistent contribution to local authorities than is presently attained through existing Section 106 arrangements.

However, in the greater scheme of things such reforms – while welcome – are both piecemeal and insubstantial within the context of general land inflation. The measures are also not broad enough to encompass the contribution of non-state actors in the increasing price of land – and retain or claw back any of the added value introduced through them.

The prospect of achieving a significant increase in the availability of land, or a reduction in its cost, is doomed to fail without a serious reappraisal of the deeply inflationary nature of global market investments, the banking system and government subsidies and investments. Equally, without controls on speculative practices associated with land, a never-ending cycle of investment is likely to continually drive up the price of land, further inflating the costs of construction and reducing the affordability and quality of new housing.

The failure to deliver

Taken in its entirety, government's entire approach to increasing the delivery of new homes fails on multiple accounts, both in recognising the causes of under-delivery and in developing policy solutions which at best are ineffective, and at worst actively damaging. Government's obsession with tinkering with the national planning system is at best window dressing, at worst a damaging distraction in unlocking the country's capacity to deliver the homes we need. The planning system may not be perfect, but builders have failed to convincingly evidence that it is a substantial barrier to the delivery of new sites. Given the failure of the sector to build on granted planning permissions, caution must be taken before removing the democratic oversight and accountability which is currently present within the system to empower communities over the types of designs and construction that is appropriate in their areas.

The UK desperately needs more new homes to service its housing demand – to do so, the central role of local authorities as developers in the housing market needs to be enshrined, if we are ever to hope to reach the scales of house-building seen in previous generations, and sufficient to achieve present targets. Local authorities as builders have many unique traits which make them invaluable to the development and maintenance of a healthy housing market.

In the first instance, their capacity to build and sustain at a loss for many years means they are able to build in areas where demand for housing is not met by the ability of an existing population to pay. In other words, homes are able to be built where they are needed, as opposed to where they are most profitable.

Similarly, local authorities as developers are able to prioritise wider savings to the public purse through the provision of housing, such as reductions in temporary accommodation bills, hospital waiting lists and improvements to population health in order to justify the development of new properties, in a way which private developers cannot.

Government policy not only entirely neglects to focus on the centrality of local authorities to solve its delivery crisis, it is proactively pursuing policies to restrict the abilities of local authorities to borrow, and increase subsidies for Right to Buy which operate as the key block to the viability of new local authority developments. Without a substantial change in focus from government, enabling rather than crippling the ability of local authorities to contribute to solving the crisis, the delivery question will not be resolved.

The UK also has a particular problem with expensive and costly development. A significant amount of supply chain inflation in recent years has emerged due to the progress of international events, not unique to the UK, and with limited relevance to our specific housing policy. However, it has to be recognised that the country's fiscal policy in response to generalised inflation is worsening the inflation of material costs for building specifically. The particular nature of the UK's outsourced construction industry also adds substantial cost to the process of delivering not just housing, but physical infrastructure in general – an issue which relates back to the fundamental structure of the UK's construction industry as well as that of many of our public services, and even commercial businesses. This disjointed approach to the development and maintenance of our physical environment not only adds direct costs to construction, but also feeds into a lack of strategic oversight of the health and long-term interests of the construction sector as a whole, as evidenced by poor workforce planning within the sector and emerging issues as regards the availability of labour and shortage of skills to deliver the scale of building we need.

Equally, government's failure to confront the failure of existing large volume developers to deliver the homes we need, and instead focus solely upon tinkering with the planning system, amounts to a fundamental failure to address the core reasons which sit behind the under-delivery of new homes. Large developers are quite open in the reasons they refuse to build at a rate which would bring down housing demand and prices. The business models of these organisations are not secrets, but publicly available knowledge. To continue to rely on these organisations to resolve a problem which they expressly refuse to resolve is an egregious renunciation of state responsibility to resolve the housing crisis.

Lastly, the failure of government policy to recognise the centrality of land and its increasing role as an instrument of financial speculation in house prices reveals a fundamental lack of comprehension over the matter of fixing our model of housing delivery. Without steps to remove speculation from the process of house-building, costs of construction will continue to rise and vast sums of inflationary investment will continue to be ploughed into land and housing through the form of mortgages and other investments, crippling our ability to access land for the delivery of new homes.

6
Regional and political iniquities in policy making

A key failing of government policy in responding adequately to the housing crisis has been an inability to tailor policy, funding and support to the specific issues being faced in different regions – each of which are facing their own chronic housing issues. Additionally, in many instances an apparent lack of reasoning or methodology sits behind many government initiatives.

In particular, much of our current policy appears to be designed and modelled on housing conditions in and around Greater London and the South East, emphasising the areas of the greatest absolute house prices and values. Treasury 'Green Book' appraisals for the spending of public money often expressly demand evidence of 'value for money', measured in profitable returns, or the growth of high 'gross value added' sectors such as financial or other commercial services. Such demands favour areas of the country which are already experiencing the highest levels of property prices and economic growth, against those experiencing the least – often areas where demand for affordable housing is not the greatest, at the expense of areas where it is.

But this regional inequity is not restricted to Green Book appraisals; it manifests itself through many strands of policy making. In this chapter, we will address each area of government housing policy impacted by the phenomenon of regionally unequal policy focus, to better understand the variable impact which government frameworks and assessments for investment, politically motivated decision-making and regional ignorance have on the successful rollout of housing policy across different areas of the country.

Planning

In many areas of the planning system, the expectations around values and outputs are based on London-centric models which simply do not fit in other areas of the country. From expectations on expected developer profits to assessments of value which implicitly favour London and the South East's existing economic situation, planning is a huge area in which one-sided policy fails to appreciate the real differences between regions of the UK.

Value capture and Section 106

One key example of this is through expectations of 'value capture' levies such as 'Section 106' agreements. At present, the only powers through which councils are able to require contributions to affordable housing or infrastructure is via Section 106 agreements. Section 106 agreements are presumed in Local Plans and form an expectation that where a locality's infrastructure requirements are impacted by a development, or where there is a need for specific infrastructure such as affordable housing, that a contribution towards those requirements can be met either in cash or in kind by the developer.

However, since 2012 reforms introduced the National Planning Policy Framework under the government of Theresa May, a 'presumption in favour of sustainable development' has been introduced under planning guidance which makes it impossible for councils to enforce these requirements unless a 'sustainable' level of profit is reached (this is broadly considered to be a rate of profit around 20 per cent of a total development).

In Greater London and areas of the country with significant land values, the profit threshold regularly exceeds 20 per cent by a substantial margin, given the values associated with development. As such, there are councils which are able to effectively leverage Section 106 as a tool to drive significant sums of investment into infrastructure in their areas via development.

In much of the country, land and development values are significantly lower – to the extent that derisory sums of Section 106 can be gleaned from a development without reducing said development below that 20 per cent profitability threshold.

In part due to the London-centric modelling used by government in drafting policy, this differing situation for councils remains a blindspot in government policy and is replicated consistently, including in ongoing discussions within government about implementing reforms to improve 'land value capture' on behalf of local authorities (allowing local authorities the powers to benefit from the difference in land before and after planning permission has been granted). In the last swathe of White Paper planning reforms from the Department for Levelling Up and Communities in 2022, a new Infrastructure Levy (IL) has been proposed to take the place of Section 106, as a non-negotiable contribution from developers to councils as part of gaining planning permission. The IL is an evolution of the Community Infrastructure Levy (CIL) which has been an alternative method of value capture for local authorities since 2010 following its introduction in the Planning Act (2008), whereby cash proceeds from development are transferred via the levy into community groups. However, neither the CIL nor the IL take much account of the question of variable values in different areas of the country – and the fact that in many areas, developers cannot be compelled to contribute towards such levies without bankrupting their projects as the margins are too tight.

In June 2023, representatives of 30 organisations including the Royal Town Planning Institute, the Chartered Institute of Housing, the District Councils Network and the National Housing Federation co-signed a joint letter to the Secretary of State for Levelling Up, Housing and Communities opposing the introduction of the IL as outlined in the technical consultation of the Levelling Up and Regeneration Bill.[1] The signatories expressed anxiety over several areas of the proposals, including a continued lack of clarity over 'how IL rates and thresholds will sufficiently uphold the economic viability of projects, protect the delivery of affordable homes and homes for social rent and return enough money to fund the infrastructure growing communities need'.

The signatories to the letter further believe that the new reforms will impede the ability of local authorities to 'secure the benefits of new development', making it harder to provide new affordable housing and adding significant bureaucratic burdens to the process of bringing new projects to site. Specifically referenced by the partners are the added complexities to the charging schedules of the IL as opposed to the CIL, which will be difficult for local authorities to enforce given strained resources, as well as the costs of the upheaval of the present system, creating risk and uncertainty for all parties.

Government have yet to clarify details on their proposed method of IL to derive more value from developments – but as it stands, in large areas of the country the proposals are widely perceived to be unworkable from across industry, trade bodies and local government.

Housing numbers and the Home Counties

Housing numbers, too, are an issue on which there is substantial mismatch between different areas of the country. The government's 300,000 new homes a year target was set in 2017 by the then Chancellor Philip Hammond, and has since been interpreted as a duty by local councils to release a 'Five Year Forward' land supply (a land supply calculated to provide five years worth of development) distributed in different areas of the country through 'Objectively Assessed Housing Need' (OAHN) figures, which are geared to generate a developable land supply requisite for an overall total of 300,000 new units per annum across the UK.

One may question how a truly OAHN methodology might equate quite so perfectly, year on year, with government's set target. OAHN is purportedly calculated through population projections – projecting the overall number of people and age structure of a given area, and household projections (which project the rate at which certain people (by age and gender) will form households). Such projections already skew housing numbers heavily towards urban areas in a self-reinforcing cycle of development and growth – meaning that those urban areas necessarily take on a much greater share of the requirements for development.

Within the National Planning Policy Framework the OAHN is to be calculated through the compilation of a Strategic Housing Market Assessment to be compiled by a given local authority area, alongside a Strategic Housing and Economic Land Availability Assessment utilising a 'standard method' formula provided by government. In calculating overall housing need, additional Planning Practice Guidance suggests the use of databases such as household projections published by the Department of Communities and Local Government and Office for National Statistics population estimates. While on paper, a fairly non-prescriptive approach to housing need is articulated within government documentation emphasising the uncertainty and geographical particularity of the figures, in practice the guidance is heavily weighted to a fairly standardised approach to calculating OAHN utilising nationally collated datasets to define its parameters. To define the final figure, planning authorities must subsequently review their available land holdings to assess how much of their OAHN they are able to provide over a given time period.

In parallel to this process, a separate methodology for calculating affordable housing need sits alongside the methodology for calculating overall housing need, incorporating a four-stage process:

1. Estimates of the numbers of households currently in need (lacking suitable housing and unable to afford suitable housing within their market sector).
2. Future anticipated demand from households 'falling into need' (taken from DCLG projections).
3. The current and future supply of affordable housing.
4. Current and future need, minus current and future supply, equals the net affordable need over a given plan period.[2]

The calculation of affordable housing need presents planners with a single-finite figure of housing which must subsequently be incorporated into the Local Plan.

Several major methodological issues have been identified throughout this process, which each bring into question the rigour of the current methodology and its effectiveness at identifying true need.

First, regarding the relationship between overall calculations of housing demand and demand for affordable housing, the difference in methodologies creates pressures which trend towards a disjuncture between the two sets of figures. At present, the 'standard method' for calculating housing need presently takes no account of affordable homes whatsoever, and creates a number solely based on national datasets (such DCLG household projections) combined with local circumstance around land availability. In theory, the affordable housing methodology should calculate a proportion of that figure which should be reserved for affordable housing (for instance, 30 per cent, or 300 out of 1,000 homes). However, in areas where land and property values are low, the numbers of affordable properties which may viably be delivered by developers may be lower than this figure – say, 10–15 per cent. In this instance, the legally correct approach for a given planning authority would be to increase its overall housing need figure to accommodate for the absolute figure (300) required by its affordable housing targets. Yet, this expanded figure is not necessarily realistic or practical given the anticipated future growth or demand for housing in a given geography. Furthermore, in such an instance a planning authority may be required to encroach upon protected space – such as green-belt land – in order to achieve expanded targets. Government's messaging on this question has been erratic at best, with 2022 guidance explicitly stating that release of green-belt land is not required to meet OAHN targets.[3]

Second, the Standard Method reinforces existing patterns of economic growth and market overheating – particularly in urban centres – and fails to distribute house-building (and thus, demographic movement) across the country in a manner which might help to redevelop areas of the country which are falling behind. Through its attempts to meet demand in areas of historically high population growth, a self-fulfilling cycle of supply and demand determinism emerges through which areas requiring the instigation of growth and regeneration are not determined to have adequate housing supply for their needs, and urban areas in which economic growth, population growth and associated issues with affordability and overcrowding receive increasing amounts of investment.[4]

In 2021, the OAHN methodology took another hit to its credibility as the top 20 urban centres had their housing need projections revised suddenly with a 35 per cent uplift – requiring those areas to discover thousands of additional plots overnight.[5] No methodology or dataset was provided to justify the uplift, which was widely perceived to be a plain case of electioneering. The impacts of these changes also revealed numerous inconsistencies in government's approach to its OAHN methodology. As planning and development consultancy Lichfields noted in its blog in January 2021:

> Take Manchester: only Manchester City Council gets the 35% uplift. While this LPA does cover the central area of Manchester, applying the uplift just to the City means that other areas close to the centre (such as parts of Salford and Trafford) are not subject to the same uplift. That is despite them potentially having more brownfield land

or central locations for development than areas in the very south of Manchester City's boundary. Equally, what is it that makes the Greater Manchester urban area (comprising Manchester City, Bolton, Bury, Rochdale, Salford and Stockport) different from the way in which all 33 of London's Boroughs and the City were treated by the method?[6]

Perhaps the reasoning for this move was illustrated by the subsequent disastrous defeat for the Conservatives in the Chesham and Amersham by-election to the Liberal Democrats in June 2021 (a result widely attributed to local anger against development on green belt). By 2021, OAHN figures and their adoption into the local plans of rural Conservative authorities was becoming a clear election issue and source of back-bench frustration. By late 2022, a Tory back-bench rebellion resulted in the dilution of housing targets.

Both the origin of and the methodology behind the OAHN figures are subjects for correct criticism and discussion, providing a clear example of high-handed and politically generated decision making which has little bearing on the realities on the ground. The truth is, for the sake of sparing political trouble in the Home Counties, the previous Conservative government skewed the housing figures to place a greater burden on urban centres. This is no way to conduct policy development, yet both rural shires and urban centres have now suffered under a decade of policy which has failed to adopt a serious methodology for calculating future housing demand and need.

Funding

Models for government funding in relation to housing are patchy, inconsistent and often delivered without thorough methodology. Unsurprisingly, this also leads to huge disconnects in regional funding which are not dictated by genuine housing need. This is an issue which affects all areas of government funding – not just in relation to housing. Yet with housing, the impact of these flawed approaches often contributes to the stacking of inflationary housing investment in certain parts of the country, leaving others without adequate support for bringing land and sites to market, or delivering affordable homes. Problematically, these funding pots are often connected with the wider economic and growth ambitions set by government, which as has been detailed in other sections, contribute to (rather than offset) many of the major issues of affordability and access to homes which are central to our current housing crisis.

Another problematic element to equity and parity of government's approach to funding is their emphasis on competition for different funding pots as opposed to evidence-based grant. Since 2010, government have consistently moved away from the previous model of area-based funding initiatives driven by particular infrastructural and economic challenges, towards ring-fenced pot funding for government-led initiatives, through which local authority areas or other public bodies must 'bid in' to 'win' grant. This process leads to a colossal waste of public resources through additional administrative burdens for public bodies – and implicitly favours local authority areas which have the additional resources required to invest in bid-writing teams.

Related to this problem, government's approach to ring-fenced project funding also lends itself to short-term funding arrangements for limited projects, as opposed to the sustained and consistent funding which is required to impact serious long-term change in areas of the country suffering from compound and complex social and economic decline.

This approach particularly impacts the areas of the country most in need of 'levelling up', particularly deindustrialised areas such as the Midlands and North of England where chronic deprivation and below average standards of social mobility, educational attainment and employment are endemic.

Housing funding is specifically plagued by government's emphasis on subsidising areas of the country with the highest absolute house prices. Either by default or by design, this approach funnels the overwhelming majority of funding into the most wealthy areas of the country, further inflating already overheated property markets.

From the outside, it seems that in most instances funding and formulas for funding are drawn up primarily from the perspective of addressing issues faced in London and the South East, with other areas of the country left as an afterthought. The end result is that money is sent to the areas which need it the least, contributing to and worsening their affordability problems while areas of the country desperately in need of that support are ignored.

The 80:20 ratio

In 2018 the cross-party local government lobbying body Key Cities released heatmap research showing the regional distribution of five separate Homes England funding schemes equivalent to £5 billion over a five-year period.[7]

The graphic provided showed the stark North–South divide in funding – and also elucidated several other anomalies.

At a glance, when compared to a visualisation of the index of multiple deprivation, with the exception of London, funding appears to inversely map almost exactly. In other words, those areas facing the highest levels of deprivation and housing need are those least likely to draw down government funding and subsidy to ameliorate them.

The study highlighted the Treasury's use of what has come to be known as the 80:20 ratio, a ratio which dictates that 80 per cent of available funds must be sent to the areas of the country facing the greatest affordability pressures, that is, those areas where there is the highest absolute gap between average wages and average house prices.[8] Between 2016 and 2019, of the £2.6 billion handed out by the Home Building Fund, 29 per cent went to London alone while the North West, North East, Yorkshire and the Humber and the Midlands combined only received 25 per cent.[9]

Perversely, this reasoning is applied across the board in relation to housing. Through the government's affordable homes programme for the building of truly affordable housing, monies are restricted again only to areas which also possess this 'highest affordability pressure'. In Greater Manchester, this means that only five local authorities of ten are eligible for the government's Affordable Homes Funding to build affordable housing products such as social housing. Furthermore, it is those most deprived local authority areas which are denied this funding – while those which have enough economic activity and growth to sustain their own local housing booms (tending to correlate to less relative deprivation) are successful.

The ratio has since been highlighted by the Northern Research Group of Conservative 'Red Wall' MPs, who themselves have discovered the systemic bias against formerly industrial and deprived areas of the country in accessing funding. In 2020 the Northern Research Group raised concerns about the 80:20 ratio. In November 2020 the Conservative MP Kevin Hollinrake stated of the issue: 'If we genuinely want to level up we need to do things differently. ... Housebuilders would rather build where it's more expensive in London and the south-east, that's more profitable, but we want more construction and infrastructure and wealth generation in the north.'[10]

The ratio is just a symbol of the thinking behind Treasury distribution of funding – based on an incredibly crude and reactive assessment of the problem of funding for housing and housing affordability. Money and prices are seen as the primary indicators of the need for investment and support, rather than any kind of holistic assessment of human need.

The Towns Fund and the politicisation of funding

The Towns Fund was a £3.6 billion fund announced as part of Boris Johnson's Levelling Up funding, designed to invest in towns outside of London in a bid to level up the British regions. The fund received widespread criticism when it became clear that monies granted through the scheme were being directed towards target Tory marginals in the 2020 local elections.

Jennifer Williams reported on the Towns Fund allocations for the *Manchester Evening News*, pointing to the success of the wealthy area of Cheadle in achieving £25 million of 'Towns' funding despite being registered as 'low priority', while a litany of deprived townships such as Swinton, Rawtenstall, Romiley, Irlam and Wigan received nothing. *Manchester Evening*

News' research found that among 11 such townships in low priority which received government funding, all were Conservative target swing seats.[11]

This research was further corroborated by a study from the London School of Economics, entitled 'The Pork Barrel Politics of the Towns Fund'. The paper, written by London School of Economics Professor Chris Hanretty, further found that 'funding decisions were driven by party-political considerations, not by need', stating that 'Conservative-held' towns were much more likely to receive funding. And that 'the success rate for Conservative towns was ten percentage points higher than the rate for all other towns, and very close to twice as high'. The paper discovered these discrepancies throughout multiple layered assessments of the awarded funding, finding that:

> [T]he success rate for Conservative-held towns in the low priority group was actually higher than the success rate for all other towns in the medium priority group. The bias in favour of Conservative-held towns was sufficiently large to over-turn civil service recommendations not just on fine distinctions within broad categories but concerning the drift of the scheme as a whole.[12]

The Towns Fund is only one in a long line of instances where funding decisions appear to have been taken with primarily political decisions in mind, over and above need. During the early years of austerity, eyebrows were raised when 'Transitional Grant' funding was awarded to primarily Conservative towns to help them cope with the early impact of austerity, and when 'Sweetheart deals' on financing were granted to Surrey Council following extensive back-room engagement between the council leader and senior Conservative Cabinet members.[13,14]

In recent years, with the introduction of requirements that applications for Levelling Up grants need the backing of several local MPs, the increased politicisation of funding decisions is becoming even more explicit. Needless to say, such processes are not effective ways to distribute money and investment into much-needed infrastructure required to sustain local economic growth or new housing.

7

Existing stock condition

With 38 per cent of the UK's houses built before 1946, the country has the oldest housing stock in Europe, and possibly the oldest housing stock in the world. The UK's first stock condition survey was conducted in 1967 amidst the huge post-war slum clearances and house-building initiatives of that era. The results of that survey were worse than had been expected – of the 40 per cent of the nation's homes at that time which had been built prior to 1919, a quarter had no access to hot water, nearly 20 per cent had no indoor toilet, and 5 per cent required maintenance exceeding £1,000 in value (more than £15,000 in 2024).[1] Since then, the UK has held regular housing surveys and, today, has some of the most comprehensive data based on continuous inspections of trained professionals in the world.

The slum clearances and huge house-building programmes of the post-war era paved the way for a gigantic leap forward in the quality of British housing stock, yet in recent years, as new house-building has fallen behind, the country is once again falling behind in standard benchmarks of success. The 2021 Census found that 73.8 per cent of households in England and Wales still used mains gas as their primary source of heating, compared to 23 per cent in Spain, 22 per cent in Ireland and only 17 per cent in Denmark and Greece. Comparatively, the UK competes poorly in floor space (with an average of less than 84 square metres per house) than its European neighbours, and higher heating bills.

But despite the clear need for investment, remarkably little in the way of concrete policy currently exists to address low standards in this sector. This hasn't always been the case – over the past 30 years, several flawed schemes designed to address the issues of declining standards in housing stock have been undertaken, though in recent years, the few areas of public policy which were focused on improving stock standard have been rolled back, meaning even less in the way of a strategic response to worsening standards. In this chapter, we will discuss the history of government policy towards the improvement of housing stock since the millennium, exploring the present absence of policy and plan towards the rejuvenation of the country's housing.

Housing Market Renewal

Under the previous Labour government, £2.2 billion of investment was made into Housing Market Renewal schemes designed to allay the deterioration of Britain's housing stock between 2002 and 2011.[2] Since the end of the scheme under the 2010 Coalition government, there has been no serious attempt by government to address the issue of the substandard quality of existing British housing stock at scale.

Housing Market Renewal was the birthchild of the Urban Task Force, established by the New Labour government in 1998. The Urban Task Force, headed up by Lord Rogers, produced a series of papers which foreshadowed the 'Our Towns and Cities' White Paper in 2000, and then the Scottish Cities Review in 2003. Both 'Our Towns and Cities' and the Scottish Cities Review articulated a vision for 'lively cities' with an emphasis on 'liveability'. The 2001 budget announced several reforms designed to facilitate this process, including:

- an exemption from stamp duty for property transactions in disadvantaged parts of the UK;
- 150 per cent tax credits to cover the costs of remediating contaminated land;
- reducing VAT to 5 per cent on conversion of houses of multiple occupancy into single properties.[3,4]

In addition to these measures, Urban Regeneration Companies were established with compulsory purchase powers and a remit to deliver housing and environmental regeneration.

In 2002, following that year's Comprehensive Spending Review, Housing Market Renewal (or Pathfinder) was launched with a particular focus on deindustrialised Northern areas, and a mission to create housing markets in areas where they had not previously existed, attracting a wider array of social groups (encouraging 'social diversification'). From its introduction in 2002, government identified nine 'Market Renewal Pathfinders' in the North of England and the Midlands – areas which suffered from high vacancy rates, increasing population turnover, low sales values, abandonment and market failure.[5] From our present vantage point, it is difficult to imagine that one of the primary concerns of early 2000s policy makers was abandonment and low values in post-industrial urban conurbations, but it is easy to forget that these issues came alongside those of crime and extreme poverty and their association with economic failure following deindustrialisation in these areas.

The Housing Market Renewal Fund was established to service this agenda, with an aspiration to ensure that housing market restructuring would proceed alongside improvements to the environment and economy. The 2004 paper for the Joseph Rowntree Foundation, 'The Road to Renewal' by Ian Cole and Brendan Nevin, elucidated the scope and aspirations for the project:

> Although the Housing Market Renewal Fund was made available on the basis of evidence suggesting a strong connection between housing

market weakness and a progressive cycle of urban decline, it has become apparent that there are different causes and manifestations of the problem in those areas experiencing the most profound changes. The larger metropolitan areas are characterised by more widespread problems of neighbourhood abandonment than the medium-sized settlements that often form part of an industrial hinterland for the major cities. However, outside the larger cities, a progressive loss of function and form can be witnessed, as the original economic rationale has disappeared and a new economic future has yet to be defined.[6]

Despite some familiar stories of an affordability crisis, at the time Housing Market Renewal was introduced widespread 'market failure' was occurring in particular areas of the country, with often stark and severe consequences. Cole and Nevin note:

> Where the market has collapsed it has tended to be a rapid process. In the West End of Newcastle, for example, neighbourhoods become abandoned within a three year period (Keenan, 1998) with properties subsequently being offered for sale for 50 pence (Blacklock, 1999). In North Manchester, an area of 5,000 pre-1919 terraced properties, vacancies increased by 40 per cent and house prices fell by 25 per cent over a five-year period (Manchester City Council, 2001).[7]

These collapses were often horrendously wasteful, as well as socially catastrophic. Cole and Nevin write in relation to the innovations in public sector investment into housing that:

> The need for a fundamental review of the way in which public sector investment was being deployed in areas with weak housing markets was thrown into sharp relief with the announcement that 50 units of social housing were being demolished in the North East only three years after they were built, having never been let (Housing Today, 1999).[8]

Responding to these events, the thrust of Housing Market Renewal was designed to arrest market failure in low-value areas. In addition to this, a wider and more ambitious objective of the programme was to 'correct' the UK's dysfunctional housing market, which the authors criticised for its lack of reflexivity to housing demand. The overall intention was considered to be an agenda to improve affordability. They note:

> At the time of writing, the British economy is experiencing its longest period of economic growth since the Second World War. This period of growth has been accompanied by a prolonged bout of house price

inflation, which has seen house price–income ratios reach even higher levels than those that preceded the peak of the last housing market boom at the end of the 1980s. The economic impact of the current national housing shortage has recently been delineated by Kate Barker (HM Treasury, 2004) in her report on future investment. This report concluded that the market for housing in Britain was 'abnormal', as the supply of dwellings did not respond to changes in price. Additionally, Barker estimated that some 120,000 extra houses would need to be added annually to the supply to ensure that, in the long term, house prices were restricted to the European annual average of 1.1 per cent real growth.[9]

Despite this, Housing Market Renewal became publicly and politically synonymous with the demolition of social and council housing, the displacement of working-class communities and the beginning of the 'gentrification' of many urban districts. In 2008, Peter Hetherington reported for the *Guardian* that the sum total of Pathfinder achievements (following £2.2 billion of spending) was that '10,200 properties have been demolished, 40,000 refurbished and 1,100 new homes built. Initial plans to demolished 90,000 houses have been scaled down, although 37,000 are still scheduled to go'.[10] In a withering piece, Hetherington notes that Pathfinder schemes were widely subsidising private landlords and property speculators:

> In fact, batches of houses – perhaps whole streets – have been bought by these speculators and filled with people on housing benefit. The unscrupulous, receiving a tidy pile in taxpayer-funded rent, subsequently received compensation from the public purse when the houses were compulsorily acquired; easy money if you can find it![11]

Academic Rowland Atkinson, writing in the *European Journal of Housing Policy* at the peak of Pathfinder in 2004, observed that through emphasising social diversity, Pathfinder had 'created a pathology in which existing residents are cast as part of the problem', referring to Newcastle's Pathfinder scheme

> in which 6,600 homes will be demolished in areas predominantly made-up of council housing and replaced with construction by private developers and registered social landlords. Neither is this process envisaged as being about the re-housing of the existing population, documentation showed that a new, middle-class population was to be encouraged.[12]

Despite a focus on fixing the housing market to create more affordable housing products, the Pathfinder schemes presided over a near trebling of house prices in their designated areas between 2002 and 2006. Author and architectural critic Owen Hatherley described Pathfinder as 'slum clearances without the socialism' in a *Guardian* article in 2010.[13] Hatherley posits that the scheme amounted to an attempt to replicate the supplanting of industry with housing markets as a profit-making force in the deindustrialised North, as had occurred in the South East. Further criticising the scheme, Hatherley observes that Pathfinder replicated many of the socially corrosive features of post-war slum clearances: the demolition and removal of long-standing communities, and razing of their homes. But while post-war, such clearances made way for new homes targeted towards the same communities which had been displaced, with Pathfinder new homes were generally designed for well-paid young professionals. A key example of such a Pathfinder scheme can be found in Chimney Pot Park, Salford, where following renovations by Urban Splash, a series of formerly dilapidated terraces were marketed towards media professionals, advertised under the banner of 'own your own Coronation Street home!'[14]

Housing Market Renewal was in many ways a flawed scheme, reflecting the hegemonic concerns of its era regarding urban decline – arguably attempting to reverse the over-correction of post-war planners in successfully depopulating urban areas. However, throughout the duration of Pathfinder, the under-provision of new housing stock across the country overcame the particular problem of market failure in many Pathfinder zones, increasing values across the board through sheer increases in national demand. In that context, many Pathfinder schemes found themselves contributing to rapidly inflating house prices, perversely, in areas of the country which traditionally had provided affordable dwellings for working-class people.

However, in its removal, government has since failed to recognise the crucial importance of any route to delivering improvements to Britain's ageing homes. At the very least Pathfinder signalled an awareness that stock condition – particularly in certain areas – was something which required government intervention.

Removal of insulation grants

Between 1990 and 2013, the UK government had provided targeted assistance towards renovating and increasing the fuel efficiency of homes, contributing significantly to the gradually improving standard of British housing stock. In 1990, the Conservative government first introduced the Home Energy Efficiency Scheme through the Social Security Act which provided insulation grants for an estimated two million homes until 2000, when it was replaced by the Warm Front grant scheme under New Labour.[15] Warm Front operated between 2000 and 2013, targeting households in receipt of certain benefits (generally, Child Tax Credit, Disability Living

Allowance and Pension Credit) with grants for the installation of insulation and modern heating systems. Between 2005 and 2013, approximately 1.5 million households were assisted through the scheme – and further evidence from the post-scheme parliamentary evaluation report suggested that the initiative also had a measurably positive impact on the supply chain and business for installers of modern insulation – particular smaller enterprises.[16] The evaluation report on Warm Homes particularly noted that:

> It was widely acknowledged that Warm Front created a huge amount of work in the industry, promoting turnover growth and job creation in many installer firms. Such was the volume of work, however, that some smaller installers reported becoming dependent on the scheme. They reported the challenges this created for their organisations as the scheme first of all reduced in size following budget cuts, and ultimately came to a close.[17]

In 2013, following David Cameron's apocryphal imperative to 'cut the green crap', the scheme was unceremoniously scrapped to be replaced by the Green Deal home efficiency programme, in which grants were replaced by loans to be paid back via savings on energy bills.

The scheme had barely any takeup, and was scrapped less than three years later alongside a damning National Audit Office report which stated that the scheme's primary impact had been to drive energy bills even higher for those who engaged. Anyas Morse of the National Audit Office said: 'Green Deal not only failed to deliver any meaningful benefit, it increased suppliers' costs – and therefore energy bills.'

Removal of insulation grants in 2012 was catastrophic – causing a 90 per cent reduction in insulation installation.[18] Following this failure, there has been no consistent or strategic approach to consistently delivering improvements to insulation or heat efficiency in British households – contributing significantly towards the country's lagging record relative to comparative nations. In recent years, the lack of progress on this agenda over the past decade has become a topic of national focus, with campaigning group Insulate Britain raising awareness of the importance of the insulation agenda in achieving the nation's zero carbon ambitions, calling for a 'legally binding national plan' for low energy and low carbon retrofit of all homes in Britain by 2030.[19]

In September 2021, Boris Johnson's government announced a 'Green Homes Grant', allowing homeowners in England to apply for vouchers of up to £10,000 to improve energy efficiency following the installation of a 'primary measure' – such as a solid wall, cavity wall, underfloor heating or roof insulation or low carbon heating systems. Grants would subsequently cover 'secondary measures' such as triple glazing, energy efficient doors or smart heating controls. The scheme barely lasted a year, primarily due to a lack of credited installers recognised by the scheme to make improvements, and after only 15,000 homes had benefited from the grants.

The failure of the Green Homes Grant scheme highlights, among other factors, the secondary impacts of the withdrawal from previous insulation schemes particularly in relation to the lack of accredited and trained professionals able to install new heat-saving technology. When the Warm Front scheme was closed, it didn't simply lead to a loss of progress on retrofitting homes – it also led to the collapse of a sector of the British economy which had been sustainably increasing its workforce and skills base to accommodate for state-led demand.

This collapse continues to mire the progress of new schemes today. In May 2023, a complex series of new grants have been announced by government to facilitate the installation of residential green infrastructure and insulation, under the banner of the Great British Insulation Scheme.[20] Under the scheme, homes with an energy rating between D and G, in council tax bands A to D, may apply for grants to install wall and loft insulation for their homes. However, over the course of the first nine months, only 4,648 homes have received any help.

Having lost the ecosystem of skills required to fit insulation, as well as disrupted the supply chains around the industry, it will take substantial time and investment to once again grow the sector to the point where it has the capacity to deliver at scale.

Lack of regulation in the private rented sector

The private rented sector (PRS) is the worst performing housing sector in terms of quality, and the standards of maintenance and housing stock in this sector are falling most quickly. These features of the UK's PRS should highlight the lack of regulatory oversight in the sector, including protections for tenants or enforcement powers. At present, and in advance of new reforms via the Renters' Rights Bill, almost all disputes between PRS tenants and landlords in England and Scotland class as civil disputes, meaning that enforcement of standards is left to tenants to pursue through civil court action. However, with the existence of provisions for Section 21 no-fault evictions, no legal obstacle to renegotiating contracts mid-term and within the context of an acute shortage of available rental accommodation, tenants are normally in no place to argue. As such, outside of ethical appeals to landlords (or grant subsidy schemes) no effective enforcement powers exist to ensure privately let properties meet a required standard.

There are some exceptions to this. In 2006, 'selective' or 'landlord licensing' was introduced in law. In landlord licensed areas, many local authorities have made a real impact on the quality of PRS provision, given full enforcement power to raid inadequate properties, levy fines on the owners and sometimes submit Compulsory Purchase Orders against the worst offenders. Despite the success of such schemes, by law landlord licensed areas are arbitrarily limited to 20 per cent of a local authority area, without explicit permission from the Secretary of State.

In Wales, since 2014 all privately let properties require a licence and terms of private renting are now enforced by government agency Rent Smart Wales (RSW). Additionally, through the Renting Homes (Fees, etc) Act (2019) a rent cap has been introduced. Though data on the progress of the regulator is still limited, a survey of lettings agents from the professional body for lettings agents, Propertymark, suggests that RSW has landed positively within the Welsh PRS, with interviewees citing RSW as 'a positive force in improving the regulation of the PRS in Wales'.[21]

In Scotland, a commitment to establish a new regulator for the PRS within the next parliament has been made, expected to be brought into law by 2025. In England, the newly elected Labour government have also revived Michael Gove's Renters Reform Bill (now Renters' Rights Bill) and, with it, a commitment to establish a new Ombudsman and mandatory landlord registration. However until these reforms are engaged, there is presently little to no regulatory power to enforce standards.

Many of the promises laid out in the Renters' Rights Bill are set to make significant improvements to the experience of renting in the UK, with promises to scrap Section 21 'no-fault' evictions, banning 'no DSA' lettings which refuse tenancies to individuals on benefits, and the creation of a national landlord register to monitor standards. Under the previous government, however, huge doubt was cast over commitments to fully scrap Section 21 evictions, with an 'indefinite delay' announced on the measure in light of concerns regarding the court system's capacity to process complaints.[22] Thankfully, the commitment has been resuscitated by the incoming Labour government.

In any case, to truly benefit from the positive aspects of the Renters' Rights Bill, an adequate regulatory regime will still be required to achieve maximum benefit for renters. Selective licensing schemes are, at present the only such regulators operating within the UK's rental market – designated areas assigned by local authorities in which the standard of rented accommodation and the activities of landlords require licensing by the local authority. Until late 2024, such schemes were arbitrarily limited to 30 per cent of a local government's geography without express permission from the Secretary of State to expand them.[23] This arbitrary restriction needlessly limited the enforcement powers of councils, preventing the effective enforcement of standards across PRS.

And yet, following the previous government's amendments to the Renters' Rights Bill, even the existing limited powers to deploy 'selective licensing' (as per the Housing Act of 2004) were under threat, with 'New Clause' NC1 on page 28 proposing to remove 'the ability of local housing authorities to designate areas as subject to selective licencing'.[24] In Parliament, MPs argued that the creation of the new landlord register removed the need for selective licensing schemes, with Conservative MP Andrew Mangnall stating landlord licensing has become 'redundant'.[25]

The new register of landlords proposed in the Bill will have no enforcement powers directly attached to it. Within current proposals, an Ombudsman has been proposed to act as a regulator: however the Ombudsman will have no resource or capability to perform the regular property checks, such as those provided within selective licensing zones, requiring tenants to bring cases against their landlords themselves. In recent iterations of the Bill, these limitations have been somewhat addressed with the movement of enforcement responsibilities to Councils, including a responsibility to enforce 'Awaab's Law' enforcing emergency hazards within social rented accommodation, as well as oversight compliance of the new register. To achieve these ends, Councils have also been granted new powers to enter properties without a warrant, and levy new fines and charges.

The renewed Renters' Rights Bill also offers significant changes and advantages for tenants, including abolition of 'no fault' (Section 21) evictions and a movement away from Assured Shorthold Tenancies towards 'period tenances' (which automatically renew unless consciously breached). Additionally, there are proposed improvements to tenants rights under Section 8 evictions (on the grounds of anti-social behaviour and rent arrears).

But other half-way houses reveal some of the limitations of the Bill. For instance, the Bill promises to restrict rent increases to once per year. This is, of course, a welcome move in the context of renters experiencing bi-annual and sometimes even month on month rental hikes. However, annual rent increases still offer far too little security for tenants and continue to allow far too much flexibility to landlords to increase prices, contributing to general inflation of rents.

As a growing portion of the UK's housing supply that appears to be here to stay, policy makers need to get serious about reshaping the country's PRS to be suitable for a society in which lifelong renting and tenancy is increasingly the norm. To these ends, we should look to examples from countries in which lifelong renting is a more established part of the culture to find functional solutions.

A 2018 paper for Warwick University compared the UK's tenancy cultures with those of Europe, Australia and the United States. The researchers found that, particularly in England, tenancy rights compared unfavourably with most other jurisdictions.[26] The average length of an English Assured Shorthold Tenancy is between six and 12 months – compared with four to six years in Italy, or often lifetime tenancies in Germany. In England, tenancies are renewed at the volition of the landlord – in most other jurisdictions such as New Zealand and Australia, tenants are able to automatically renew their tenancy once the previous agreement has expired, unless the landlord provides notice. In most nations, there are substantially greater protections for tenants against any form of eviction than in the UK – in Australia, tenants often may not be evicted until the end of their fixed term. In Germany, tenants deposits accrue interest which must be repaid upon the termination of a tenancy – a huge disincentive for evictions. In most comparative nations, rent increases are capped or controlled – unlike within the UK.

Even within the UK, if we compare the average length of tenancy between social or council housing tenancies and the PRS, we see huge discrepancies. Seventy-eight per cent of social housing tenancies in England are lifelong tenancies, alongside 95 per cent of council house tenancies.[27] Such long-term tenancies allow tenants to invest in their homes, and develop their community, without fear of being moved on periodically as their tenancies end.

At present, the Renters' Rights Bill still fails to counteract some of the most pressing issues facing renters – namely, the length of tenancy, rent increases and effective regulation of standards. An effective approach to the regulation of private tenancies would have to address seriously the following issues:

- Granting surety for longer-term tenancies, up to several years, where wished for by tenants. Ideally, this security could be delivered in a manner which still allows maximum flexibility for tenants in the instance they wish to move (that is, avoiding a situation where they are bought into a fixed-term tenancy and must pay off the remainder in order to move). In Germany, the security of long-term tenancy is combined with the flexibility of periodic tenancies, by disincentives to the landlord to evict or end the tenancy agreement for their tenant. Such measures must be complemented by measures to increase protections for residents against eviction.
- More effective rent controls to limit rent increases for multi-year timescales, as opposed to the 12-month period currently proposed. Renters need to have surety over their rental payments over longer periods to attain any kind of financial security. Landlords should also be able to justify rent increases on the basis of improvements to the property, or other criteria regarding the value of their property, and a guidance framework should be developed to establish valid reasons for rent increases. In the past, the UK successfully utilised direct rent controls from 1915 with the Increase of Rent and Mortgage Interest Act until the Housing Act in 1988. A corollary benefit of the 1915 Act was also to curtail mortgage interest inflation, by freezing interest rates on mortgages for properties covered by the act. Furthermore, tenants could only be evicted if they had 'committed waste or caused nuisance and annoyance to neighbours' or 'that the premises were reasonably required by the landlord for his own occupation, or that of an employee'. From the 1965 Rent Act, direct rent fixing was replaced with rent regulation from 'rent officers', introducing

the principle of property valuation into the question of ascertaining 'fair rents' based on the age, character, locality and state of repair of the building. This system remained in place, broadly, until its removal in 1988, and provided a stable rate of rents and rent increases throughout this time.

- Greater enforcement against indecency, poor standards and malpractice from landlords must be realised through the creation of an effective regulator. The Ombudsman proposed through the Renters' Rights Act is a relatively toothless body, in comparison to the proven and effective role in regulation performed by local authorities through selective licensing areas. A universal form of landlord licensing would provide a clear route through which to establish such a regulatory body, with the authority to makes checks on and fully enforce decency standards across the rental sector, and particular the PRS where standards are consistently lowest.

8

Homelessness

According to government figures, rough sleeping has almost trebled since 2010 – numbers which shocked many British people as huge numbers swelled on pavements and in alleyways, with new tent cities springing up across the country. A decade on from the explosion in numbers, rough sleeping now has an established presence in the streetscene of Britain's major cities and has initiated a national debate on the crisis – and how to deal with it.

But the problem of homelessness goes beyond rough sleeping. The Local Government Association believes that there has been a 430 per cent increase in the use of temporary accommodation by councils since 2010, with 10,510 households across the country currently being put up in B&Bs, and over 95,000 people living in temporary accommodation of all kinds across the country.[1] In March 2024, the News Agents reported that this figure could be under-reported, with claims that 140,000 children alone are currently living in temporary accommodation.[2] Following a shocking investigation conducted by Dan Hewitt of ITV News which uncovered widespread homelessness among pupils, The News Agents interviewed Daniel Moynihan, the chief executive officer of the Harris Academy of London-based school academies, the reality of temporary accommodation for these children is articulated in horrendous detail. Of temporary accommodation, Moynihan states:

> That accommodation is overcrowded sometimes. You can have a whole family living in a room. It can be inadequate accommodation which can't be heated properly. Accommodation without cooking facilities, or living in cheap hotels where children are having to share toilets and kitchens with unknown adults where it's a safeguarding risk.[3]

The extent of the temporary accommodation crisis in parts of the UK is reaching crisis point. Moynihan claims that in one Harris Academy primary school in Peckham, 50 per cent of the children are currently living in temporary accommodation.

> We'll have kids, particularly if they're primary, who will have travelled two hours to get to school. They're exhausted. ... We'll have children coming in who are hungry because they can't cook, or their parents haven't got money for food. We're feeding children, and they can't cook in the evenings. We often provide food which doesn't need cooking so

that they can take it home. They can't wash sometimes so we provide washing machines for some children so they can wash their clothes. In school. We provide facilities to shower.[4]

Between August and December 2018, Jennifer Williams of the *Manchester Evening News* chronicled the 'Dickensian conditions' of 'Manchester's grim private guesthouses', in which children live amidst flea infestations, drug abuse and prostitution in a network of B&B accommodation procured as an emergency measure by the local council.[5] Figures from Greater Manchester show a 77 per cent rise in temporary accommodation between 2020 and 2023, with 5,014 households presently residing in temporary accommodation across the conurbation.[6]

According to government data, in 2021 over £1 billion was spent on homeless services of one form or another in England alone.[7]

This crisis has led to many government initiatives, promises and commitments – united by a failure to deal with homelessness as a systemic issue, driven by the wider housing crisis and not resultant from personality defects, mental health crises or criminality and drug abuse. The measures also fail to recognise the central role of welfare reform in instigating a large part of this rise, in particular policies such as the Bedroom Tax and Local Housing Allowance caps which caused havoc with significant numbers of financially vulnerable families.

The numbers of rough sleepers appear, for the time being, to have stabilised at their new higher level – however our temporary accommodation lists continue to grow and councils and other responsible authorities are at breaking point. As our housing crisis continues to dovetail with the homelessness crisis, the social costs of homelessness are growing to inordinate levels.

Legislation: the Homelessness Reduction Act

Following a recognition of the severe increase and severity of homelessness in the UK, in 2017 the Homelessness Reduction Act was passed by government establishing a new set of statutory responsibilities for local authorities in identifying and providing housing for homeless individuals.

Under the Housing Act 1996, councils already had duties to secure available accommodation for 'priority need' and 'unintentionally homeless' applicants for support – unless they had 'unreasonably refused to cooperate' or had already refused a final offer of 'suitable accommodation' (either social housing or approved private rented accommodation).

In addition to previous responsibilities, the 2017 act also introduced a 'Duty to prevent homelessness' and a 'Duty to relieve homelessness', powers which required councils to seek accommodation for applicants who are 'threatened with homelessness within 56 days', assess the causes and circumstances of homelessness as well as the particular needs of family members, and develop personalised plans for each homeless individual to help guide them into housing.

These provisions were welcomed by many homelessness advocacy organisations, however they were extremely limited by the inadequate levels of funding provided by government for authorities to cover their newly acquired statutory duties. Only £73 million, nationally over three years, was provided to local authorities to manage these duties – and in 2019, two-thirds of councils surveyed by the New Local Government Network stated that they did not have sufficient funding to fulfil their legal duties to prevent homelessness under the act.[8]

Funding was significantly increased through the Homelessness Prevention Grant in 2021, and again in 2022 up to £315.8 million – however the money still fails to tackle a central issue in preventing homelessness, the availability of suitable accommodation.

Traditionally, those in need of a home would most likely have been placed in council or social housing – however in many instances due to the declining number of available council or social homes, this is no longer an option. Nationally, 1.16 million households are on local authority waiting lists for housing today – however National Housing Federation estimate that this figure could be as high as 1.6 million households, or 3.8 million people.[9] Suitable private sector accommodation is difficult to come by – and a by-product of this is the explosion in the use of temporary accommodation.

This shortcoming was noted in the Ministry for Housing, Communities and Local Government's 2020 evaluation of the Homelessness Reduction Act, in which, discussing the new relief duties, it noted:

> This [the duty of relief] was the element of the Act where reported effectiveness varied most between different local areas. The ability of local authorities to relieve homelessness was strongly mediated by the local supply of affordable housing. Local authorities in areas with relatively good supply described cases where suitable accommodation had been secured either straightaway or after a short stay in temporary accommodation. Those in areas with limited supply were much less likely to describe such positive outcomes under the relief duty.[10]

The evaluation noted that 50 per cent of local authorities 'cited *insufficient access to affordable housing* as a significant challenge', 43 per cent struggled with the new administrative burdens and 39 per cent cited concerns regarding the 'sufficiency and certainty of future funding' as a major concern in their ability to continue to enact the act's provisions[11]. Despite these provisions being noted, no actions to help improve the supply of affordable housing were made in the recommendations of the paper for Ministry for Housing, Communities and Local Government.

Money spent on initiatives to tackle homelessness is more often seen as an investment in drug and alcohol services, dealing with the by-products of homelessness rather than the root cause. Yet a stream of consistent evidence points to access to housing as the most effective solution to homelessness. Until a supply of safe, suitable and affordable homes is attained, the legislative changes brought about by the Homelessness Reduction Act will be impossible to fulfil.

Welfare reform: the Bedroom Tax and Local Housing Allowance caps

In 2013, as part of a raft of welfare reforms, David Cameron's government brought through the 'Removal of the Spare Room Subsidy' or what became colloquially known as the 'Bedroom Tax', aiming to reduce spending on social housing by removing a portion of benefit from Local Housing Allowance claimants if they occupied a property with a spare room.

The reform impacted an estimated 660,000 working age social housing tenants, reducing weekly incomes by an average of between £12 and £22.[12] The Bedroom Tax followed the first significant shakeup of the benefits system announced in 2012, the introduction of Universal Credit as part of the Welfare Reform Act 2012, which merged the six different benefits of Employment and Support Allowance, income-based Jobseeker's Allowance (JSA), Income Support, Child Tax Credit, Working Tax Credit and Housing Benefit. As part of these reforms, a new 'sanctions' regime was also introduced in which pecuniary fines could be levied against the total sum of an individual's benefit for indiscretions such as lateness or absence for Jobcentre meetings, refusal to attend interviews or failure to hit applications targets agreed with jobseeker supervisors.

The raft of reforms have been widely criticised for their severity. Under the new system, penalties of 100 per cent of an individual's JSA entitlement for up to three years are possible – with claimants missing even one of their Jobcentre appointments having their payments reduced or removed for 28 days (following three incidences, the penalty is 91 days).

In 2020, a paper published by Sharon Wright, Del Roy Fletcher and Alasdair Stewart for the *Social Policy Administration Journal* documented that nearly 25 per cent of JSA claimants were sanctioned between 2010 and 2015 – and often for trivial reasons.[13] The paper further notes that initially through a 1 per cent inflation limit increase annually, and subsequently through a freeze from 2016, JSA has been steadily reduced in real terms for claimants, stating:

> In 2018, JSA was worth only 12.8% of median wages (IPPR, 2019). Many unemployed people are also affected by wider cuts to housing benefit, the 'bedroom tax' (spare room subsidy), and the household

benefit cap. The benefit claim process has also become 'digital by default,' which erects a digital barrier that obstructs individuals' access to their entitlements (Alston, 2018). All of which has succeeded in instilling 'fear and loathing' of the system in many claimants (Alston, 2018, p. 6).[14]

Among other effects, the paper finds that the cumulative impact particularly of the new sanctions regime has been to pressure many welfare recipients into insecure or inappropriate employment: 'Some had been pressured with the threat of sanctions to apply for an unrealistically high number of jobs (up to 30 per week) or instructed to pursue job opportunities that were inappropriate or would entail prohibitively expensive daily commutes for low paid, chronically insecure work.'[15]

Unsurprisingly, the study also found a connection between insecurity through the new welfare regime and homelessness: 'Sanctioned claimants are more likely to be disadvantaged, for example, homeless (Reeve, 2017), than those who are not sanctioned and genuine barriers to employment, rather than resistance, often prevent compliance with requirements (Hasenfeld, Ghose, & Larson, 2004).'[16] And in 2019, changes were also made to the traditional Housing Benefit claimants, creating a new Local Housing Allowance which was to be capped at a set rate.

The combined consequence of these reforms has been widely understood to have contributed significantly to the homelessness and rough sleeping crisis. In Crisis' 2019 Homelessness Monitor, Universal Credit was named as 'compounding existing affordability issues' for residents unable to sustain rent payments through either errors with their Universal Credit payments, or sanctions,[17] and a 2019 report by the Greater London Authority has shown that welfare reforms have impacted on homelessness numbers particularly acutely in the capital, increasing the number of rent arrears, observably higher numbers of evictions from Universal Credit claimants, and a significant increase in in-work poverty.[18]

The Greater London Authority report also notes that these reforms have compounded issues with temporary accommodation, as since welfare reforms have been implemented private sector landlords are less willing to agree for their properties to be let to welfare recipients.

This last point illustrates one of the most significant compounding impacts of welfare reform in limiting the supply of appropriate 'move on' accommodation for those currently held in temporary accommodation. For several years now, homelessness advocacy groups such as Shelter have conducted well-publicised 'No Department for Social Security (DSS) Discrimination' campaigns, to support tenants being discriminated against on the basis that they are in receipt of benefits. Increasingly, landlords and lettings agents have begun to operate a 'no DSS' policy refusing to allow prospective tenants to view affordable properties, refusing to consider them as prospective tenants and advertising properties for working professionals only.

No DSS bans have been ruled unlawful in the UK since July 2020, however the practice is still widespread and often operated informally.[19]

Due to the generally higher dependence on welfare and benefits among those at highest risk of homelessness, these cumulative welfare reforms have served to substantially increase the risk of homelessness and rough sleeping for large numbers of UK citizens and, as of February 2022, government policy has been to double down. As of February 2022, claimants may now be sanctioned after only four weeks if they do not search for and accept a job outside of their chosen field. Furthermore, the current Labour Government has prioritised further cuts to welfare payments as a key tenet of its spending plans.

If we are to be serious about tackling homelessness and rough sleeping, this will not be achieved without significant reform to the current welfare system. When combined with inadequate access to affordable housing, welfare reforms aimed punitively at punishing those in receipt of benefits for minor infractions, or those within council properties for possessing an extra spare room, are clear contributors to the homelessness problem.

Schemes and initiatives

Alongside legislative change the government has also introduced a myriad of schemes and initiatives to deal with the issue of homelessness and rough sleeping.

Housing First

Housing First is an internationally recognised approach to homelessness rehabilitation which focuses on getting homeless people into secure, permanent and safe accommodation as a first step in tackling homelessness – above providing support for drug, alcohol, mental health or other commonly aligned issues related to homelessness.

The Centre for Social Justice notes in its 2021 evidence review on Housing First:

> Evidence from the UK and abroad shows that Housing First works in ending and preventing rough sleeping for the vast majority of people with high and complex needs. Typically over 80 per cent of Housing First tenants retain their tenancies, with 88 per cent of those housed by the city region Housing First pilots by September 2020 doing just this.[20]

Within the UK, the scheme was first adopted by Turning Point in Glasgow in 2010, and has boasted of great success rates since. But despite boasting impressive rates of rehabilitation, government has been slow off the mark in committing to the scheme nationally – instead funding pilot partnerships in areas such as Greater Manchester, the Liverpool City Region and the Midlands which were last formally reviewed in January 2024.[21]

The review found that a year after entering Housing First, 'the majority of clients were living in long-term, largely social rented, accommodation', stating:

> 84% were living in long-term accommodation at the point of the six-month interview and this rose to 92% after a year. This represented a significant shift in their living circumstances compared to prior to being part of HF. The long-term housing secured for HF clients largely suited their needs and approval, with clients rating highly their 'satisfaction' with various aspects of where they were living. A year after entering HF, very high proportions were satisfied with the autonomy they had in their accommodation (e.g., 94% were satisfied with the control they had about who could come round).[22]

However, a steady supply of housing to sustain Housing First beyond the pilot stage was identified as a key factor in the limitations of the programme. The 2021 evaluation paper of Housing First concluded that:

> Securing a sufficient supply of suitable properties for service users was considered the main risk in each Pilot area. … Ideally this would mean having access to a property supply from the start. In some areas, a greater focus on facilitating PRS access earlier in the programme development and mobilisation would have been beneficial.[23]

A reliance upon private rented sector homes to fulfil Housing First's provisions is clearly not ideal. In Housing First England's FAQs document, a preference for social housing as a more suitable form of tenancy is expressed:

> Just under 50% of services source housing through the private rented sector, which can be challenging when considering the Local Housing Allowance and use of Assured Shorthold Tenancies. Social Housing seems to be a more stable and affordable form of housing, and is sourced through agreements within local authorities (i.e. social housing allocations are given for Housing First residents) or through partnerships (i.e. a service will partner directly with a social landlord or is part of a larger organisation which has its own stock). However it can be more difficult to access, with longer waiting periods, and there may be less flexibility in offering people the option of moving to a different property if needed.[24]

As professional and political opinion continues to be won over by the growing evidence base of Housing First, the prevailing question over the sustainability of the scheme remains an accessible supply of truly affordable housing – which in the most successful schemes is provided partly through a readily available stream of council or social housing. However, with no prospect of significantly increasing those council and social housing numbers in the near future, it is unclear how the scheme may develop before reaching a natural buffer.

'Everyone In'

For a brief period during the COVID-19 crisis, street homelessness was rendered effectively nil following the 'Everyone In' policy announced by government in March 2020. Through that policy, funding was provided to all local authorities to secure accommodation for any and all rough sleepers on the streets of UK cities. Much of this accommodation was in hotels and B&Bs – unsuitable long-term accommodation but from a homelessness prevention and Housing First perspective, an exciting opportunity to engage with high need individuals and get them off the streets.

However, two months later, in May 2020, the scheme was quietly and unceremoniously wrapped up without any official communique or recognition from government.[25] In many local authority areas, former beneficiaries of Everyone In were able to retain a roof over their heads through alternatively funded arrangements – but a huge opportunity was missed. In report by Shelter one year on, the extent of that missed opportunity is spelt out clearly:

> The Government's ambition to get 'everyone in' during the pandemic showed us just how much can be achieved with the right political will and funding.
>
> Though not perfect – with many still stuck on the streets during the deadly pandemic – 'Everyone In' represents a watershed moment in this country's history.
>
> It has shown us that we have the power to end rough sleeping for good. With many people brought in off the streets in this pandemic, we have an opportunity like never before. And we can't afford to squander it by failing to make sure people can move on into permanent accommodation.[26]

The opportunity that came with housing nearly 100 per cent of chronic rough sleepers, housed even in temporary accommodation, was huge. The fact this opportunity was not seized indicates a lack of strategy and commitment from government to its own pledge to rid the streets of rough sleeping within the space of the last Parliament (up to December 2019). As the report notes:

Government state that 37,000 people have been helped under 'Everyone In', with 26,000 helped into longer-term accommodation.

But this report details new research that finds that fewer than 1 in 4 (23%) people had moved into settled accommodation of at least six months – that's an estimated 8,600 people.

This means that more than three-quarters (77%) of those initially accommodated under 'Everyone In' had not moved into settled accommodation. This equates to an estimated 29,000 people.[27]

Siloed and short-term funding

For those working on government-funded schemes to tackle homelessness, there is little in the way of a coherent or comprehensive approach to addressing the matter systematically or strategically – a problem exemplified by the numerous short-term funding initiatives which provide the bulk of resource for homelessness support.

In local government in Greater Manchester, as one example, councils must work to deliver homelessness and homelessness-adjacent services through a huge variety of programmes and grants from various departments; the 'Changing Futures Development Grant', the 'Community Accommodation Services' programme, 'Discretionary Housing Payments', the 'Homelessness – Out of Hospital Care' programme, the 'Homelessness Prevention Grant', 'Homelessness Transformation Fund', 'Housing First' programme, the 'Household Support Fund', 'Rough Sleeping Accommodation Fund', 'Rough Sleeping, Drug and Alcohol Treatment Grant', 'Rough Sleeping Initiative' and the 'Winter Pressures Fund'.

In addition to this huge plethora of grants and programmes – each provided temporarily, on its own separate timescale and with its own funding criteria – various housing grants and programmes are also utilised for homelessness prevention, while not being directly related, such as the 'Affordable Homes Programme' and 'Brownfield Funding' programme.

This is just the list of funding sources taken by one local authority area – not incorporating the separate funding initiatives and programmes which are funnelled through NHS England or other public services.

Taken as a whole, the impact of this hugely varied programme for tackling homelessness leads to the development of professional siloes, in which heavily related work takes place concurrently, running the risk of duplication and inefficiency – and the short-term nature of the funding means that strategic, long-term planning is often difficult if not impossible.

Both of these issues point to the fundamental reactivity of the government's approach to funding for homelessness prevention – as well as the lack of an objective evidence base. Where data provided through schemes such as Housing First clearly shows the underlying requirement for a steady supply of truly affordable homes in tackling 'complex needs' and chronic homelessness, instead the schemes we utilise tend to emphasise tackling other esoteric traits associated with homelessness such as unemployment, substance abuse and educational attainment, with the provision of housing provided in isolation. Homelessness is treated as though it is a pathology or series of character defects, as opposed to the lack of having a home. As has been clearly established, the single most effective programme of response to chronic rough sleeping is Housing First, in which rough sleepers are provided secure tenancy in their own home with wrap-around social support. Given the clear evidence base for Housing First, it remains a mystery that so little time and resource is spent providing such accommodation as opposed to the myriad of initiatives directed towards addressing the symptoms of street homelessness.

Lack of long-term commitment and strategy

In total, the UK's approach to tackling homelessness is characterised by a paucity of long-term vision or strategy on behalf of central government, and an unwillingness to engage with evidence-based policy.

Too many of the UK's homelessness programmes focus on remedying character deficiencies such as substance abuse, criminality or 'complex needs' – neglecting the direct experience of Housing First that, primarily, a home is in the vast majority of incidences the first port of call in tackling the multiplicity of issues associated with chronic homelessness and rough sleeping.

For every policy initiative and funding pot dedicated to tackling homelessness as it manifests itself on our streets and in our cities, there is a policy which is proactively damaging to the cause of containing homelessness and ultimately ending it.

Welfare reform has been one of the single biggest contributors towards financial insecurity among those at highest risk of homelessness, but rather than seek to mitigate or turn back on those reforms, instead the direction of travel is to double down.

Equally, the laws around tenancies make English renters unique in Europe in their vulnerability to eviction – issues which will remain even once Section 21 evictions are put to an end due to our lax approach to short-term tenancies and security of tenure.

Meanwhile, policies such as Everyone In, the Rough Sleepers Initiative, Social Impact Bonds and others are siloed and piecemeal – and based on short-term funding arrangements which grant no security or consistency to service providers either in local government or the charitable sector. And while government does – through these schemes – recognise at least an imperative to tackle rough sleeping, the far wider issue of those living in temporary accommodation is broadly neglected.

Further complicating the issue of the government's response to homelessness is the unintended consequences of many of its programmes in worsening access to affordable accommodation in the private sector. Through schemes like the Community Accommodation programme, the Everyone In scheme, Rough Sleeper Accommodation programme, Rough Sleeper Initiative and the Next Steps programme all rely on the private housing market to provide temporary accommodation at a heavily subsidised rate. To do this in the context of hugely limited supplies of accommodation in general is to pump billions in inflationary investment into the system, embedding higher rents and worsening the issues of affordability.

Considering that an acute shortage of reliable, affordable, safe and suitable accommodation is the golden thread uniting each of the government's initiatives on tackling homelessness together, the absence of a strategy for funding and delivering social and council housing is puzzling, and highly negligent. The social rented sector is the only portion of the housing market capable of consistently delivering these services – and its absence is referred to repeatedly in evaluations and surveys of different homeless initiatives and services – yet discussion on the topic from government remains mute. Indeed, as discussed elsewhere, the number of new council and social houses continues to atrophy and decline.

As opposed to delivering more social rented homes, government's solution is instead to continue an array of unconnected initiatives which perform the function of pumping more and more money into the private rented sector – leaving councils and housing services to manage what are effectively agencies of private landlords offering bonds and cash incentives for them to take on tenants, who they can evict with six months' notice.

Tales from the coal face of homelessness provision

Molly Bishop worked for four years as the Strategic Lead for homelessness at the Greater Manchester Combined Authority between 2019 and 2023, before moving on to work on homelessness at Westminster Council, then to her current role as Head of Implementation for the Centre for Homelessness Support. She spoke with me about her experiences working in homelessness prevention, the demoralisation prevalent within local government around addressing homelessness and her frustrations with national government's approaches to systemic problems:

> I've got a funny relationship with it [local government] because I think even though I've worked sort of alongside it and briefly in it, there's a sense I've never really felt like part of the local government, like part of the furniture. And I think some of that is that a lot of people who are working in homelessness in local government have reached a point where they are just trying to make the wheel

turn. And that isn't because they don't care or they didn't come into the role wanting to achieve the best outcomes for people. But that is the only way that they can find of doing their job day to day, which is just to keep things ticking.

I think local government is a space where you paper over a lot of the gaps that are left in poor government policy, while also trying to shine a light on the fact that they're there and that if you don't do anything about them, they'll get bigger and bigger. Local government officers have been doing that work for a very, very long time. When I first started working at GMCA, some of the local government officials that I talked to really just wanted to give me a history lesson on why things were the way they were, and why we weren't going to be able to make them better. And I think there was a huge amount of scepticism, given the length of time and the kind of hollowing out of public services generally, but also the specific neglect for the issues that that drive homelessness, which leads to a lot of people to feel like it's just not possible to really turn the corner on this.

And obviously, what's you know, the last ten years have been absolutely brutal to both people, households, families, people experiencing homelessness … but also to those professionals and officials who have been trying to make things better, who had their jobs made worse year on year, and felt like what they're lobbying for and what they're saying, and the evidence that they have and the experiences that they have just aren't being taken into consideration.

National government frequently addresses homelessness as a standalone issue and a system that exists, a set of laws and services and experiences that exist beyond or are disconnected from wider system failures. And even when that has been evidenced, i.e. that Home Office policy is driving households to destitution, government department to government department are often not able to wrestle out those issues and find a coherent policy which supports a reduction in homelessness. Other things trump homelessness outcomes and there are departmental hierarchies.

There's a real knowledge and capability gap on what works to implement policy well. You see it between civil servants and when you get to public servant local government level. Knowledge of how to make policy work in practice is largely locally held as every place is different. With something like the Homelessness Prevention Act [2017] it has become an administrative task, rather than being implemented to drive homelessness prevention in real terms. We've had funds that government literally has to go on a road-show to sell. … They can't get local authorities to bid for this money because they know it's so difficult to implement, like the early rounds of the rough sleeper accommodation program (RSAP), which, over time, they've tweaked and improved, and there's now the supported housing accommodation program (SHAP). But it's an example of designing something from the top down that is just completely not fit for purpose.

You've only got so much time in the day, and you can't overestimate the amount of time that's put into bidding and negotiating and then mobilising to somebody else's timeline, and then reporting to somebody else's reporting expectations, within the full knowledge that the funding will also end, probably within 12 months, definitely within three years. That's the cycle. So, yeah, there are always calls to be made when government releases new policy and new funding as to whether it's actually the best use of time to draw down on it. And local authorities have got commissioning cycles, this doesn't seem to be something that national government take into consideration in the release of funding and services are being crippled by the short-term sporadic funding approach.

I remember, and I'm struggling to put a year on it (which makes it difficult to identify which homelessness minister it was because we've had so many). But there was a letter that was sent out to local authority chief execs, pre-Christmas, sort of saying, 'this is such a difficult time', 'everyone's doing amazing work', 'this is the winter funding that we've given, you know, however many millions'. And then it said, 'we really want everybody to take a really focused approach to lowering the numbers of rough sleeping this Christmas' and I can't remember how the sentence was phrased, but the meaning of it was 'it would be really great if you personally could focus on the outcome of just one person rough sleeping in your area to sort of sponsor their journey off the streets'. And I remember a meeting had with all of the heads of homelessness across the region, and one of my colleagues described it as a 'sponsor of donkey campaign', which just cut across the disregard for the amount of work that was going on and the complexity of the challenge. You know, the idea that actually, if you just paid a little bit more attention, or if you pulled some strings a bit harder, that the outcomes for people would be different, was, was just quite incredible.

I think that's what's so difficult about working in homelessness, and why it kind of has a particular feel to it, which is often quite kind of heated and emotive. There are a lot of big characters, and because the policy is dealing with people's lives at the point where it is people are at their worst, or people are having the hardest possible time, it makes bad policy all the more distressing.

9

Delivering council and social housing

From the introduction of Right to Buy in 1980, new council-house building dropped to negligible levels under consecutive governments – but it was not simply the numbers of new council homes which were at issue. Equally as significant to the demise of council houses as the drop in production was a prevailing policy hostility to the delivery of council homes, and an emphasis on moving ownership of these homes out of local councils and towards private individuals and social housing providers.

Not only were millions of homes sold at a huge discount following the introduction of Right to Buy, but millions more were transferred into social housing providers particularly under New Labour. Since, there has been a steady loss of housing from the social housing sector as well as from homes lost through Right to Buy, particularly in the last decade as the funding model for social housing providers has become less reliable and housing associations have been forced to adopt more overtly commercial business models.

Throughout most of this period, political discourse paid little heed to the loss of council and social housing, and a general culture of stigma developed in which council estates were associated with poverty, deprivation and violence. Very little political appetite to build more came either from the Conservative or New Labour administrations in government with numbers of new council houses falling to a nadir under New Labour in 2004 (ONS).

However, as the housing crisis has become more and more acute, and as the increased size of the private rented sector (PRS) has seen significant deprivation and poverty persist in PRS with often higher rents and less security of tenancy, public attitudes towards council housing have begun to shift.

Additionally, more and more evidence continues to be compiled from housing programmes illustrating that the absence of an available supply of housing is hampering our homelessness relief efforts, as well as causing bottlenecks for move-on accommodation, downsizing homes and reducing the numbers of families being housed in temporary accommodation.

Since 2016, under Theresa May's government, government policy has begun to talk of the necessity of council housing as an important element of the housing mix and small measures to enable council and social house building (such as the affordable homes programme and the lifting of the cap on Housing Revenue Accounts) have been announced.

Despite these measures, however, council and social houses are still not being built at remotely the scale required to resolve Britain's housing crisis.

Right to Buy

By far and away the biggest obstacle to large-scale council-house building is the Right to Buy legislation first introduced by Margaret Thatcher's government in 1980, through the Housing Act of the same year. The Right to Buy granted all tenants of council houses a right to purchase their home from the local authority at a discount of up to 70 per cent (with other variable rates for different types of properties). To facilitate the purchase, local authorities were obliged to provide a mortgage with no requirement for a deposit.

Only 50 per cent of the money raised through Right to Buy was returned to the local authority itself, and that money was ring-fenced for the paying down of debts as opposed to reinvestment in new properties.

The impact of the reform was immediate. Within the space of seven years, over 1,000,000 homes had been sold under the legislation – and it became economically unviable for councils to replace them, both for the loss they had made on the original house but also the risk of losing further stock. The numbers of council-house completions plummeted, and by the mid-1990s council housing was no longer a significant net contributor to Britain's housing stock.

The terms of Right to Buy legislation are particularly egregious to local authorities, creating huge financial risk for any committed to building and maintaining such properties.

Since that time, the terms of Right to Buy have been altered slightly by different governments. On their election in 1997, the incoming Labour government reduced the rate of discount available to tenants in areas which had severe pressure on their housing stock – and in 2005, five years' tenancy was required before tenants were able to qualify to purchase the homes.

In 2012, David Cameron once again raised the upper threshold of discount to 70 per cent and suggested that revenues raised should go towards new affordable homes – although the scheme's clear lack of economic viability prevented any success. In the same year, borrowing caps were placed on Housing Revenue Accounts well below the levels at which it would be possible to finance new builds.

From 2016, the Housing and Planning Bill extended the Right to Buy to housing association tenants, although turning this pledge into reality has proved legally tricky (Housing and Planning Bill, 2016).

However, the broad impact of Right to Buy remains as a severe dampener on local authorities' ability to deliver new homes at any kind of scale. Even if there were not discounts on the value of the homes sold and receipts were returned solely to the local authority in question, the underlying concept of Right to Buy presents several logistical challenges for local authorities as developers:

- In the first instance, replacing individual homes 'like for like' is often less economical than providing a high volume of homes on large developments – which account for many of the homes being sold. When set against generally increasing costs of construction for new builds, replacing homes sold piecemeal under Right to Buy is in the overwhelming number of cases not a viable proposition with monies gained from their sale.
- Second, in general, the first generations of council properties were built in choice locations close to transport amenities, schools, sites of employment and with access to shops and other services. In most cases, particularly in built-up areas, councils now must choose from less choice sites – infill areas left out from previous development, and sites further away from central locations and amenities. In many instances, councils landholdings have suffered greatly as many local authorities have been encouraged to sell them off through the past decade of local government austerity – as such, new land for development must be bought at a premium.
- Finally, and most significantly, the insecurity that Right to Buy poses to council assets means that sourcing finance to build new homes becomes next to impossible. In the absence of the generous grant funding regimes of the past, profiling debt and repayment schedules on council homes which could be sold at any minute becomes unworkable, as certainty around the asset, its projected revenue and expenditure is severely diminished.

Of all the houses sold under Right to Buy since 1980, Shelter believes that less than 5 per cent have ever been replaced. Over 40 per cent of homes sold under Right to Buy are estimated to have either been sold or converted into PRS housing – and in some areas, this is even more acute, with Milton Keynes estimating that a huge 70 per cent of its former council stock is now being let privately.[1,2]

The impact of Right to Buy on the development of new housing is revealed most starkly when the devolved decisions of the Scottish Government (2014) and Welsh Government (2017) to abolish Right to Buy are considered. Scotland is currently in the middle of a £3 billion scheme to deliver 50,000 council houses. In 2019, Adam Montgomery, the former leader of Midlothian Council, was able to claim that despite being 'one of the smallest local authorities in Scotland … we are building more council houses than the whole of London' – this, despite Scotland reflecting only one-tenth of the population of England.

In addition to the removal of Right to Buy, Scottish councils also enjoy fewer restrictions on their borrowing capacity, and a more generous grant regime. John Mills, Head of Housing for Fife Council, gave a frank assessment of the situation in a 2019 article for *InsideHousing*. Mr Mills commented:

> There was little point in our investing over £125,000 in a property and after a period of time having to sell at a significant discount.
>
> You are not able to get the rental income you need over a 30-year mortgage, for example, if you are having to sell at Right to Buy discount. The rest of the tenants and the Housing Revenue Account have to pick up the tab.[3]

In Wales, the new rules have allowed councils like Cardiff to announce a £800 million plan for 4,000 new council homes by 2030.

While recent proposed reforms to Right to Buy, including restricting the sale of new-build council homes in the first 35 years, will hugely alter the balance in the economics of developing new council homes, they fall short of attaining the full benefit of removing Right to Buy altogether. The existing stock of council homes will continue to bleed out and be sold, and even with 35 year pauses on sale, new units lack the capacity to be utilised as long-term assets which could assist in borrowing and more strategic planning of housing capacity.

Why don't housing associations build more?

The historic answer to the decline of councils as developers has been the rise of housing associations as an alternative provider of 'social rented' properties. Housing associations have a history as philanthropic, non-profit bodies – many of which emerged in the latter half of the 19th century – to provide subsidised housing for the poor. However, most existing housing associations expanded, or were created, following the introduction of Right to Buy and the channelling of grants for affordable housing to housing associations as an alternative to councils.

Many housing associations were formed as part of 'stock transfer' agreements, through which councils would bulk transfer their existing council houses to these new entities. Such 'stock transfers' were also legally facilitated by the Housing Acts of 1985 and 1988, with the 1988 Act further redefining housing associations as non-public bodies which therefore had unrestricted access to private finance. Many councils saw transfer of stock as the only way to both protect their assets from Right to Buy, but also to access the required finance for repairs and maintenance. The Joseph Rowntree Foundation has estimated that as many as 1.3 million council homes were transferred directly into housing association ownership between 1988 and 2008.[4] But despite access to private finance, and despite a fairly impressive track record at upgrading transferred stock, housing associations have never provided substantial numbers of new housing units comparative to their local authority predecessors.

Many commentators criticise the housing associations for this failing, pointing to the increasingly commercial model taken on by housing associations as time has passed, citing large commercial surpluses and high rates of executive pay as evidence of misallocation of resources. However, there are core, structural obstacles to the delivery of social rented homes by housing associations at the scale required to meet our housing needs, which must be considered.

Particularly over the past decade, the fundamental funding model of housing associations has been called into question. Traditionally, housing associations secure income through several different streams – government funding, rents and private finance. Following the 1988 Housing Act, the proportion of grant relative to the cost of new builds by housing associations was reduced, leaving borrowing as the primary source of investment. While grant regimes were still generous, this situation was tenable; however upon achieving power in 2008, the Conservative government quickly set about reducing grant funding for affordable housing by 60 per cent, pushing housing associations into further reliance on private sector funding.[5]

Up until 2008, housing associations were regulated by the Housing Corporation that had been established under the 1964 Housing Act (which was split into the Tenant Services Authority in 2010, then the Homes and Communities Agency in 2012, replaced again by Homes England in 2018). Following the 2008 Housing and Regeneration Act, a new 'Regulator of Social Housing' was established, and in 2011 the government introduced 'affordable rent', permitting rents 'to be set at up to 80% of market rent' in a given locale.[6] The foundation of the Regulator of Social Housing allowed, among other powers, government to set the rate of social sector rents. This power was first utilised in 2016, when government announced moves to cut social sector rents by 1 per cent each year for four years (the 'social rent reduction').[7]

At the time of this announcement, it was clear to the industry that such moves would mean a restriction on the numbers of units of social housing being completed. Quoted in the *Guardian*, then chief executive officer of the National Housing Federation, David Orr, said that '[a]t the very least, 27,000 new homes will not now be built, though that figure could be much higher'. In the same year, in an excoriating statement, the Institute for Fiscal Studies scathingly reported that the reductions would be 'of little or no direct benefit to most of the 3.9 million households in England living in social housing', stating that '[b]y reducing the annual rental income of social landlords by £2.3 billion, the cut in social rents could reduce the amount of new housing supply. The Office for Budget Responsibility assumes that 14,000 fewer social sector properties will be built between now and 2020–21 as a result'.[8]

The Institute for Fiscal Studies further noted that the benefits of the rent reduction were likely to confer to the Exchequer, rather than social tenants – as many of the social tenants would have had their rent increase covered through receipt of Housing Benefit, and that lower social rents would increase 'the incentive to seek access to social housing' and therefore increase demand.

Two years into the 'social rent reduction', the government announced its plans to allow rent increase on both social and affordable rent properties by the Consumer Price Index plus 1 per cent each year for five years, from 2020. However this limit was again curtailed in 2023, following high levels of inflation, capping rent increases at 7 per cent. But despite these changes, government fiddling with the formula for social rent increases hugely impacted the delivery pipeline of social rented properties from 2015 onwards.

In addition to such cack-handed manoeuvres from the Treasury, housing associations have also found themselves hamstrung by changing market conditions, which leave their model of relatively affordable housing provision particularly vulnerable to economic shock. In a 2018 study on under-delivery by housing associations by Network Homes, researchers found that the average build cost for a new housing unit had increased by 42 per cent in the previous ten years, with only one-third of the grant received per home between 2011 and 2018 as had been received between 2008 and 2011. With grants of £60,000 to £80,000 per social rented home, researchers found that an additional £200,000 was still required from 'borrowing, reserves or cross-subsidy from sales' equivalent to 75 per cent of the total build costs.[9] In short, the grant and funding regime for social homes no longer matches the construction costs for building.

More recently, since the inflation crisis following the Russian invasion of Ukraine and the Bank of England's decision to raise interest rates, housing associations have faced difficulties in making their model of affordable housing delivery stack up. In April 2024, the *Financial Times* reported that 'higher interest rates ... have stretched the financing model for affordable housebuilding'.[10] The article notes that between 2023 and 2024, housing associations across England had cut their five-year building forecasts by 64,000 homes, with Paul Hackett, the chief executive officer of Southern Housing, claiming that government grants funded only one-fifth of the cost of new housing.

On top of these unfavourable economic conditions, housing associations have also had to contend with repeated threats from government to introduce Right to Buy to housing associations, alternatively known as the 'Right to Acquire'. Since the 1996 Housing Act, repeated Conservative governments have attempted to end the era of subsidised social rents altogether through a final act of privatisation; the right for housing association tenants to purchase their homes at a discount. However, legally the extension of the Right to Buy to housing associations has proven tricky, given the independent legal status of housing associations as private charities. Given that housing associations have been financed primarily by private sector debt since the

1988 Housing Act, the Right to Acquire for housing associations cannot be achieved without causing a default on the loan securities taken against housing association properties, causing catastrophe for lenders and tenants as homes are seized by lenders and returns lost. In addition to this, housing associations themselves would be ruined by the policy, and have to shut up shop. Despite the self-evident unworkability of the Right to Acquire proposals, the Conservatives have repeatedly included a pledge to introduce the measure in their 2005, 2015 and 2019 manifestos, as well as in advance of the 2022 local elections.[11] Though the measures have yet to take any substantial toll on housing associations, the repeated attempts to foist Right to Acquire onto housing associations is a clear marker of the Conservative Party's ongoing contempt for the housing association sector, and its refusal to engage seriously in measures to increase the sector's effectiveness in delivering homes.

It must be noted that even in the more favourable grant conditions of the 1980s and 1990s, housing associations were unable to replicate the huge numbers of new developments delivered by councils over the previous few decades. Fundamentally, the nature of housing associations' dependence on private finance for delivery has pushed housing associations down a road on commerciality against which the underlying purpose of their organisations – to provide discounted rents – is perpetually in conflict. New development has often been unrewardingly costly for housing associations, measured against the risks of commercial exposure to increased costs and unforeseen obstacles to development. As the organisations have been forced into commercial development by a restriction of their core funding model, the costly, affordable accommodation they provide as the basis of their organisations becomes a more and more difficult element of their model to deliver.

Housing associations provide a hugely important route to house-building and development, and it is imperative that the financial and legislative chains cast upon them be unshackled. However, consistent policy initiatives from government fail to unlock the potential of this sector to provide homes that the country truly needs, implementing obstacles which must be removed if we are in any way serious about dealing with our housing crisis.

The Housing Revenue Account

Traditionally, councils have used Housing Revenue Accounts – accounts which exist solely for the construction, maintenance and management of council-owned homes – through which to borrow and build new housing. Housing Revenue Accounts have always been required in law to set balanced budgets and have required approval to borrow, however historically they had no absolute borrowing limit and were able to service large amounts of debt (historically also facilitated by more generous grant regimes).

However, in 2012 the Coalition government imposed a cap on borrowing within Housing Revenue Accounts which remained until the Theresa May premiership in 2018. During this time, a key source of finance for the development of new council homes was removed, and in conjunction with reductions in grant and impositions of rent caps on social rents, had a inhibitive effect on the construction of new social housing.

Though the cap has been lifted once again, access to finance is only one small part of the problem facing councils, particularly in light of the huge negative impact caused by Right to Buy on the ability of councils to replace stock. As such, the repeal of the borrowing cap has had a negligible impact on the delivery of new numbers of council homes since.

Replacement of homes

Alongside the Right to Buy measures adopted at the 2015 budget, the Conservative manifesto of that year committed to the replacement of council and social homes lost through Right to Buy utilising Right to Buy receipts – involving providing a larger share of the sale price back to local authorities. This policy was not costed or thought through from the beginning, and in large areas of the country outside of pockets of London (where values were inordinately high) was entirely unfeasible. The Local Government Association estimates that since the commitment to 1 for 1 replacements of council houses, there continues to be a net loss of council and social houses, as many as 7,449 in 2022–2023 alone. Furthermore, the Local Government Association believes that an average of 24,000 council homes a year have been lost since 1991.[12]

Receipts by themselves are entirely insufficient to cover the building costs of replacing a property. Partly, this is a by-product of rising land values, but also the concurrent costs of breaking up former council estates and the associated economies of scale with which they were once managed, and the redevelopment of new homes in areas which are not close to amenities or sites of employment. The question of replacing council homes lost through Right to Buy has never been realistic or practical, nor has government ever truly delved into what would be required to make such a scheme stack up.

Affordable Homes Grant

In recent decades targeted grants towards the delivery of council and social housing has been entirely insufficient to build at scale – grants which, as noted earlier, are essential in the business model for delivering these units.

One fund which is related (though not devoted) to the delivery of such homes is the Affordable Homes Programme, which between 2021 and 2026 commits £7.39 billion to deliver 130,000 affordable homes outside of London.[13]

Within the category of 'affordable homes', homes for social rent comprise one strand out of six. Other forms of affordable homes funded through the scheme include:

- Affordable Rent – rents set at 80 per cent of the local market rent for an equivalent property.
- Shared Ownership – allowing the purchaser to acquire a share of the home and pay rent on the remaining share, starting at a rate of 10 per cent.
- Homeownership for people with Long-term Disabilities (delivery of specialist homes for the disabled).
- Older Persons Shared Ownership – shared ownership available only to the over-55s.
- Rent to Buy – rents set at 80 per cent of market value to allow the tenant to save for a deposit.

Among the competing categories, social rented units struggle for space and the issue is further complicated by the distribution formula which sits behind the scheme. The formula, as standard under the previous Conservative government, weights funding towards areas of the 'highest affordability pressure' – that is, those areas of the country where the absolute difference between wages and house prices are most significant in absolute terms. In general, this formula directs what small amount of social housing provision that there is to areas of the country where there is the most wealth and where there is the least concentrated deprivation. When rolled out in Greater Manchester, a city region in which over 50 per cent of children live in poverty, only the five wealthiest regions of the city (Manchester, Salford, Stockport, Trafford and Bury) were deemed eligible for the funding while the incredibly deprived boroughs of Tameside, Oldham, Rochdale, Wigan and Bolton were not.

With huge sections of the most deprived areas of the country ineligible for the available sums to build social rented properties, the prospect of delivering the scale of social and council properties required and across the right stretch of geography is futile. The July 2025 Comprehensive Spending Review has announced a huge increase to Affordable Homes Program funding, rising to £39 billion over 10 years, and further specifies that of the 300,000 new homes it intends to build in this period, at least 180,000 are to be for social rent.[14] While welcome, the details of both the distribution mechanisms for this funding are yet to be fully determined, and the social housing sector is still cautious about integrating the fund fully into their business plans given the uncertainty of the scheme operating over multiple parliaments. Despite these misgivings, the fund is substantial enough to be a real game changer for social housing delivery in the coming years. The issue of distribution, however, remains unchecked, and without further specification, the new money risks being again sent into the areas of highest absolute values, away from areas of highest deprivation.

Dérive and the difficulties in delivering social rents

In 2017, Salford Council established a wholly-owned subsidiary housing development company, Dérive, for the purpose of delivering social housing. The name Dérive (French for 'drift') was inspired by the Situationist philosopher Guy Debord and his 'Theory of Dérive', a process of spontaneous travel through urban landscapes. The purpose of this process, for Debord, was to encourage playful interactions with the physical and built environment, as a method for overcoming the alienation of life under capitalism, and as a tool for the study of urban pyschogeography. The company was named by the late councillor Paul Longshaw, a former housing officer himself, who as lead member for housing on the council was determined to deliver true social rented accommodation in the city which had been absent from new housing development for decades. I interviewed the City Mayor Paul Dennett, former Director of Place from Salford Council Peter Openshaw and Dérive Director Councillor John Merry about Dérive and the story of the challenges in establishing the organisation. Openshaw notes:

> This goes back to Paul Longshaw, now sadly deceased, and the mayor who had a vision to do something about the housing social housing challenges within the city. Massive waiting lists, burgeoning rents, all the rest of it, and basically not enough properties for people to get hold of affordable rent. So Paul [Longshaw], supported by the mayor and others, decided he wanted to do something about that.

Dennett also recalls:

> Housing Associations at this time were pursuing this cross-subsidy model, using the proceeds of that to build truly affordable housing, but the numbers weren't stacking up. It wasn't happening. As far as I was concerned, we needed to use our land holdings, our borrowing powers, we needed to take commuted sums from private development happening in the city to set up this company and to get on with building truly affordable housing.

Councillor Longshaw was appointed as director of the company in May 2017, a role tragically cut short by his passing in September the same year. Longshaw had always been passionate about housing and homelessness, and was an active volunteer in homelessness charities across Greater Manchester. These activities were highlighted in a tribute from his ward colleague Councillor John Warmisham in the council chamber following his passing:

He was committed to Salford working tirelessly to improve the quality of life for people through housing. His particular concern was homelessness so much that he did voluntary work at night shelters, slept out overnight to raise money and was currently working with Coffee4Craig [a GM-based homelessness charity] looking at a Salford base.

In Councillor Longhsaw's place, Councillor Merry was appointed chair of the company and continued to develop the organisation. Dérive was initially established with £2 million in 'commuted sums' from a Section 106 negotiation (a financial contribution towards affordable housing from a developer who was unwilling or unable to provide affordable housing 'on-site'). Merry recalls:

> We had a £2 million fund for social housing, which we could spend as we wished on new housing stock, and building that new housing stock, and that's what we decided to do. We identified a site, built the units which were almost immediately snapped up, and we were able to recycle the money.

From day one, a significant obstacle to the building of new homes was Right to Buy, through which homes built by the council with public grant could be sold. A key focus for Dérive was avoiding this outcome, allowing the council to borrow to build. But this wasn't easy, as Openshaw notes:

> They [councillors] didn't want a situation where those houses that came under the Dérive banner could be subject to the right to buy. And really the only way to do that was for the council to put in all the money. The only problem was it wasn't financially viable in the long run, because the money, which was a heck of a lot of money that was needed, only produces a fairly low level of rents.

Ultimately, Openshaw notes, public subsidy was needed to make the figures stack up:

> Very quickly we established that the only real way to get more properties delivered was to find a way where we can access Homes England [government] money. Generally speaking, you need 35–40 per cent of the cost of a property, something like £70,000 a unit.
>
> So we needed a setup that enabled us to access that money. The council did have registered provider status [as a regulated provider of social rents] so we could access money that way, but it would trigger the Right to Buy. Obviously, with Right to Buy people can buy them after a certain amount of time, get a big discount, and we'd lose the housing.
>
> We settled on a model where Dérive itself became a registered landlord, then could bid for the money itself. Yes, that still attracted the Right to Acquire. But the Right to Acquire is much less advantageous [to the recipient] than the Right to Buy.

Avoiding Right to Buy on the new properties would require more, however, than simply establishing Dérive as a social landlord. A complex and innovative company structure had to be established to ensure the properties remained safe from unwanted sales. Openshaw continues:

> Dérive needed a housing company and a load of subsidiaries where the council could still exercise some control over operations (albeit the registered social landlord element had to be completely independent of the council). That sounds really easy, it was far from it. When I took over from my predecessor, they had spent a lot of time and effort working with legal colleagues trying to come up with a structure that would work. They got external legal advice to do that, and got absolutely nowhere.

Openshaw also believes he faced internal opposition from council officers to establishing the company:

> Usually when a project is struggling people say 'there's political opposition to things'. Well, there was no political opposition here. They [the politicians] really wanted it to happen.
> The biggest battle here was internally with legal and financial colleagues who weren't wholly supportive of what we were doing. So we would have a way forward, but at every stage this was challenged with 'we don't think this is [legally] right', or 'this is too risky, or it'll cost the council lots of money'. I could never get my head around it. Politicians wanted to do something clearly a no-brainer in terms of the benefits it would bring, and yet we had a group of people who were trying to derail it at every opportunity.

City Mayor Paul Dennett also recalls having to deal with internal opposition to the company:

> The setting up of Dérive was happening at a time when the direction of travel since Thatcher had been to hollow out local government, to turn local government into a commissioning and contract based entity, and not really to meddle in what they perceive as public services and public good being delivered by the market.
> So we were trying to set up Dérive against the backdrop of outsourcing, commissioning, contracting, that is inevitably going to bring you up against some sort of resistance. And inevitably, in those early years, we did see resistance. I think officers of the City Council in those early years quietly wanted to just talk up the importance of our housing association partners as the only vehicle for delivering truly affordable housing.

In the face of intransigent internal opposition, Openshaw recalls reaching outside of the council for additional support in setting up the company:

Lots of other people across the country were doing similar things, but all slightly different. So we were checking them out to see which ones might suit Salford's aspirations and ideals, and none were really quite a perfect match.

But just by chance, we noticed one chap who had advised two different councils, and was obviously a bit of a specialist in this area. He had a housing background, but he also had a financial background. I rang him up and said, 'Listen, we've got this problem in Salford. We can see you've done all this for people, if we would speak to you and get you on board, do you think you could have a look and see if you can come up with something that meets our needs?'. And literally, on that phone call, he said, 'Well, it's not too complicated. You just do this, this and this.' So we got him in.

The new company was structured with the council-owned 'Dérive Group', beneath which sits 'Dérive Registered Provider (RP)' to run the houses. A further company exists to hold the first 65 homes built by the group without public subsidy, and another to manage private rented homes Dérive is set to build on new sites in conjunction with more social rents. Openshaw believes the company mission and structure could be expanded further in future: 'So Dérive PRS provides, hopefully, an ethical private renting market. And then there's other boxes that, in time, could be filled. So Dérive Regeneration, do we want to get involved in wider regeneration and development? Do we want to start building a workforce that can actually deliver these properties?'

With the company structure in place, Dérive was finally able to scale up its operations. Openshaw recalls:

That's when everything started in terms of setting aside council land instead of selling it to private developers or other registered providers. A lot of land was set aside. We did a big trawl of everything, tried to work out what the land bank was that could be made available.

We had about 60 houses at the time I got involved, and around 190 in the five years to now. The vision is for 3,000 over the next ten years, and we're well down the road with what's in the pipeline already to delivering about 1,500.

As for the misgivings within the council, both Dennett and Openshaw agree that the council is now fully on board with the project, driven in no small part through pride in the end quality of Dérive's finished units. Dennett notes:

Because not only are we delivering truly affordable housing, i.e. social rents and rents capped to Local Housing Allowance, we're also delivering this housing to fabric first standard, which is amazing. We've placed the importance of energy efficiency at the heart of the housing types and the housing build we bring forward, and it's been a massive learning curve. And Salford now, I'm proud to say, probably something in Greater Manchester, is it the vanguard of delivering truly affordable housing, but also at that energy efficient standard.

Openshaw concurs:

> We were building and are still building the very best quality housing that's being delivered in Salford, sustainable, accessible, you know, ticking all the boxes right at the very top of the list in terms of home. Homes England standards, you know, sustainable low energy, low cost.
> We won some local awards, we won some regional awards, and then we actually won a bloody national award for what we were doing. It's like, wow, from a standing start three years before.

But while Dérive is in its own terms a success, in and of itself, it cannot resolve Salford's housing crisis. Dennett refers to Dérive as playing a role in convincing the wider development market to engage in affordable housing, as a proof of concept:

> People are talking to our partners. Housing associations have come on this journey with us. ... We've had Salix [a stock transfer housing association in Salford] build passive house standard housing in front of the cathedral, rents are at social rents as well in the mix there. People are starting to come on the journey. And we've always been very clear, one of the reasons why Salford wanted to do this was to put pressure on the market, and the housing associations.

Openshaw also ponders on the scale of the challenge ahead: 'The waiting list [for social rented houses] is still around 6,000 households in Salford. So, you know, even 3,000 it gets you some way down the road, but it only starts really scratching the surface.'

Given the scale of the challenge in Salford and nationally, the story of Dérive illustrates both the extents and limitations of what can be achieved within the present legislative and funding environment. While the determination of Salford to work through these barriers is laudable, it is clear that the process of delivering social units is fraught with difficulty and risk.

10

Homeownership and house price inflation

Encouraging homeownership was a flagship standard of the Conservative government since its election as part of the Coalition government in 2010. In that year, Housing Minister Grant Shapps said:

> The Government are committed to helping those who aspire to own their own home. ... The coalition agreement included a commitment to promote shared ownership. While grant funding under the new investment model for affordable housing announced in the spending review will primarily target the new affordable rented product, there may be some scope for delivery of low-cost home ownership as part of the contractual arrangements with providers where this is appropriate for local circumstances.[1]

Further measures were introduced in the 2013 budget to assist first-time buyers, including Help to Buy – and in 2015, then Prime Minister David Cameron announced the Conservative Party's intentions to create a 'property owning democracy' and announced a raft of initiatives and investments to help first-time buyers onto the property ladder. The agenda has been central to Conservative messaging on housing ever since, under the premierships of Theresa May, Boris Johnson and Rishi Sunak. But despite this, rates of homeownership have been declining now for the past two decades. The 2021 Census reported that 62.5 per cent of UK residents owned their own homes either outright or via a mortgage, down from a high of 70.9 per cent in 2003.

By far and away the largest commitment of the last government to supporting homeownership was the Help to Buy scheme announced by Chancellor George Osborne in 2013, aiming to help first-time buyers and those looking to move home purchase a residential property. Through a mixture of equity loans, mortgage guarantees and Help to Buy Saving ISAs the scheme focused on allowing access to mortgages and other financial support with a reduced deposit (usually 5 per cent).

Yet since its peak of 71 per cent in 2003, the Office for National Statistics reports that homeownership has dropped to 62.5 per cent in 2021. For young adults between the ages of 25 and 34, that figure dropped from 59 per cent to 41 per cent. A report taken to the House of Lords in 2022 concluded:

The increased cost of owning a home is reflected in the fact that, between 1991 and 2003, about 40% of people whose parents were homeowners had become homeowners themselves by the age of 30; this dropped to 25% between 2004 and 2017. Over the same period, the figures decreased from 19% to 9% for those whose parents were not homeowners.[2]

Escalating house prices

Clearly, government is failing in its agenda for increasing rates of homeownership. Fundamentally, the root cause of the stagnation of homeownership is the increasing cost of housing. Government's own research[3] concludes that affordability of housing is the central issue preventing people getting onto the property ladder – citing numerous concerns. In the period between 1997 and 2004, the average deposit required from first-time buyers rose from 8.8 per cent to 21.7 per cent. A report by Halifax in 2021 found that the average cash sum of a UK deposit in that year was £59,000. In 2020, a report by the Affordable Housing Commission found that the average deposit required for a first-time buyer in London was £147,000.

The UK Collaborative Centre for Housing Evidence has said that 'the main constraint on achieving home ownership remains an inability to save the required deposit, a goal that becomes increasingly out-of-reach if house prices rise faster than savings'.[4]

In short, the schemes set in place by government are failing to subsidise first-time buyers to the extent at which prices are increasing – and to a sufficient level that the majority of potential first-time buyers are eligible for a mortgage.

Making things worse?

A report given by the House of Lords Built Environment Committee in 2022 has even suggested that government's investments into first-time buyers may actually be making the situation worse, by inflating prices. The report notes: 'We find that the Government's Help to Buy scheme, which will have cost around £29 billion in cash terms by 2023, inflates prices by more than its subsidy value in areas where it is needed the most.'[5] The report further argues that '[i]n the long term, funding for home ownership schemes do not provide good value for money, which would be better spent on increasing housing supply'.

The wisdom of using financial incentives to increase homeownership was questioned throughout the report, as a key component in the cycle of house price growth. Speaking to the committee, London School of Economics Professor Christian Hilber noted that: 'Demand side housing policies (such as the Help to Buy Equity Loan scheme) may increase housing construction, but only in locations where it is comparably easy to add new housing supply (such as near the English/Welsh border).' Adding that, in areas where 'jobs are located and housing is severely supply constrained (such as in Greater London)' the scheme has 'led to a substantive increase in house prices, with no statistically significant effect on construction numbers'.[6]

Policy fellow Laurie Macfarlane from University College London has argued that 'it was clear from the outset that the policy (Help to Buy) would do more harm than good', noting:

> Help-to-buy was premised on the idea that the problem of unaffordable house prices could be solved by making it easier for potential buyers to access a mortgage. But given that mortgage lending is a key driver of house prices, the scheme always risked pushing up prices further, thus benefiting existing owners rather than new buyers. Predictably, this is exactly what has happened.[7]

Macfarlane also argues that the scheme is poorly targeted, quoting findings from the National Audit Office, which state that as many as 63 per cent of those who benefited from Help to Buy initiatives could have still bought a home without assistance.

Help to Buy has not been the only initiative by government to help first-time buyers onto the property ladder, but it is reflective of a wider set of policies which effectively boil down to pumping more and more cash into an already inflated market. Although these measures are not solely to blame for the increasing rise in house prices and deposit requirements, they are ultimately counterproductive and feeding the problem they were intended to solve. Help to Buy was ended in March 2023 and has not been revived by the current government. Instead, the recent Comprehensive Spending Review has introduced a decidedly more modest Mortgage Guarantee Scheme to help buyers with small deposits.[8] The changes reflect a move away from the more inflationary elements of Help to Buy, with a demand-side focus on assisting buyers, as opposed to investment in new properties.

Second homes and short-term lets

Another significant source of house price inflation is driven by domestic and international buyers, either investing in properties as financial assets or as business opportunities for short-term lets. Such investments have a particularly acute impact on affordability in areas dependent on tourist economies and urban centres.

Internationally, this phenomenon has been coined as the 'Airbnb' effect, named after the short-term letting giant, which with over 7 million online listings is by far the largest webhosting platform for short-term lodgers globally. International studies have shown clear links between house price inflation and short-term lets, with one study from Barcelona suggesting a clear contribution to rent price increases, with 16.8 per cent of all residential flats removed from renting stock in Ciutat Vella and rents increasing to 9 per cent more than the Barcelona average (having been 3 per cent lower in 2007).[9] In America, the Economic Policy Institute directly links house price increases to the expansion of Airbnb, through the removal of available housing supply. The paper suggests that Airbnb rentals may have added a full US$400 annually to the rental cost for the cities' residents.[10]

In the UK, the issue of short-term lets has become particularly acute in the South West, and areas of Wales, where communities are being eroded in place of temporary tourist residencies pricing locals out of the housing market. In 2022, ITV reported that 20,688 active Airbnb and Vrbo rentals advertised in August, with only 240 advertised rentals on Rightmove. In Devon, 15,732 Airbnb and Vbro rentals were recorded, as against 936 Rightmove rentals.[11]

According to the Department for Culture, Media and Sport a 'plausible estimate' for the number of short-term lets operating in England in 2022 was 257,000 – though researchers believe this to be an underestimate. Another report from the BBC in 2022 estimated that the number of holiday lets in England had risen by 40 per cent in just the previous three years – an astonishing increase. It can't be excluded from our assessment of house price inflation that in particular areas of the UK, demand from tourism is playing a significant role in removing housing supply, and pushing up prices. At present, there are few limitations on short-term lets in England, as opposed to much more robust regulations in Wales and Scotland.

Similarly, investment properties such as luxury apartments in urban centres or holiday homes help to feed a general climate of investment, increasing property values often well beyond what most local residents can afford. From the ITV report in Cornwall, the Harbour Housing representative also touched on the impact facing communities from huge numbers of second and holiday homes in the county:

> It is worth noting that particularly during the period where stamp duty was removed for certain housing purchases, there was a notable increase in the number of rental properties becoming sold to purchasers, a number of which were from outside Cornwall, further reducing the supply of housing available to people living here.
>
> To us, it does not seem right or fair that where there are thousands of properties available for short-term rentals at a price which is as much per week as a residential letting is a month, there are sometimes less than a hundred properties available to rent and call home and it is a phenomenon which is disproportionately affecting popular areas such as Cornwall.[12]

Cornwall contains some of the most deprived areas of the UK, with 17 Cornish neighbourhoods classed as in the most deprived 10 per cent of the country, so such upward pressure on prices is felt acutely. A 2022 blog post by Tom Woodman, chief executive officer for the Housing Association Cornerstone and on behalf of the Chartered Institute for Housing, witheringly describes the impact that such short-term lets are having on local communities: 'Holiday lets are houses not homes; they are zombie houses that are hollowing out our communities.' Woodman further elucidates the problems faced by present attempts to regulate the sector and draw down value into communities: 'Proposals to levy double council tax don't touch many of them; registered as businesses, they don't pay any council tax at all, and in many cases won't pay any business rates either. They enjoy huge short-term letting fees, combined with tax reliefs unavailable to the private rented sector.'[13]

Figures from the Ministry of Housing, Communities and Local Government in 2018–2019 estimate that 772,000 UK households reported having a second property for the purposes of holidays or leisure, the highest proportion of which were in the South West (27 per cent).[14] The number of second homes is growing, and hugely exacerbating the housing crisis in specific areas of the country. The scale of the challenge is beginning to be recognised: as part of the Levelling Up and Regeneration Bill (2023) powers for councils to charge an additional 100 per cent premium in Council Tax on second homes have been announced – however the measures still go substantially less far than similar programmes under the devolved governments of Wales and Scotland.

The Scottish and Welsh examples are indicative of the more robust approach to this issue which is possible – with owners of second homes in Scotland charged double Council Tax, and owners of second homes in Wales required by law to let their property for at least 182 days a year (on pain of being required to pay 300 per cent Council Tax on that property). In both countries, a mandatory licence is now a requirement for all short-term lets. To curb this growing problem in England, similar policies should be introduced to control and curb the numbers of second homes (particularly in areas where such homes have taken up a substantial portion of the local housing supply) and licensing should be required for short-term letting properties with an eye to controlling the numbers coming through the system.

International investment properties

Increasing amounts of evidence show that foreign international investment in UK property has had a substantial impact on house price growth over the past two decades. In a 2017 paper by Filipa Sa, foreign investment directly accounted for 19 per cent of all house price growth between 1999 and 2014, estimating that for every 1 per cent increase in the share of property transactions in the UK by foreign companies and individuals, there is a corresponding 2.1–2.3 per cent correlated increase in house prices.[15]

At present, in key UK markets this trend is continuing. In 2021, the Centre for Public Data reported that foreign ownership of UK property had increased by 200 per cent over the past 11 years, with 1 per cent of all UK properties owned by overseas entities.[16] In 2023, as many as 20 per cent of new-build homes in London were sold to overseas buyers,[17] rising to 53 per cent in Central London.[18]

While evidence suggests that the vast majority of these properties are rented out (as opposed to standing empty) evidence from Lisbon suggests that a substantial number of 'buy to let' investments are subsequently used for short-term lets, such as Airbnb. In their 2021 article for the *Economy and Space* journal, Cocola-Gant and Gago assess the role played by the Portuguese government in spearheading global investment into Lisbon, particularly following the 2008 financial crash, with the government specifically targeting international second-home buyers. In 2009, the Non-habitual Residents programme was introduced, offering lower rates of taxation to European Union citizens – and in 2012, the 'Golden Visa' programme was approved offering freedom of movement within the Schengen area and promises of Portuguese citizenship to non-European Union applicants who bought properties worth over €500,000.[19]

The researchers focused their studies on the Alfama area of Lisbon, a historic working-class neighbourhood in the city. Between 2015 and 2016, the proportion of short-term lets as a proportion of the property market leapt from 16 per cent to 25 per cent of the housing stock. Within these figures, the proportion of international individual and corporate landlords rose substantially – with investors making up 78 per cent of Airbnb landlords in Alfama and mobilised primarily through lettings agencies, advertising their services abroad. This phenomenon forms part of what researchers describe as the 'professionalisation' of short-term lets, as represented by 'Hostmaker', an international lettings agency managing over 550 properties across London.[20] Through both Airbnb and other short-term lettings platforms, a significant portion of international investment is not facilitating the growth of domestic housing supply, but rather providing tourism-led gentrification and further exacerbating price increases.

Such findings may make for awkward reading, given that attracting overseas investment and investors is a central plank of many local authority regeneration strategies. In many areas, international investment is proactively sought as a method through which to 'regenerate' derelict areas of a city, or drive new patterns of economic growth in regions which have deindustrialised or are otherwise struggling to find economic avenues for profitability. However, the evidence is clear – and mounting – that acquisitive international property investment is a key driver of house price inflation, particularly within tourist hotspots, and measures must be taken to dilute its impact if we are serious about controlling house price inflation more broadly.

In recent years, government have taken some steps in the right direction. Since 2013, companies owning residential property worth over £500,000 have been required to file Annual Tax on Enveloped Dwellings returns. Since 2015, capital gains made by overseas entities on residential UK property held as an investment has been taxable in the instance of any sale. Following the Russian invasion of Ukraine, these measures were further built upon with the establishment of a 'register of Overseas Entities' to track overseas owners of UK-based land and property, with an intention to enforce new sanctions against Russian interests. Overseas Entities (either individuals or organisations) must now register, annually, a declaration of their governing documents, and the address and country of origin of their controlling interests. As of October 2023, over 29,000 overseas entities have been registered reflecting compliance of 90 per cent with the new legislation.

Additionally, since April 2021 an addition 2 per cent Stamp Duty surcharge has been placed on non-UK buyers of residential property in England and Northern Ireland, on any property in excess of £40,000.

But positive though these measures may be, it must be recognised that international investment is still seen to have a central role in the redevelopment of British towns and cities – with many new-build properties designed for international investment and buy-to-let markets. If government is serious about dealing properly with this issue, restrictions need to be brought to the table on new development designed for international purchasers, particularly as investment properties or for buy to let. Additional charges should also be levied against international investment into UK-based property – and alternatives from other nations should be considered as well.

In 2018, the government of Jacinda Ardern in New Zealand introduced an outright ban on foreign purchases of particular types of residential property, restricting purchases to new-build apartments in large developments. And in Canada, the Liberal government under Justin Trudeau introduced an outright ban on foreign purchases of Canadian residential property, which has just been extended to 2027. Explaining their rationale for the move, a communique issued by the Canadian government states that:

> For years, foreign money has been coming into Canada to buy up residential real estate, increasing housing affordability concerns in cities across the country, and particularly in major urban centres. Foreign ownership has also fueled worries about Canadians being priced out of housing markets in cities and towns across the country.[21]

While the success – or otherwise – of the New Zealand and Canadian examples is still in dispute (prices in Canada have reduced by a modest 1.3 per cent since the ban,[22] however factors such as increased interest rates set by the Bank of Canada will undoubtedly played a role) the measures show the extent to which the question of foreign investment can be taken seriously, with the requisite political will.

11

A failed growth model

Since the 1990s, governments of all stripes in the UK have sought to resolve the problems facing many of the country's deindustrialised cities, particularly as regards depopulation of once bustling metropolises, large-scale vacancy of plots, sites and old buildings, and plunging land values. The answer that has been provided by policy makers to these issues has been what we now know as 'urban regeneration', an attempt to rejuvenate economic growth in formerly industrial urban areas through construction, the transition to service-sector economies and the cultivation of cultural centres and activities.

But these self-same policies for urban regeneration have laid the cornerstones of our current housing crisis today, and given rise to the modern incarnation of 'gentrification'. We will address two of the clearest case studies around this failed growth model in the UK to illustrate the point.

London

London is the UK's prime example. The situation in respect of housing affordability in London is widely perceived as getting to crisis point. In 2021, a PricewaterhouseCoopers study reported that London's population was set to decline for the first time since 1988 – driven mainly by economic fallout following the COVID-19 pandemic, but also due to the cost of accommodation.[1] 2019 data from Halifax shows that the average deposit from a first-time buyer in London was £110,656, or 26 per cent of the total value of their new home. This figure had increased three-fold from 2008, where it stood at £38,335.[2]

In the early 1990s, London was a fairly affordable city, with large areas of empty properties and space, particularly that which had been vacated through the deindustrialisation of the city centre. A semi-detached home in London, in 1990, would have cost on average £79,900. By January 2024, that figure would stand at £480,000.[3] But London's economy was impacted particularly acutely by reforms to the UK's banking system, enabling a revolution in banking services which would transform the face of the city.

Beginning in the 1970s and through to 1986, a series of reforms to the UK's banking system would upturn the traditional distinctions between domestic commercial, international and mortgage finance. As a result of these acts of deregulation, London became an international centre of novel financial services and instruments, absorbing vast quantities of international investment.

These changes were most immediately and visibly seen in the redevelopment of centres of banking and finance in the city, and in the creation of an entirely new centre for banking and financial services at the site of the old docklands, Canary Wharf. From the 1980s, the London Docklands Development Corporation had already begun work patching up the former dockland at Canary Wharf for redevelopment as a financial hub, and a project was sold to Canadian company Olympia & York for construction to begin in 1988. Despite a faltering start, declaring bankruptcy in 1992, it was soon revitalised by an international consortium of investors, and its continued growth since has fostered huge amounts of economic growth, and house price growth, across the East End of London.

On the other side of the river, within the boundaries of the ancient walled City of London, the Square Mile (London's traditional financial district) also began to massively expand its commercial activities, using the new easing of regulations to invest in a complicated array of innovative international financial services. This huge growth in commercial activity drove significant inward investment, growth of demand and increase in house and land prices. This process saw the beginning of London's property-price boom, which has continued to this day.

Thea Gasparyan, in a study on behalf of Uppsala University, notes on the pre-history to London's move to gentrification that:

> In 1960 London still had a large manufacturing base and working-class population. Inner London consisted of Victorian terraced houses and the housing market was privately rented with only a few council estates and some owner-occupancy. Ethnic minorities lived outside the middle-class residential areas of St John's Wood, Hampstead and South Kensington. Notting Hill was a rundown residential area with a West Indian population and Aldgate and Whitechapel had a large Jewish population. The boroughs surrounding City of London, such as Clerkenwell, Shoreditch, Hoxton and Bethnal Green, were dominated by the working classes and some industries. Tower Hamlets, Camden, Islington and Kentish Town were rundown inner-city boroughs and Holloway had some of the worst housing conditions.[4]

Gasparyan particularly traces London's gentrification to the redevelopment of Canary Wharf and the former docklands as centres for financial services.

> The docks and warehouses are now financial centres in Canary Wharf and luxury apartments. The manufacturing industry and its employees have disappeared from London and have been replaced with the service

sector. Ethnic minorities are around a third of the population of Inner London. Notting Hill and Islington are now among London's most expensive residential areas. The old East End is being gentrified and turned into expensive residential area for city workers.[5]

For Gasparyan, the development of post-industrial parts of London as financial centres is central to the question of gentrification, and its linkage to policies of urban regeneration. In the transfer between an industrial and a service-based economy, working populations have become more mobile and Western countries such as the UK have seen a growth in high-wage 'knowledge economies' around industries such as financial services. In the case of London, the growth of a financial services economy has driven an influx of wealthy individuals to London into the heart of formerly industrial areas.

London is an example of a city in which 'gentrification' has occurred, for the most part, organically and in an unplanned manner. Increasing land values in London were not pre-planned, but rather a side-effect of the growth of financial services and 'regeneration' initiatives undertaken in ad hoc recognition of the increased commercial viability and anticipated return on property investment. Regeneration of formerly industrial areas accelerated the process of increasing land values, contributing direct investment and general improvements to amenities which fed and extended the emerging property boom.

But though the process of gentrification in London has been spurred by the development of the financial system, the model for urban growth and regeneration has been internalised by local planners and policy makers as a tool for attracting investment – particularly in redeveloping former industrial parts of the city. Citing Damaris Rose (2004) on urban policy and regeneration, Gasparyan notes that modern cities 'are trying to achieve the "liveable city" image in order to compete in a globalised knowledge-based economy.[6] This is done by targeting young people that work in "new economy" professions as well as promoting "family-friendliness"'.

As part of this process, a quite deliberate process of raising values in low value areas is undertaken by planners which includes the demolition of low value properties, the enticement of luxury or expensive brand shops and retailers, and marketing developable 'plots' internationally as 'growth hubs' to attract inward investment. In 1999, Southwark Council's Head of Regeneration Fred Manson articulated the thinking behind deliberate gentrification quite frankly, explaining the council's hostility to new social housing units: 'Because social housing generates people on low incomes coming in and that generates poor school performances, middle-class people stay away.'[7]

What began as an unplanned process in cities such as London, through which commercial activity through an expanded role for financial services fed a property boom in formerly industrial areas of the city, has become an end in and of itself for many city and urban planners. As a route to growing out of post-industrial decline, the pull of the 'London model' is as a route to developing a hugely profitable enterprise for the construction industry and international investors, which in an era of restricted public finance also offers a path to investment in and redevelopment of public amenities such as footpaths, parks, and the removal of vacant derelict sites which had become hubs for crime as well as eyesores.

London is indeed remarkably changed since the start of this process. However the social cost of a model built on ever-expanding property prices is more than beginning to make itself felt as the affordability of the city to even middle to upper tier earners becomes more and more remote.

Financial deregulation and urban regeneration schemes in and of themselves are not the only sources of gentrification in the capital. Throughout the past few decades, numerous changes to policy on housing from government have contributed to the displacement of low-income Londoners from central districts in the city. The introduction of Right to Buy had its own unanticipated role to play in this process. Following the introduction of Right to Buy in the 1980s, the 'Lawson boom' erupted in the property market following the then Chancellor Nigel Lawson's cuts to income tax and the interest rate, prompting a 20 per cent increase in house prices. Significant numbers of lower-income Londoners took their opportunity through Right to Buy to purchase their homes, many of which were repossessed as the Lawson boom made way for the economic shocks of the 1990s, further socially stratifying the capital. Right to Buy has had, in general, a huge impact in the displacement of lower-income residents from central urban areas in London as many as 40 per cent of homes sold under Right to Buy are sold on again either into further private ownership or the rental sector.[8]

However, on the macroeconomic scale, the increase in values we have seen in London could not have happened without the gigantic sums of inward investment seen following financial deregulation, and the proactive redevelopment of large areas of the city to facilitate its growth.

The end result has been huge social stratification, enforced by rapidly increasing land and property prices. As Matthew Engel has written for the *Guardian* in 2016:

> In the past 20 years, an era of low general inflation, the Halifax house price index shows that values in London have multiplied by almost six. The Office for National Statistics figures, which started later but dig deeper, suggest that in some of the richest areas of inner London, the 20-year increase is tenfold. Over 70 years, that £5,000 house might have gone up to £5m or £10m – one or two thousand-fold.[9]

Even the benefits of the economic growth underpinning these astronomical increases is in some cases coming full circle. Engel argues that the increasing use of properties in London as vehicles for investment is killing high streets in high value areas such as Chelsea, where property prices are now so high that depopulation has begun to set in. His article further documents the genesis of gentrification from the arrival of penniless artists and bohemians in dilapidated areas of town, followed by middle-class professionals, and onwards – chronicling the rapid decline of communities and businesses which served them. Referring to a 2013 opinion piece by Michael Goldfarb, Engel quotes:

> [Goldfarb] point[ed] out something that had not then been widely understood: how the most expensive London homes had ceased to be places to live and had become a store of global money. 'Almost nothing has changed,' says Goldfarb now, 'except that all the stresses in the system have got deeper. It will take an epochal catastrophe – like the great depression followed by a war – to allow ordinary people to get into the housing market. But no one will say this. It will be a London without Londoners.'[10]

In many former industrial or deprived areas of London today, the main surviving groups of long-standing deprived communities remain in subsidised council housing, which, due to controls on rental values, have preserved zones of affordability. Beyond this, cost pressures are increasingly forcing poorer residents towards the suburbs and beyond – with an exodus from London to other parts of the country.

Manchester

Manchester, and Greater Manchester, is a key example of where the London model has been expressly and consciously adapted for the purpose of regeneration – and where outside of the capital, the housing and homelessness crisis is the most acute.

Significantly more so than London, Manchester from the late 1970s and 1980s was depopulated. In 1901, the population of the City of Manchester had been 700,000. Between 1961 and 1981 it is estimated that Manchester lost almost one-third of its population to migration – and 2001 Census data showed that the population of Manchester had dropped to a nadir of 392,000. By 2021, this figure had risen to 586,000 – and is projected to continue to grow substantially over the coming decade. Within Manchester city centre – the population in 1990 stood at just 500 people – by 2025, it is anticipated to be over 100,000.[11]

Manchester is heralded within the construction industry and by government as a model to follow – with huge numbers of housing units constructed over the decade, and significant growth in both jobs and business activity in the city and wider city-region. From a city centre populated by vast empty Victorian warehouses, huge patches of wasteland where criminal activity was rife – to a sparkling Mecca for shopping, eating, nightlife and cultural activity – the transformation of the city is clear for all those who have witnessed its development.

And yet despite economic growth, and the construction of huge numbers of housing units, Manchester is second only to London in its increasing housing affordability crisis and associated issues such as homelessness and rough sleeping. There are clear signs that the benefits of new housing and job creation have failed to benefit many of the long-standing residents of the city, with key measures such as life expectancy and deprivation statistics showing harsh divides and stubborn entrenched poverty.

Unlike London, Manchester in the 1980s didn't have a burgeoning financial sector driving city centre growth – but a very conscious attempt was made by the city council to court financial services and other high wealth economic sectors as being central to the vision for Manchester's rejuvenation. From the 1980s, the rehabilitation of the city centre was driven by the pursuit of high-end cultural 'anchor institutions' such as the redevelopment of Manchester Central Railway Station into high-end conference and exhibition venue the 'G-Mex' (1986), the Royal Bridgewater Hall (finished in 1996), and strategic partnerships with the university on projects such as the redevelopment of the Whitworth Art Gallery in 1995. Much of this was driven by the Central Manchester Development Corporation which was in existence from 1988 to 1996.

Similarly, decrepit housing in low-value areas of the city was demolished and redeveloped – most notably in Hulme, where the Hulme Crescents (which had housed around 13,000 residents) were demolished in 1992. The urban regeneration of Castlefield was also undertaken between 1988 and 1996, including the construction of Merchants' Bridge (1995). In 1995, Manchester won the bid to host the 2002 Commonwealth Games. The announcement attracted huge amounts of capital to invest in sporting infrastructure, such as the Etihad Stadium in North Manchester (the start of Manchester's 'Northern Gateway' regeneration project) – as well as providing a huge opportunity to showcase its transformation from a crime-stricken, desolate post-industrial city to a thriving, modern metropolis.

In 1996, the IRA bombing of Manchester flattened a huge section of the city centre, including 500,000 square feet of retail space and 600,000 square feet of offices. Following the blast, public-private taskforce Manchester Millennium Ltd was formed and raised £83 million of public funding to put towards the regeneration of the city centre – a further £500 million of private sector money was raised between 1996 and 1999.[12] This 'post-bomb' era was critical in the future growth trajectory of the city, opening up a huge central area of prime land to be redeveloped and redesigned to facilitate the continued growth of the city.

In the early 2000s, the Greater Manchester Combined Authority began sending delegations to the international property investment conference, MIPIM – advertising the city as an international development and investment opportunity. From hereon in, Manchester's skyline began to change drastically as thousands of luxury investment properties and flats began to be developed. From this point on, the transformation of the city centre began to emerge as a political issue among residents, increasingly alienated and concerned by the rapid alterations to the built environment in the city centre and the beginnings of its impact on rents and prices.

In 2006, 'New Economy' was formed as a semi-independent research group focusing on the redevelopment of Greater Manchester's economy – loosely connected to 'Manchester Enterprises' (a Manchester Council-controlled economic growth agency which was a fore-runner to the Greater Manchester 'Growth Hub' which sits beneath the Greater Manchester Combined Authority). New Economy took on the mission of providing an intellectual and academic framework through which to articulate Greater Manchester's growth model, particularly in relation to reducing Greater Manchester's dependence on central government finance.

Key to New Economy's focus was an approach which centred around reversing what was considered to be Greater Manchester's net cost to the Treasury through demand for public finance and services. The organisation combined a desire to become an international city with a supply-side approach to the labour market and job creation (emphasising early years education to provide an educated and well trained workforce). In 2009, New Economy facilitated the creation of an extensive collection of essays and studies, the Manchester-led Independent Economic Review (MIER) which would become a body of analysis and information informing growth policy around Greater Manchester for the next decade, particularly informing the creation of the first Greater Manchester Strategy document in 2010. Fundamental to this approach was the drive to develop the urban core of Greater Manchester's conurbation, from which the benefits of growth would 'trickle down' (or in the parlance of the MIER, to 'trickle out').

It's hard to overstate how much of Manchester's subsequent city strategy has been intertwined with this strategy of courting inward investment. One central example of this is the beginnings of Manchester Council's relationship with the Abu Dhabi United Group of investors and the Far East Consortium, crystallised by the purchase of Manchester City by Sheikh Mansour in 2008 and the movement of the club from Main Road Stadium to the Etihad Stadium in 2011. The Etihad is now at the centre of a gigantic regeneration project, known as the 'Northern Gateway' project announced in 2018, financed by the Far East Consortium, which is intended to bring up to 15,000 new homes and 35,000 new residents, connecting much of a former industrial land in North Manchester to the City Centre.

In 2017, Jennifer Williams wrote an article for the *Manchester Evening News* chronicling some of the 'unease' afflicting Manchester residents in relation to the rapid development of the city centre:

> As London's housing market flatlines, Manchester's is booming. Its economic growth is starting to outstrip the capital's and hundreds of millions of pounds are flooding into the city from all over the world, investment that would have been unimaginable even five years ago.
>
> For Manchester's leaders, this has been a long time coming. It is an economic moment they have worked towards ever since heavy industry shut its doors in the 1970s and 1980s. They have pushed for decades to build up the city centre's profile and finally make it punch its weight.
>
> Yet the rising cranes have also brought unease in a climate of growing angst over economic inequality.
>
> Many Mancunians look on in bafflement as thousands of upmarket apartments shoot up, taking rents skyward along with returns for overseas investors. For every willing young professional tenant, there is also a willing first-time buyer barred from buying homes marked 'investor-only'.[13]

Through the article, Williams interviews property journalist David Thames who gave an unambiguous assessment on the impact this investment was likely to have on Manchester's housing market:

> As a result investors are undoubtedly benefiting, says property journalist David Thame, who has been covering Manchester's housing market since the 1980s.
>
> 'Amazing' amounts of money are now coming into the city in quantities that are 'very, very rare', he points out, but with rents predicted to rise by up to 4.5pc every year between now and 2021, investors are not doing it out of the goodness of their hearts.
>
> 'If you're chasing income, you get out of London and into Manchester,' he says.
>
> 'Why buy a declining asset at an expensive price in London when for a much lower price you can buy a rising income in Manchester?
>
> They are not investing to provide cheaper space, it's to push house prices up as close as they can get to London prices. At which point, when it reaches its peak, they will move on somewhere else'.[14]

Yet despite the inordinate amounts of money which have been flowing into Manchester and Greater Manchester throughout this period, the city region has failed to shift the dial on entrenched issues of poverty and deprivation.

In a London School of Economics paper written by Professors Folkman, Froud, Johal, Tomaney and Williams in 2017,[15] the authors argue that Greater Manchester has yet to pull away from other 'core' UK cities even in terms of its own metrics around the growth of 'gross value added' (GVA) per capita, stating that growth has been stacked in geographically limited areas of the conurbation and sits side by side with areas of stubbornly low GVA, and high rates of deprivation. The paper argues:

> Using the Gross Value Added (GVA) measure as the standard measure of city region achievement, London GVA per capita is twice that of Greater Manchester; Manchester City GVA per capita is twice that of northern boroughs like Oldham, while Manchester City itself has many deprived districts. Using the same GVA measure and time series, the inconvenient truth is that Greater Manchester has not pulled away from other British core cities. Greater Manchester has done no more than hold its position against other British core cities and the internal relativities between the central City and the northern boroughs have hardly changed since de-industrialisation in the 1980s.[16]

The paper further assesses the geographical spread of job creation across the city region, finding little evidence that the growth in city centre economic activity had filtered out ('trickled out') to the surrounding boroughs.

> In the pre-2008 period, job creation was heavily dependent on the public sector which was creating jobs in the centre. The public sector accounted for more than half of the 46,000 extra jobs created in the ten Greater Manchester boroughs between 1998 and 2008. Because of the concentration of hospital, university, and administrative functions in central Manchester, Manchester City claimed 16,000 of these jobs, accounting for 40 per cent of its total job creation.
>
> The post-2008 story is dismal. The outer northern boroughs of Oldham, Rochdale and Tameside are in a dire plight because they are now net losers of both private and public sector jobs. Once again, the net gains are concentrated in the central city and the inner south-west quadrant. From 2008–14, Manchester City gains 30,000 net new jobs, while four of the ten GM boroughs see job loss.[17]

This economic stasis has progressed hand in hand with steadily increasing property prices and rent increases, driven at least in part by the huge amounts of capital flowing into the city centre. Increased prices and rents, combined with static incomes and deprivation, is a perfect recipe for gentrification.

In a 2019 Manchester University study by Buffel and Phillipson studying the impacts of gentrification, the South Manchester district of Chorlton is used as a case study on the process and impact of these changes.[18] Chorlton had, traditionally, been a low-income neighbourhood with a large working-class Irish Catholic population. Between 2001 and 2011, Chorlton's population grew by 26 per cent, drawn mainly from younger, white-collar professionals. Between 2001 and 2018, the average house price in Chorlton increased from £100,461 to £311,305 (data from Rightmove updated in April 2024 suggests that the average price of a sold house in Chorlton was an enormous £656,857 that year).

Reflecting these overarching statistical trends, Buffel and Phillipson found significant tension among older, long-standing residents of Chorlton as regards the changes which had occurred in their community, with words such as 'invasion', 'yuppies' and 'snobs' used to describe the new influx of professionals. One resident of 69 years expressed his concerns that his children had been priced out of the neighbourhood in which they had grown up.

> Like my kids, they can't afford a house in Chorlton. The house prices around here have been pushed up to unrealistic figures, so my two sons moved out and live in other parts of Greater Manchester. That's what's happened, the younger generation has dispersed, and it's become property for professional people.[19]

Another resident of 42 years suggested that long-standing residents had been alienated by the demographic changes that had occurred in the suburb, which had lost its original cultural character and community: 'It's not the old Chorlton anymore but it's still Chorlton and I consider myself to be a Chorltonian anyway, I'm proud of where I live.'[20]

Throughout the survey of residents, researchers found that not only the increase in house prices but also the businesses and services operating in Chorlton had changed in a way which excluded long-term residents of the area. Residents spoke of new opportunities for aerobics classes and wine tasting events which did not appear directed towards them, often operating out of commercial premises which once housed social spaces, pubs and bowling greens. The local Wetherspoons was referenced by many respondents as a holdout for longer-standing Chorlton residents, valued for affordable food and an informal atmosphere.

Palpable among the interviews not just of Buffel and Phillipson, but of many comparative studies of the impact of gentrification, is a clear sense that the 'new' city is not designed for the pre-existing residents, but for the new population of well-heeled professionals. In many senses, it remains to be said that this perception is accurate – and in the case of Greater Manchester, not an unconscious by-product of urban growth, but a conscious process of deliberately inflating property values to generate economic activity and attract a new professional population.

The battle for affordable housing in Greater Manchester

From the 2008 economic crash through to the mid-2010s, rough sleeping exploded on the streets of central Manchester, in the context of the huge boom in property development and prices which had begun to transform the city's landscape. While tent cities bloomed under motorway bridges and in public squares and parks, homelessness and rough sleeping began more and more to dominate the political discourse – and formed a central plank of Andy Burnham's successful campaign to become the city region's first directly elected mayor in 2017. Paul Dennett, the City of Salford's directly elected mayor (currently Deputy Mayor of Greater Manchester) was appointed to the critical role of portfolio lead for Housing, Homelessness and Planning following Burnham's election victory. He recalls that policy through Greater Manchester took a while to catch up with the scale of the problem: 'I think we've always known there's been a looming housing and homelessness crisis of some form or another, but I think it's fair to say, over the period I've been involved in politics, things got significantly worse.'

Dennett recalls his appointment under Mayor Burnham, and reflects on the struggle to develop a serious policy response to the crisis:

> Things did get really, really bad. There's no doubt about it. People on our streets across Greater Manchester, numbers going through the roof. And I think in the early years when I became the mayor, there was almost this denial of how serious this was, if I'm honest, or if it wasn't a denial, it was certainly this belief that somehow we could just quicken supply and that will solve all of our problems. But the quickening of supply meant the building of the private rented sector. It didn't mean the quickening of council houses being built, or housing associations building for social rent or local housing allowance, so people on housing benefit could access all of these. And at the same time, you know, the labour market and the economy wasn't quickly transitioning to being a highly paid, highly skilled one, either, you know, the foundational economy was ballooning.

Yvonne McDermott is a chartered surveyor, who has worked in the field of social housing development for 25 years, and recalls Manchester Council's hostility to affordable housing provision during this period, particularly in relation to the planning applications for social housing, and specifically one-bedroom units which were in high demand in the sector following the introduction of the Bedroom Tax:

> [A]ny planning applications that came forward for just one-bed units was met with resistance and wouldn't even be received by the planning authority. And we understood that the thinking behind that was that it would be too much of a concentration of single people, you know, people in social, affordable, rented

housing with complex needs who would be detrimental to the regeneration that was going on in the city.

Ben Clay, housing activist and former Labour councillor for Burnage in Greater Manchester, was elected in 2018, and recalls that the council at this time had an idea of the 'type' of person they wished to cater for with new housing:

> One explicit part of the strategy for developing the city centre of Manchester, not just as a destination for leisure and tourism and the night time economy, but as a site of significant new accommodation, was to ensure that it was made attractive to graduates, young professionals and residents who would be economically active, well qualified and well paid, who would therefore be net contributors to council funds through higher rates of Council Tax, and contribute to economic activity through spending of higher disposable income in city centre businesses.
>
> While that may all be very laudable, there was also an unstated counterpoint to this. People who were active at the council in that time as elected representatives and also as staff members, relayed to me that ... the prevailing policy under the auspices of Richard Leese (the Council leader) and Howard Bernstein (the Chief Executive) was to get Manchester away from a culture of [welfare] dependency.
>
> There was a period of deindustrialisation and economic decline that Manchester has had for many decades, and still has huge numbers of people who are very disadvantaged and recipients of unemployment and disability benefits, long-term sickness benefits etcetera. So what that meant was a general disfavouring of organisations [catering to them].
>
> 'Culture of dependency' was the phrase that was used, the message being that if you provide these sorts of services, and if you focus on that kind of support, you're encouraging people who presumably might otherwise be able to 'get on their bikes and look for work' or whatever the feeling was.

McDermott notes that the impact of these restrictive planning policies went further than the city centre, having wider ramifications on the social housing sector as a whole:

> So for a number of years in Manchester, this policy of no one-bed [units], certainly in the affordable housing sector, meant that the demand for one-bed [units] went through the roof and we couldn't meet the demand and any turnover within our existing houses. Stock for one-bed [units] was fulfilled by almost internal transfers, because the Bedroom Tax had such an impact on the demand for one-beds.

An additional squeeze on demand was caused in 2015, when the city council passed over £2 million in cuts to homelessness provision, primarily within the city centre, despite a six-fold increase in homelessness presentation since 2010. The closures of long-standing homelessness provision such as the Salvation Army and YMCA in the city centre contributed enormously to the visible tide of street homelessness, McDermott notes:

> So YMCA, Salvation Army in Manchester were closing, which were often city centre, types of housing that have been there for decades. And there was a prediction within my colleagues that we would see a massive spike in street homelessness and real chaos from this. And it all came true. It all came to bear. My supported housing colleagues would say, 'Well, we told you so you can't actually go and close all of these facilities'.

Despite the huge public outcry over the burgeoning number of rough sleepers, Manchester Council remained bullish on restricting new affordable provision arguing that land values made affordable provision unviable. In 2015/2016, not a single affordable home was built in Manchester, and the city's planning panel continued to uphold developer objections to affordable housing provision in most city centre developments up until 2018. Former Councillor Clay recalls the intransigent position on affordable housing held by many of his colleagues on the council:

> The people that I spoke to in Manchester, they talked a lot about the past. To be completely sympathetic to the positions of people like Richard Leese and Bernstein etcetera, they seemed to imagine Manchester like the L.S. Lowry paintings and be very mindful of that bleak industrial or post-industrial heritage. And that was what they were trying to get away from.
> Both physically and spatially in the geography of Manchester, but also socially and culturally there was a desire for Manchester to be an international city, thrusting and dynamic, a kind of place where people want to live and to invest and stuff. And that was often, I think, the trade off. You know, if there's some of this other stuff that needs to be pushed out, well, overall there's a benefit.

Throughout his successful campaign for mayoralty, Andy Burnham picked up on the public anger over affordable housing provision and commitment to challenging the lack of provision in the city centre was placed front and centre of his bid for the Labour Party's selection. Following his success in the selection process, Burnham commented to the *Guardian* that '[t]here was an anger about housing policy in Greater Manchester and a sense that Greater Manchester hasn't been focused enough on affordable housing'.

Salford's Mayor Paul Dennett had only recently been elected on a manifesto which had centred affordable housing, and particularly council housing in the city. During a housing conference in July 2017, Dennett had made critical comments regarding the conurbation's growth trajectory, and the free market logic underpinning it. Speaking to the conference, Dennett said: 'The theory is that you reduce obstacles for developers and in turn, they build the homes you need. But that simply isn't happening. The pipeline of housing developments in Greater Manchester, and elsewhere in the country, is stacked full with luxury flats and accommodation for wealthy young professionals.'

Dennett's appointment to the portfolio of Housing and Homelessness, and particularly the announcement of his remit to deliver a city-regional housing strategy, ruffled feathers in Manchester. During a prickly interview with the Manchester Council leader Richard Leese in the *Manchester Evening News*, Leese intimated that Manchester Council may refuse to enact the strategy if it deviated from the existing policy direction:

> If it's a Greater Manchester housing strategy, as long as it's based on what we are doing that's fine … but if there's an attempt to impose, for example, more detailed numbers or the type of housing that should be built in Manchester, then I'm not going to support it.

Dennett did go on to oversee the introduction of the city region's first joint Housing Strategy in 2019, which substantially changed the focus of Greater Manchester's housing priorities and which crucially included a commitment to deliver 50,000 'affordable' homes, 30,000 of which were for social rent. Dennett muses on this achievement:

> [F]or me, this journey has all been about incrementalism, you know, slowly chipping away to get policy strategy, both locally, city, regionally and nationally, into a much more progressive space than it's been for many, many years. And we won the argument, but we didn't just win the argument on political conjecture or emotive discourse, we won the argument empirically because we laid bare to Greater Manchester that the housing and homelessness crisis we're facing is fundamentally as a consequence of us not building truly affordable housing.

But despite these successes, battles continued on Manchester's planning committee over the allocation of affordable housing units. Councillor Clay recalls some of his experiences as a member of the city's planning committee from 2018 to 2019, and as a councillor instrumental to organising a push for changes to housing policy from the back benches towards the end of Leese's period as leader:

> Over and over again, we were told that affordable housing couldn't be delivered because of viability.
> Changes were made through motions to council from backbench councillors to ensure that viability assessments became not public, but available to the planning committee.
> Some of us on the planning committee were quite clear that we weren't happy with what was being offered and the use of Section 106 money.

Section 106 are agreements made between developers and planning authorities, where developers offset the costs of their development to the council (for instance, increased demand for school places, bus routes or strains on physical infrastructure) through the use of cash or in-kind payments. Clay continues:

> The policy in Manchester was for all Section 106 money for affordable housing to be used off-site. ... The argument was made that by taking the Section 106 from city-centre adjacent development, you could build a lot more social housing in the less desirable parts of Manchester. But the research that has been done demonstrates conclusively that for a significant period of time, almost no social housing at all was being delivered (certainly on a net basis) in the City of Manchester.

Clay believes this failure was in part due to a series of connected policies which were deployed, preventing the delivery of affordable units elsewhere in the city:

> There were policy reasons here. It was by policy that they [Manchester] never asked for units of affordable housing at all, ever. They only asked for Section 106 financial contributions to deliver off-site affordable housing.
> And this is one of the battles that we had in the council with planning policies. They always talked about how they wanted mixed communities, but things that were seen to favour social and affordable housing were seen as inimical to developing mixed communities in the more peripheral parts of Manchester, because they already had lots of social housing.
> As well as giving the planning committee access to the viability assessments, we also managed to start getting on site affordable homes, along with wider changes to the council's strategic housing policy, with much more ambitious targets for social home building within the Housing Revenue Account (HRA) and also through use of land in agreement with Registered Providers.

Clay believes that while there has been a change in tenor at the council since councillor Bev Craig took control of the council in December 2021 (and the planning committee does now take some on-site affordable housing) the dial is still to be shifted enough to make a substantial impact:

> I don't really see any indication that there's been a serious challenge to the developer-led model from the new leadership. Within the council, I think it's probably seen as in some ways a benefit, in other ways a beast that's uncontrollable. And maybe you should try and ride the tiger to some extent and get what you can from it. But I still don't believe that the challenge has been made strong enough on Section 106 and on-site affordable housing. [The Council] has serious land interests. You've got the choice to have the negotiation. You don't need to take the cash. You could say to a large development vehicle, with billions and billions of pounds, that if you want to build 10,000 homes on this sector of land in North Manchester we want 2,000 of them to be council homes.

The case study of Greater Manchester is instructive, in that the Greater Manchester model is seen as the pinnacle of a regional UK success story both within the construction industry and among policy makers in Whitehall and Westminster. It is also unusual, in that Greater Manchester's approach to development and growth is taken very consciously and deliberately, predicating itself on the most current received academic and economic wisdom available. Through the work of New Economy and the MIER, a thorough intellectual and evidential basis was created through which to pursue international capital and investment as a means to pursue the agglomeration of economic activity in the city core.

Yet Greater Manchester still hugely underperforms in educational outcomes, particularly in early years education. The high-paid jobs which city-centre growth was anticipated to attract have been introduced to a degree, however there is little evidence they have benefited the long-term population of the city region and appear to have primarily been taken by inward migrants. The creation of a low-skill, low-pay economy in services and the tertiary sector has indeed boomed within the city centre, while growth in the regions has stalled and in some cases reversed. As an alternative to the multitude of well-paid and highly skilled manufacturing jobs the city once boasted, it is clear that the growth model has failed to deliver prosperity or opportunity to those in the city region who need it most.

In addition, the huge success in attracting inward investment has created a huge affordability crisis most acutely felt in housing, which is further squeezing incomes. Greater Manchester's homelessness problem is second only to London's, and with thousands of families in temporary accommodation across the conurbation, the crisis in available accommodation is becoming acute. If housing affordability is the main pillar of the country's housing crisis today, then a policy for economic development predicated on the conscious and deliberate inflation of property prices could hardly be designed more effectively to worsen the situation.

Legitimate questions must be asked as regards the efficacy of the model of growth which has been pursued in Greater Manchester, both from the perspective of housing policy and also its wider benefits. For whom is this policy geared? Removing and replacing the existing population of the city has been a feature, not a bug, of the approach to regeneration adopted in the city – as well as being one of the central features of our ongoing housing crisis. If improving the lives of the pre-existing population of Greater Manchester, and other areas of the country, is the primary target of our goals from the perspective of local and city regional governance, then in the context of housing at least, our approach to growth appears to be aggravating rather than mitigating the symptoms.

Compounding the problem

The overheating of the housing market is driven itself by multiple factors. We have previously discussed the role of the financial system, and particularly the increasing business-emphasis of commercial high street banking networks on mortgage lending, in driving billions of pounds in inflationary investment into the housing market each and every year (all but guaranteeing year on year price inflation). This near guaranteed return on investment creates several other feedback loops, such as the increasingly common phenomenon of 'investment properties' – speculative investment driving further asset-price inflationary spirals within the housing market.

The question of fiscally driven asset-price inflation spirals in housing shouldn't be new to policy makers. In the early 1970s, the most rapid increase in house prices in history occurred, immediately precipitating a market crash, following an easing of credit and fiscal policy under the Conservative Prime Minister Edward Heath, first following fiscal deregulation in 1971, and latterly as a result of his 'dash for growth' budget in 1972. What followed was the so-called 'Barber Boom' (so-called after Anthony Barber, the Chancellor of the Exchequer). Following the slashing of interest rates and the release of credit (on top of increased pensions, benefits and tax reductions), house prices for new homes increased by 37 per cent, and 45 per cent for second-hand homes, in the space of just two and a half years, causing huge hardship for millions of families.[21] Where credit and new money was released into the economy without adequate increases in the supply of new homes, inflation was the inevitable result. Lessons from the past continue to go unlearnt, and the impact of inflationary credit and mortgage lending on ever-expanding house prices, alongside a raft of complementary spending propping up house prices such as Help to Buy and Housing Benefit, continue to go unnoticed as significant contributors to house price inflation.

In 2022, the government spent around £9.6 billion on schemes relating to the development and delivery of new homes – including monies determined for the remediation of brownfield land, the provision of housing infrastructure and the assembly of small sites.[22] Yet in part due to methodological failures in its distribution, that sum has fallen far short of what has been required to enable the numbers of developments in the places they are needed to achieve significant increases in housing numbers. In 2018, the local government lobbying organisation Key Cities published research on the geographical distribution of £7 billion worth of government investment through five separate housing programmes – finding that £5.6 billion of that money was directed into the South and South East of England.[23]

The reason for this geographical slant was the Treasury methodology deployed to target the monies, which relied on a ratio of median house prices to median workplace-based household incomes to determine the areas of 'highest affordability pressure'. The resulting formula determined that 80 per cent of the available funding was directed towards areas of the country where the housing market was at its hottest, and prices were already rising the most. The outcome here is perverse for several reasons; first, that in such areas the value of development is such that assistance in the delivery of new sites is far less acute than in areas of prevailing low values. Second, that money spent in an area where the housing market is overheating goes far less distance than in an area of low value. Third, that investing in areas where the market is overheating most drastically further increases the value of land, which in turn inflates prices for land and properties.

Councillor Judith Blake of Leeds City Council, and chair of the Core Cities lobbying group, said of the research:

> The way funding for housing and infrastructure is currently being prioritised is already putting many of our major towns and cities at a disadvantage. We should be moving away from competitive and ultimately counter-productive drivers of investment such as mortgage affordability and land value uplift towards a collaborative and place-based approach where national and local governments work together to tailor cross-tenure solutions to meet local demands and opportunities.
>
> The current proposal is likely to further consolidate the economic gaps between London, the South East and the rest of the country.[24]

Such are the deficiencies in government pots designated towards the construction of new homes – however from the wider perspective of government housing policy as a whole, a parallel crisis also becomes apparent. In addition to the £9.6 billion spent on development in 2022, the annual spend for Homelessness and Rough Sleeping in 2024 is £2.4 billion,[25] of which there is a significant overlap with Shelter's estimated costs for the UK's temporary accommodation bill of £1.2 billion each and every year. Almost all of the money spent by government on temporary accommodation is an inflationary investment into the private property market, made in payments to businesses, hotels and landlords to home the country's most vulnerable people.

But far greater an expenditure even than this is the country's Housing Benefit bill, which in 2022 amounts to a colossal £23.4 billion.[26] For reference, this is more than the country's entire policing bill, and in real terms has doubled since the 1990s. In very real terms, the £23.4 billion spent on Housing Benefit is an inflationary investment into the private rental market each and every year – which in turn is sustaining huge numbers of private rented units which would otherwise have to either reduce their rents or in many cases sell their properties. Buy-to-rent purchasers are in most instances in direct competition to other house buyers.

Taken alongside the findings of the House of Lords Built Environment Committee on the Help to Buy scheme referred to earlier, a picture begins to emerge of a network of inflationary government schemes which are pumping billions into the housing market each year, sustaining artificially high prices for homes and for rent, in addition to domestic and global capital markets which see housing as a safe asset in which to invest.

Stagnating wages

In addition to price inflation, the UK has witnessed stagnant wage growth since 2008. Between 1970 and 2007, real wages grew on average by 33 per cent each decade. However, according to Office for National Statistics data from 2023, they are now back at the same level as 2005. Following the Brexit referendum in 2016, Andy Haldane, the chief economist at the Bank of England, attempted to make sense of the result, noting that the stagnation of real terms wages up to that point amounted to 'the longest period of flat or falling real wages since at least the middle of the 19th century'.[27] During the same speech, 'Whose Recovery?', Haldane referred to the growing gap between incomes and housing affordability:

> [C]onsider the impact of housing tenure. This has undergone seismic shifts over recent years. ... Those under 50 have seen a secular rise in renting and a fall in mortgaged households. Among young adults, these shifts have been dramatic. In 1977, one in four 25-year-olds were renters. By 2014, that fraction had risen to two-thirds. The number of households aged 21 to 25 with a mortgage has fallen by a factor of three. While these trends in housing tenure are long-lived, the financial crisis has clearly amplified them. Since 2007, the share of renters among those aged between 25 and 34 has risen by 12 percentage points. Among 35–49 year olds, the share of renters has increased by over two thirds. By contrast, those over 50 have seen a much smaller change in housing tenures. These shifts are likely to reflect the combined effects of a rise in UK house prices relative to income and, since the crisis, a reduction in mortgage availability for the young.[28]

This lack of real terms wage growth, in conjunction with house prices which continue to rise, is in practice pushing homeownership further and further out of reach for larger swathes of the UK's population, particularly the young.

Research from the Resolution Foundation finds that one of the main reasons for the decline in real pay growth in the UK was sterling depreciation far more pronounced than that experienced in many neighbouring countries. Throughout the course of the 2008 financial crisis, sterling depreciated by 27 per cent – creating huge inflation and depressing real wage growth.[29] Emerging from this period of sluggish pay growth, however, is not an easy prospect. The Resolution Foundation conclude that tackling the UK's long-term problems with productivity growth is key to restoring strong wage growth – however such a prospect is a long way off, if feasible at all. According to the Living Wage Campaign, one-fifth of UK workers currently experience work insecurity, 56 per cent earn less than the real Living Wage and 53 per cent of shift workers receive less than a week's notice of their hours. The proportion of these low-paid and insecure jobs appears to be increasing – as increased rates of employment since the financial crash (which sit at their lowest in half a century) have failed to make a dent in poverty and child poverty statistics, or average real incomes.

The increasing shift of the UK towards a low wage economy on less secure terms of employment further compounds the ability of many to access mortgage finance and afford repayments. Without inflation-matching pay increases, or a collapse in house and rental prices, it is highly unlikely that rates of homeownership will be able to increase at any kind of scale.

Making homes affordable

There are two elements to the affordability gap in the British housing market. The first is the rapidly increasing cost of housing. The second is our low-wage economy which fails to provide incomes requisite to those costs. In short, no policies to encourage homeownership will be successful unless the price of a home falls relatively against average incomes.

One route to repairing this disparity would be to focus upon slowing or even reversing the current inflation within the housing market, allowing incomes to catch up. To achieve these ends, policy must focus upon reducing the role of speculative finance in driving the onward march of house prices, as well as increasing supply of affordable and available homes.

But there are risks associated with reducing the growth in house prices. Reducing the growth in the price of houses will in turn reduce the profitability of development – something which will likely have an impact on the already limited extent of development within the private sector. Councils and the public sector would have to have the capacity not just to deliver huge numbers of affordable housing, but also pick up some of the slack from the general housing market as private developers draw back.

And if the housing price growth is completely reversed – causing deflation in the housing market – this could have catastrophic consequences for both developers and mortgage holders as their properties are plunged into negative equity, precipitating a wave of foreclosures.

Which is why the second element of the housing affordability problem must also be simultaneously addressed: our low-wage economy and our low-income society.

If incomes can be increased at a faster rate than the growth in house prices, then a substantial portion of the political and economic damage threatened by falling house prices can be avoided. But to integrate such a 'high wage' plan into a strategy for dealing with the housing crisis, housing must be seen as one part of a much broader and more ambitious programme to remodel the economy away from low-wage sectors such as tertiary and service sectors and into higher paying sectors such as manufacturing, engineering and other forms of industry (a process which will take decades from which to see meaningful change). Public sector wage suppression – seen consistently since 2010 – must be relaxed – and in-work benefits could also be a mechanism to bolster incomes in the short term.

Conclusion to Part II

The UK's housing policy landscape is a confusing mishmash of disconnected and disjointed initiatives, without clear strategic focus or goals – often contributing (rather than alleviating) the housing crisis. Insofar as there is a purpose or thinking behind the UK's approach to housing, since the 1980s that rationale has generally centred around the assumption that planning regulations, public sector involvement and lack of financial investment have been the primary obstacles to generating often unclearly defined policy aims, such as 'regeneration'.

However, if we are to define our housing policy goals around the three pillars of affordability, availability and quality, it becomes clear that many of the initiatives and policies enacted are at best ineffective, if not actively harmful, to our objectives.

Support for homeownership has clearly contributed significantly to our general affordability crisis, which is now having a suppressant effect on the numbers of new homeowners. Similarly, regeneration programmes in our major towns and cities predicated on increasing land values have pumped huge amounts of inflationary capital into housing in these areas, contributing significantly to displacement and gentrification of existing communities, as well as homelessness. Financial reforms designed to liberalise investment have allowed inordinate amounts of speculative finance to find a safe home for investment within housing – and reforms to enable the expansion of the private rented sector is similarly contributing significantly to price increases.

Undoubtedly the greatest failure in modern UK housing policy has been the dismantling of council and social housing provision. Local authority-built homes once made up a third of new-build completions – now, the number is negligible. In removing local authorities as a supplier of new homes we have decimated our capacity to deliver at the numbers and scale required to keep pace with demand. Private developers, and particularly the large-scale volume developers on which our housing system increasingly depends, have structural disincentives from adequately addressing our housing crisis – even if they had the capacity to do so. Structural changes to the planning system, as such, are effectively red herrings – unable to unlock the scale of building envisioned. These developers, furthermore, have entirely failed to invest in the training of the next generation of builders and tradesmen, leaving an industry with a gigantic workforce crisis unable to cope with the scale of building required to address demand.

In losing our supply of social and council housing, we have also lost our primary asset in addressing homelessness and rough sleeping. The result has been the tremendous increase in temporary accommodation and its associated problems of squalor and maladaptation to resident needs, as well as eye-watering costs.

The true solution to some of the associated crisis in our housing system – such as rough sleeping, temporary accommodation and adapted homes – is a ready supply of council and social housing which can be deployed tactically and strategically to ameliorate the situation of high need groups and individuals. In the absence of this, many associated crises such as homelessness and rough sleeping are treated as pathologies – the by-products of alcoholism and drug addiction, or mental health issues – as opposed to the absence of a home. The inability to grapple with this, and many other by-products of the lack of available and affordable accommodation through council and social housing, has led by default to a dizzying number of different grant funded pots and schemes addressing the symptoms of a crisis – while often also contributing to inflating rents and worsening general affordability.

The inability of policy makers to take several steps back from this scene, recognise the twisted interconnected causes of the present crisis and their antecedents is one of the greatest obstacles to redressing the balance. Rather than a continued doubling down on individual schemes to address isolated elements of the crisis, what is required is a holistic approach to the housing system as a whole with the clear goal of universally accessible, affordable and decent quality housing for all.

PART III

How do we fix it?

Our current housing crisis is possibly the most pressing social and political issue today, and rests upon at least 40 years of disastrous decisions taken by the UK government on almost every imaginable strand of housing policy. In the UK today, there appear to be no roadmaps to achieving any clear housing outcomes beyond an array of short-term funding pots for limited objectives (such as tackling the visible symptoms of homelessness or helping first-time buyers onto the housing ladder). Many of these initiatives (as has been demonstrated in the case of the perverse impact of Help to Buy on inflating property prices) operate counter to their stated intentions and in fact worsen the overall situation. Others are simply ineffective and small scale – such as the litany of disconnected short-term funding pots for mitigating the most visible aspects of the huge explosion in street homelessness.

It remains to be said that the UK is not alone in experiencing this crisis. Globally, it is estimated that 1.6 billion people worldwide lack access to adequate housing, expected to rise to three billion by 2030.[1] In a note to the 78th session of the UN General Assembly in 2023, several universal 'systemic shifts' were identified at the heart of the global affordability crisis, including:

> [A] misguided belief in market self-sufficiency without responsible State intervention, a notable decline in public housing provision by national and local governments, limited State capacities to address affordability concerns, diminishing public support for enabling low- and middle-income families to secure sustainable housing, inadequate legal safeguards for tenants, renters and mortgage holders facing excessive housing costs, rapid urbanisation expedited by the climate crisis, increased ownership concentration among a few financial entities, escalated housing and land speculation, and the financialization of housing.[2]

Yet this country's housing crisis is particularly acute among comparable nations, a fact worthy of deep reflection. It should be self-evident that the goal of housing policy should be to provide a stream of high-quality and affordable housing options for all British residents, to ensure that no British resident is compelled to go without suitable permanent residence for any substantial period of time, and to facilitate the creation and sustainability of communities. Furthermore, these outcomes are achievable – and yet, so much of this country's approach to housing is either ineffective in reaching these goals – or even exacerbating our present crisis.

The final section of this book will be devoted to proposed policy solutions to the present housing crisis, resting on the evidence and examples set throughout the first two sections. Through these remaining pages, we will explore numerous examples of workable policy changes to fix the fundamental failings of our housing system.

12

Council and social housing

The loss of Britain's once substantial council housing stock has had huge ramifications across the housing sector, and sits behind so many of the disjunctures we now face within our housing system.

Council and social housing has historically provided three key functions in stabilising the housing market. First, as a counterweight to general rent and house-price inflation, as well as a safe haven of affordability. Second, as a controllable source of accommodation which can be improved, adapted and directed towards the most acute instances of need. Third, as a huge addition to housing delivery and source of new available accommodation (in the absence of councils taking on roles as developers, the private sector has never filled the gap in delivery that we have seen since the 1980s).

The single most important policy towards resolving this country's housing crisis would be unlocking the power of councils (and housing associations) to build council houses at scale once more. With the government's own figures from 2022 to 2023 estimating that 1.29 million households are currently on local authority waiting lists for homes,[1] a clear demand for council housing is not being met which will be crucial in resolving our present crisis. In this chapter, we will cover the two major areas required to unlock this potential, and begin building the homes we need at scale once more.

Remove the Right to Buy

The central obstacle to the mass building of council housing over the past 40 years has been Right to Buy. The right of tenants to purchase their homes at a discount, with most of the proceeds returned to the Treasury, means in most cases it is entirely uneconomical for councils to invest in new council properties which are not substantially funded through grant. Councils cannot invest in building assets which may be sold under their noses at a substantial loss within a completely unpredictable timeframe – particularly when the building is being financed through borrowing which requires debt repayments to be scheduled over a long period of time.

The Right to Buy cannot be reformed. Even without the subsidy to tenants, the inability of councils to profile rental revenue streams from properties over time interferes with any kind of long-term borrowing schedules, in addition to there being no guarantee that the full market value of the property would be able to fully finance the creation of a replacement house. The erratic sale of homes from blocks of flats or estates also creates a chaotic picture for estate management – which itself provides better value for money and service through economies of scale. Land is generally built on from the most optimal locations to the least. Many early council estates were built in central locations, well connected to public transport and sites of employment. As subsequent generations of council estates have been developed, they have moved further and further away from sites of economic activity and transport connections, creating isolated ghettos with little access to amenity and poor employment prospects. The concept that it would be possible to sustain a system of replacing homes like for like with proceeds from council housing ignores this fundamental question – where would the new homes go?

Since 2024, the new Labour government has confirmed that there is no political intention to scrap Right to Buy – however there are plans to restrict Right to Buy on new build properties, and to significantly reduce the discount available to buyers[2]. Such measures could prove transformative in unlocking the viability of future council house construction; yet without the full withdrawal of Right to Buy, the continued bleed of existing Council Housing stock is inevitable, as is the risk of relaxed rules on the reintroduction of Right to Buy in future. Instead, the government aspires to build social rented homes through housing associations. While any focus on social rents is welcome, a huge opportunity is being missed to increase development capacity. Planned reforms will certainly make the development of new council and social housing significantly more viable, with 10 years of tenancy required for existing tenants to purchase their council homes and reduction of discounts – with all new-build council homes exempt from Right to Buy for 35 years. Additionally, the £12 million proposed 'Council Housebuilding Skills and Capacity Fund' to assist councils in rebuilding their lost development teams and expertise is a clear step in the right direction. Further than this, the full removal of Right to Buy would provide active protection for what remains of our existing housing stock – as well as provide a more significant political safeguard against the reintroduction of Right to Buy under future governments. As opposed to the complete removal of Right to Buy, for the time being at least England's option is simply to dial it down.

Investment and funding

Government investment will also be required to kick-start the scale of council house building which we will need. This will entail a root and branch reform of current funding mechanisms, which presently do not reach the locales which require help the most, and instead worsen the inflationary spiral of property prices we are seeing in overheated property markets in urban areas and the South East.

At present, funding programmes for 'affordable homes' are not designed specifically for council or social rents, but for an array of 'products', many of which have dubious claims to true affordability. Under the present government definition, 'affordable housing' can mean anything from rent or sale at 20 per cent below the market average in a given location, social or council rents, shared ownership schemes with developers, or 'First Homes Scheme' homes for sale at 30 per cent under market value. Depending on the given values in many areas, percentage reductions may be welcome, yet fail to achieve a benchmark of affordability for the increasing numbers of people who have no additional disposable income. In addition, increasing amounts of evidence suggest that government-sponsored homeownership schemes inflate property prices by a greater sum than the benefits they grant to individual households, worsening the affordability crisis.

In practice, of the categories of 'affordable housing' recognised by government, only social and council rents are guaranteed to target the individuals in most need – yet such homes amounted to only 13 per cent of all 'affordable' homes (subsidised with public money) built between 2021 and 2022.[3]

The amount of government grants available for affordable housing have historically been nowhere near high enough to encourage local authorities to embark on the scale of building required to fix our present crisis, with grant of between 35 and 40 per cent of unit costs required to make social rents stack up over the long term.

The funds released have also not been distributed to areas with the most acute housing need; rather, they have been distributed to areas with the most active housing markets, leaving many of the most chronically deprived areas of the country bereft of the necessary funds to build. Present funding programmes directed towards affordable house building should be redirected towards the construction of social and council housing as a matter of urgency. This has to a certain extent been recognised with recent announcements reallocating 'Objectively Assessed Housing Need' targets more equitably across the country, and with the release of several regeneration funds for high-need 'trailblazer areas' from the Comprehensive Spending Review – but truly tackling the Treasury Green Book methodology which directs funding towards areas with the highest market values has not yet been undertaken.

Fixing the funding model for council and social housing is a necessity if we are to scale up our building aspirations, and there are several ways we might do so. Having a level of grant which is able to subsidise the build without loss to the developer is key – but calculations regarding net cost-savings to the Treasury and other public bodies through reducing dependency on temporary accommodation and reducing other costly social problems related to homelessness and rough sleeping would also go a long way. At present, there is too little in the way of joined-up thinking among public sector bodies to understand the true extent of potential savings on existing service provision from owning an adequate source of council stock – however where the work has been done, the findings are staggering. Kate Wareing, Chief Executive of Soha Housing, published a report into alternative funding models for asylum and temporary housing in 2024, which found that publicly funded capital subsidy grants of as little as £1.75 billion nationally would enable local authorities to purchase hotels and accommodation presently used to house asylum seekers, paying back the borrowing costs in as little as eight months and reducing costs of asylum-seeker accommodation per head by almost 93 per cent a year.[4] Similarly, Shelter in conjunction with the National Housing Federation commissioned the Centre for Economics and Business Research to 'assess the economic and social impacts of building 90,000 social homes' in 2024, calculating that such a project would cost around £5.3 billion, but would 'break even' for the Treasury after year three when accounting for the direct and indirect benefits to the Exchequer through employment, reduction in costs for temporary and homeless accommodation, and savings on healthcare.[5] Crucial to unlocking the Treasury's borrowing powers will be the treatment of council and social housing as assets, and understanding the complex interplay between services across the wider public sector and the aggregate savings they can bring – in addition to rental income.

New patient lending models also need to be explored. At present, much UK housing development finance is provided over a relatively short term, with significant pressure on developers to pay down their borrowing as soon as possible following completion – yet longer-term borrowing periods would benefit developers of social housing in particular, given the lower short-term yields available from lower rents.

There are also experiments with other types of arrangements. The Charities Aid Foundation Bank already provides long-term lending facilities for registered providers of social housing, with repayment periods of up to 25 years up to £10 million (significantly longer terms than most lending in the sector). But these are still fairly small sums of money in volume house-building terms. The increasing involvement of pension funds in UK housebuilding may provide some opportunities for patient capital investment, as well as innovative cross-subsidy models. In 2024, the Universities Superannuation Scheme, the UK's largest pension scheme, invested £405 million into 3,000 shared-ownership homes from a national investment of almost £4 billion on 17,000 homes (11,000 of them for social rent) from the property investor Sage. Speaking of the scheme, James Seppala of Blackstone (the parent company of Sage) boasts that:

> Through Sage Homes … Blackstone has been the largest provider of newly built affordable housing in the country for the last three years.
>
> By deploying capital to fund the development of new homes, we are proud to have created an institutional-grade portfolio which, in turn, has attracted more long-term institutional capital into the sector. This transaction will allow us to continue to invest capital into Sage

Homes to help to alleviate the structural undersupply of housing across the UK.[6]

Other initiatives increasingly see pension funds as prospective patient lenders, providing longer-term financing arrangements for the social housing sector. In January 2025, Legal and General (L&G) were tasked with managing a £100 million investment fund establish by the Greater Manchester Pension Fund aimed at developing affordable housing across the North West of England. While these private initiatives are welcome, without clear strategic leadership from the state they are still likely to fall short of the capacity and vision to deliver against the country's demand for affordable homes.

State-backed bonds to build affordable and social homes with payback periods of 40–50 or 60 years could have a transformative impact on the sector, enabling registered providers to economically build social homes at scale once more. Short of this, the state underwriting the risk for pension funds and other institutional investors experimenting with longer-term financing arrangements for social housing developers could enable the sector to innovate with solutions which are presently too risky.

What's needed for the delivery of social rents

For this book, I interviewed Charlotte Norman, chief executive officer of the housing association of Mosscare St. Vincent and chair of the Greater Manchester Housing Providers network, encompassing all housing associations in Greater Manchester (note that Norman's interview was conducted prior to the 2025 Comprehensive Spending Review and as such provides perspective on pre-CSR announcements). She spoke on the prospects for devolution to enable a significant uplift of social house building in Greater Manchester, as well as obstacles faced by the sector:

> About 12 years ago, all of the Greater Manchester housing providers came together to coalesce around a Poverty Truth Commission report that Bishop David [Walker] had sponsored. We were frankly horrified about the outcomes of that report. And so we came together loosely and to talk about that and what more we could do. We started to think, well, we could work together on a number of things here. You know, the work we do in communities, on growth, development, repairs, work and skills, that kind of thing. And we've [Greater Manchester Housing Providers] just grown and grown organically as a 'coalition of the willing', what we refer to ourselves as.
>
> We signed an MOU with Greater Manchester Combined Authority in 2017 when Andy [Burnham] was elected, I remember being at all the hustings for the first GM mayor. We could already see that we were well aligned with Andy and his priorities around health, public service reform, growth and homelessness in

particular. And we set up our Social Impact Bond, which turned into Housing First in Greater Manchester. Then we signed another deal, the tripartite agreement in 2021 which brought in health – because there's health devolution in Greater Manchester. And we've gone from strength to strength.

So the Housing First philosophy is that everything starts at home. If you can get a decent, safe, warm home, everything flows from that. We've aligned all of our priorities around the three pillars of Housing First, which are: supply (he [Mayor Burnham] wants to build 75,000 new homes in Greater Manchester, a good proportion of which will be social homes). Standards (which is about investing in our existing homes, and things like the good landlord charter and bringing up standards in the PRS [private rented sector]) and, culture. We all saw what happened with Grenfell and the report that came out last week, and the fact that those residents just weren't listened to or treated with respect. So it's about culture as much as about investing in homes and support, and linking back to the support that and access to opportunity that people should have.

So we're organising ourselves around that. We think that the single settlement and Welsh and Scottish-style devolution can get a good pot into Greater Manchester, for investing in new homes and existing homes and supporting people, and to try and do something in Greater Manchester the rest of the country hasn't yet managed to smash. There's still not a long-term strategy for housing in the country.

Despite great optimism and enthusiasm for an increased role within a devolved Greater Manchester, Norman still has some fundamental concerns regarding the ability of the sector to scale up delivery. In particular, she notes that grant regimes are insufficient to sustainably build at social rent:

> GMHP [Greater Manchester Housing Providers] are doing a capacity piece of work at the moment to look at what's in our business plans now, both in terms of existing kinds of investment and new supply. But also what's the headroom, and what are the asks as well? Because there are barriers in our way to deliver those ambitions. Things like getting a long-term rent settlement, the Affordable Homes Programme that's stalled at the moment ... it's shocking what's happened with the Affordable Homes Programme given the housing crisis that we've got.

Norman stresses the grant rate on new builds, and its importance in enabling further social development:

> I'm old enough to remember working in the sector when we got 100% grants to build social homes. Now it's down to 20–25 per cent. Our financial model is that we borrow money on the open market from high street banks and institutional investors and pension funds and what have you. So we're raising capital on the back of our existing assets, which then we've got interest to cover issues and that kind of thing. So we can only borrow so much.

Ultimately, I think the Affordable Homes Programme and the grant regime needs to change, particularly to deliver social rent, social rent property. Because they cost more, you're going beyond 60 years to get payback on them. So the grant amount needs to move up to more like 40 per cent [of delivery cost] and beyond. And for a supported property, something like a custom designed learning disability scheme, you need grant mates going 50 to 60 per cent to make those stack up because they're so niche.

So we can keep raising capital, but then you know that we are constrained in how much we can do that, and then you've got all your interest to cover, so the grant rates need to come up, or it needs to be creative uses of funding within local authorities.

For Norman, all of these questions form part of her co-ordinated lobbying efforts with the new government around five key areas: increasing funds through the Affordable Homes Programme; regeneration and repairs funding; increasing the rent-cap for Registered Providers; dedicated support for supported accommodation; and planning reform.

So the government have changed, and they've obviously got a budget, and we've got two fiscal events coming up. We're trying to organise ourselves to pitch into that. We need (1) that Affordable Homes Programme, ideally a ten-year programme with higher grant rates. (2) Another pot for regeneration; proper regeneration, funding and investment in existing homes (because some of our homes are at the end of their lives). (3) Funding a long-term rent settlement at inflation at CPI+1 per cent, and (4) things like Supporting People [a now obsolete fund] that pot of money that we used to have that was ring fenced for wrap-around support that you put around people who've got very complex needs. That would be ideal as well as (5) planning reform. You know, there's the NPPF [National Planning Policy Framework] consultation that's out at the moment. Planning is really a big barrier in terms of supply.

The way forward

The obstacles in the way of mass council and social house building today are large, but they are not infinitely complex. The primary concern of local authorities in relation to council house building is in access to finance, and models for financing social and council housing which 'stack up'. Homes for which there is proven demand and reliable income are relatively safe investments. Through removing Right to Buy, we would remove the risks to councils of losing their asset, which in turn would remove a key barrier to accessing finance and funding, enabling a huge programme of development to be undertaken.

While the incoming Labour government has announced restrictions on Right to Buy for new properties, the lack of protection for existing properties all but guarantees a continued bleed of these properties out of public use as well as their use as assets which could be borrowed against or redeployed as tenancies end. Rather than councils, it seems the current government believes that the social housing sector more broadly must be enabled to scale up its development and take on an expanded role in new provision.

Right to Buy is reflective of a broader problem of making the economics of social housing stack up for prospective developers. Developing sustainable funding models and business cases for social housing needs to go much further. With this in mind, the removal of the rent cap in social housing, announced recently by government, is a necessary if controversial move (most rents in social housing will still fall beneath the Local Housing Allowance rate, meaning that in the majority of incidences this increase will be burdened upon the Department for Work and Pensions and Housing Benefit rather than tenants). Also desirable would be an increase in the grant rate for social builds pegged at roughly 40 per cent or more of the cost of delivering a given unit. Presently, we are nowhere near this ambition, leaving a difficult road ahead in scaling social housing delivery (though as we begin to learn more about the allocation of recent announcements for £39 billion into the Affordable Homes Program, this may become more clear).

But in absence of immediate moves on the grant rate and the removal of Right to Buy, there are other areas that could be developed. For starters, social housing developers and the wider public sector must invest in more sophisticated methods of accounting for cost savings to the public purse through the provision of social housing. Preliminary research into the savings which could be accrued through small-scale capital subsidy to enable the purchase of existing temporary accommodation suggests that the investment would pay its own way in an astonishingly short amount of time – in some cases under a year. Savings on temporary accommodation payments would primarily benefit local authorities and the Home Office – but other areas of the public sector could also accrue significant savings through the provision of adequate housing, particularly the health sector where savings could be gained from reducing the burden on intermediate care units and in reducing health problems associated with unsuitable accommodation.

And long-term lending models should be incentivised by government among prospective lenders, extending available borrowing periods for social housing developers to help the business case for social units stack up would go a long way to enabling the sector to scale up its provision. Work is already being done on the financing model across the sector – but with some strategic focus from government, the impact could be substantially increased.

13

Controlling house price inflation

The inflation of house values in the UK presents a huge conundrum for policy makers. The ever-growing value of property and housing within the UK acts as a reservoir of notional nationwide wealth. To collapse house prices to a level at which homes would become affordable would not only have an apocalyptic impact on our present construction industry, it would also have huge ramifications for inward investment and gross domestic product (GDP). In 2022, real estate contributed a total of 7 per cent of the UK's GDP, employing more than 1.2 million people[1] – and land value accounts for over 60 per cent of the UK's net worth.[2] Any rapid deflation of property prices could cause immediate crises, not to mention the disastrous impact such a collapse may have upon indebted homeowners, who could be plunged into negative equity, risking foreclosures and a worsening of the general housing crisis.

But the rate at which prices are growing is astonishing – and it is the growth in house prices which lies at the base of the increase in costs in the rental market and increasing levels of debt undertaken to finance mortgages. Growth in prices is now unsustainable – in 1997, the average UK house price was only 2.9 times the average salary.[3] In 2023, it has more than doubled to 8.3 times average salaries (ONS). Controlling house price inflation has to be a key driver of housing policy if we are to stand any chance of resolving the housing crisis – however, managing this process carefully will be key to avoiding a cliff-edge, and potential economic crisis.

Council and social housing

The widespread provision of council housing on controlled sub-market rents has a substantial role to play in the process of controlling general house price inflation. One of the most inflationary sectors of the current housing market is the proliferation of buy-to-let properties – in turn spurred by the collapse of traditional alternatives to private renting such as council homes. Since the 1988 Act and the establishment of Assured Shorthold Tenancies, buy-to-let mortgages emerged in the mid-1990s and have proliferated to take advantage of the new expanded rights for landlords. Between 1999 and 2015, the Council of Mortgage Lenders estimates that 1.7 million buy-to-let mortgages were advanced to the value of £200 billion.[4] Today, buy-to-let mortgages cover 45 per cent of all private rented sector (PRS) homes, representing £300 billion of outstanding mortgage debt (18 per cent of the entire mortgage market).[5] Buy to let has bolstered demand for mortgages, and even accelerated following the credit crunch as first-time buyers moved away from homeownership, hugely contributing to the sustained growth of house prices we have seen over this period.

However, while excess units of council housing were available to British residents throughout most of the 1980s and the first half of the 1990s, the buy-to-let market was subdued in its growth, competing directly with council and social housing on price and quality. Research from the local government network Core Cities suggests that the reduction in size of the social housing sector was a huge growth factor for PRS, with 1.2 million fewer social tenants in 2011 as there had been in 2001.[6] A 2018 paper commissioned by the Nationwide Foundation in conjunction with the University of York and the Centre for Housing Policy also concluded that the growth in PRS was substantially driven by 'demand for social housing ... far outstrip[ping] availability'.[7] The paper concludes that 'the private rented sector is primarily a commercial industry that does not currently operate in a way that adequately provides decent, affordable homes for the most vulnerable households. This is leaving many people trapped in homes that clearly fail to meet their needs'.[8]

Introducing a substantial amount of council and social rented housing into the system to compete with the private rental market would help to curb excessive rents within PRS, and begin to replace PRS in the market. The reduction in buy-to-let investment would also have a significant impact in reducing the growth of house price inflation – making homes more affordable for purchase by owner-occupiers.

Council and social rented homes would also have a related impact on curbing house price inflation; the reduction in expenditure on services from PRS. A substantial stock of social rented properties could help to replace our current systemic dependency on hugely inflationary programmes such as Housing Benefit, which each and every year pumps billions into the housing market in the form of a direct subsidy to landlords (in 2022, the cost of Housing Benefit to the Exchequer was £23.4 billion, more than the entire transport budget, Home Office budget and policing budget). In its stead, Housing Benefit would form an indirect payment to local authorities and housing associations in the form of rents, recirculating Treasury money within the public sector – as opposed to an inflationary subsidy maintaining high rents in the PRS.

Re-evaluate grant-based projects

In addition to Housing Benefit, almost every policy response to any element of the present housing crisis in some form or another is predicated on huge levels of inflationary investment: that is, investment in housing which does not increase the supply of available homes. Whether it is the Rough Sleepers Initiative, the billions spent on temporary accommodation by local authorities every year, or Housing Benefit, the vast bulk of money from these initiatives fails to tackle the root source of the issue (a lack of availability of affordable housing) and instead ply more and more money into inflating rents in the PRS. For any success in the area of controlling house price inflation, a re-evaluation of any and all initiatives and policies which invest money into the housing market without increasing availability of truly affordable accommodation needs to be undertaken, and as a system we need to wean ourselves from dependence on short-term funding pots to resolve immediate crises.

This will be difficult. Our failure to systemically challenge the failings of our housing system over many decades has left us with an endemic over-reliance on emergency funding to remediate the most acute impacts of our failed housing system. But this dependence is increasing exponentially as the crisis reaches a new threshold and is entirely unsustainable as a model.

Almost all funding currently directed towards homelessness prevention could be rendered redundant with a sufficient supply of council and social rented housing and supported accommodation, through which to place individuals with high needs. A movement towards targeting this issue would quickly begin to save money both from homelessness reduction programmes and temporary accommodation bills.

A clear strategy, including a pipeline for delivery, should be developed immediately to create a routemap to providing the new truly affordable accommodation required to tackle the housing and homelessness crisis, reducing the amount of inflationary spending currently invested into the housing system through individual schemes.

Curb financial speculation

Financial investment and speculation, including the focus of commercial high street banks on mortgage lending, is undoubtedly the central factor behind the endless inflation of house prices not just in Britain but across much of the Western world. Within the UK, a whole series of legal reforms have acted to consistently liberalise financial markets since the 1970s, making it easier and easier for consumers to finance the purchase of properties through debt. Business lending equated to around 40 per cent of GDP in most advanced economies during the early 1980s, with mortgage lending at 25 per cent. However by the 2008 financial crash, mortgage lending had grown to 75 per cent of GDP (as of 2021, this has settled to 65 per cent[9]). This in effect amounts to billions of pounds of inflationary investment into land and property which cannot be matched by increased availability of land. Josh Ryan-Collins argues that this huge infusion of cash is the largest single institutional cause behind the ever-inflating price of land – as an asset-price inflation spiral which has now been embedded into the fundamental principles of most advanced economies.

This trend has been identified as the 'housing-finance feedback cycle' by in his government-sponsored research on behalf of University College London's Institute for Innovation and Public Purpose.[10] The paper demonstrates that increases in financial flows into housing are generating both immediate price increases and expectations of further inflation – particularly among buy-to-let properties and second homes. In the immediate term, there would appear to be little within the power of governments to tackle mortgage-lending without removing the central plank through which most people are able to acquire finance to buy their homes (though the paper does propose longer-term fixed mortgages for first-time buyers, as well as compulsory mortgage insurance) – but measures could and should be introduced to remove the hugely inflationary impact of speculation within land markets and the construction of development properties which are contributing hugely to pushing up prices.

'Land value capture' and reforms to property tax

One mechanism to assist in curbing land market speculation would be to provide proper tools to public authorities to capture the value uplift in land which receives planning permission and is subsequently developed. At present, 'planning gain' speculation drives both a shortage of developable land and high prices. In 2019, estimates from the valuation office showed that while the average price for a hectare of agricultural land in England was £23,033, the average for land with planning permission for housing was over £6 million a hectare – 300 times the value.[11] The problems with this issue are multiple. With costs for land skyrocketing, in a housing market which is under-supplying units, developers are easily able to transfer these costs to consumers in the form of higher unit prices. Equally, with the value of land skyrocketing, there is a huge incentive for landowners to 'bank' their land and wait for prices to increase further, restricting the supply of developable sites. To combat this, robust measures to tackle speculation on land value need to be introduced.

Historically there is precedence for such a tax, although it has proven politically contentious. In 1947, the Town and Country Planning Act enabled local authorities to levy 'development charges' against developments where permissions had been granted to change from its 'existing use', 'equal to the value of the permission'. In effect, the act nationalised the development value of all land – simultaneously reducing the development value to close to nil for any developer. This move in a fell swoop removed speculation on development via planning permissions, however the issue revealed an over-correction. With reduced incentives for landowners to pass on land for development, the supply of developable land became too restricted and stymied new projects.[12] The subsequent 1953 and 1954 Town and Country Planning Acts removed these sections of the act.

Following this, in 1965 the Finance Act was passed, introducing capital gains taxation on windfall profits from the development of land. Following this, in 1967 the Labour government passed the Land Commission Act, establishing a Land Commission to acquire developable land with a 'betterment levy' of 40 per cent of the total net development value. These reforms were abolished immediately following the return to government of the Conservatives in 1970.

The 1974 Labour government again attempted to introduce mechanisms for land value capture through the Community Land Act (1975) and the Development Land Tax Act (1976) – raising local authority powers to acquire land for development, and levy a Development Land Tax upon the realisation of development value. Once again, the Community Land Act was removed in 1980 by the incoming Conservative government, however the Development Land Tax remained in place for another five years, after which it was removed having been widely avoided by developers.

Concurrent to land value taxes, 'planning gain' mechanisms have also emerged with more limited ambition to claw back value from development. Powers from the 1947 Town and Country Planning Act through which authorities establish negotiated planning agreements to regulate the development and use of land with landowners were translated into Section 52 powers in the 1971 Town and Country Planning Act – powers for local authorities to levy charges on, or demand contributions to, infrastructure from development to mitigate its wider impacts. Under the 1990 revisions to the act, these powers were translated into Section 106 agreements. Clarified by a Secretary of State circular letter in 2005, Section 106 negotiations were restricted to contributions to developers which were relevant, necessary for the development, directly related to the development, and fairly and reasonably related in scale and kind to the development.[13]

Section 106 agreements remained the primary mechanism through which local authorities could benefit from planning gain until 2012, when the terms were again revised with the introduction of the National Planning Policy Framework,[14] which rendered such agreements unenforceable by local authorities if they compromised the economic 'sustainability' of a given development (conventionally, sustainable development is considered to achieve a profit margin of 20 per cent or more).

At present, weak Section 106 agreements and often impractical Community Infrastructure Levies provide the only means by which proceeds of the value of development can be harnessed and reinvested by public authorities – but both are weak, and target developer profits rather than those of the landowners (which in turn risks increasing inflation as developers hike prices to recoup their costs). To help mitigate endless inflation, tools for capturing value uplift need to intercept the development process at source, removing the speculative ability to make a profit simply by buying land and receiving permission for its development.

Numerous tools for land value capture could be adopted, which could improve this process. In 1975, Harrisburg in Pennsylvania introduced a land value tax which has been overwhelmingly associated with huge improvements to the city. The Harrisburg tax, still in use today, is a split rate tax which charges one rate for the undeveloped land and a second rate for improvements or developments on it. In Australia, most state and territory governments deploy some form of land tax, particularly for rural land with residential, commercial or industrial developments.[15]

Despite the UK's difficult history with land value taxation, the concept is tried and proven and among the only mechanisms for reducing the speculative value of land, which is doing so much to drive up property prices.

Controls on international buyers and short-term lets

It is increasingly clear that international investors and buy-to-let purchasers are inflating the costs of housing both through their initial investment, and the removal of homes from the effective housing supply. Simultaneously - local and City-regional Authorities in the UK continue to chase property price-led growth models, encouraging international inward investment. Both phenomena contribute to worsening supply and affordability problems, in a vicious circle of asset-price inflation and increased profitability.

Internationally, there are examples of controls on international property investment which are effective and politically popular. Restrictions on these kinds of investment could have an outsized impact on house prices and the availability of domestic UK housing supply to residents.

While future purchases of land and property from non-UK internationals is a fairly straightforward process, greater difficulty would be posed by retrospectively applying sanctions to existing overseas investors. The previous government may have inadvertently provided one of the major tools to enforce such restrictions on existing international property owners. Following the Russian invasion of Ukraine, in an effort to bolster sanctions targeted at Russian investors the UK government introduced a new 'Register of Overseas Entities', a new legal requirement for all overseas owners of UK property to register their assets and controlling interests. A government committed to a reduction in overseas ownership of UK land and property, including international property investment and speculation, would be in a much stronger position to apply such sanctions than they may have been previously.

But efforts to curb domestic buy-to-let mortgages could also have a huge impact on suppressing continued house price inflation. Reforms to limit the amount of buy-to-let mortgage finance available would effectively curb the purchasing power of buy-to-let landlords within the housing market, relatively benefiting prospective homeowners (this is also a measure proposed in J. Ryan-Collins' paper written for the Institute for Innovation and Public Purpose).

A new approach to urban regeneration

In the face of no national strategy for housing supply, particularly one connected to a broader industrial strategy and public health agenda, local authorities in particular have developed models for growth and housing development which in many respects are exacerbating the key elements of our national housing crisis today.

The model of deliberately fostering areas of high value as a honeypot for investment, usually within urban cores, is contributing hugely to the commodification of housing and property not just in urban cores where much of the activity is located, but across the country. There is scant evidence that this approach to growth efficiently or effectively distributes the proceeds of economic activity across the areas in which it is fostered, and extensive evidence that it contributes to the crisis of affordability and availability of accommodation. Gentrification, displacement and the increasing prevalence of homelessness within the UK's urban cores are all testament to the limitations of this model.

Alternatively, a more strategic approach to economic growth needs to be fostered which accounts for housing demand. The sectors we choose to invest in as a country should not be selected merely on the basis of which sectors truncated local authorities with declining services budgets still have influence over – they should be selected on the basis of wider benefits to society in terms of jobs, wealth and prosperity. Such an approach would require a level of interconnected thinking between skills and work, infrastructural investments and housing policy areas which simply hasn't been attempted since the post-war period.

Short of this, at the very least local authorities should at least be prevented from continuing to engage with models of development that facilitate the most inflationary facets of inward investment into housing markets, and ensure that the principle of affordability and wider social accessibility is included in any and all improvements to public realm and amenity, and the redevelopment of urban areas. Ensuring social and council house provision within areas of new development is one effective mechanism for preserving affordable islands within high value areas. But similarly, covenants on public land used or sold for development, fees and charges levied by Combined

Authority mayors and an exploration of direct rent controls could be used to mitigate the negative impacts of runaway urban inflation and the creation of sustainable and truly mixed communities.

Managing property-price inflation

Given the centrality of the growing affordability crisis as a plank of the UK's housing crisis today, it's clear that controlling and managing continued house-price inflation is a necessity of any effective policy response. To do so requires an audit of almost every element of our current models for financing both new development, but also homeownership and our policy responses to housing issues such as homelessness. While supply of requisite affordable accommodation continues to be restricted, we must be incredibly wary of any financial mechanisms operating within the field of housing which are not dedicated to increasing the supply of affordable homes – as each in their own way are likely contributing to the continued cycle of runaway prices.

Where investment is needed, safeguards such as rent controls or subsidised social rents, fees and charges or novel forms of taxation should be utilised to ensure affordability is preserved even in the areas where price inflation is at its peak. Where possible, new state investment into housing support and services should be focused on increasing the housing supply – and restrictions must be introduced to prevent and curtail the use of homes as commercial assets (either as short-term lets, passive investments or for the buy-to-let market more generally). The task of controlling house price inflation is a delicate balance. A house-price crash could be disastrous, requiring far greater levels of intervention from government to prevent a wider economic crisis. But growth in house prices at the present rate is unsustainable in any case – and unless the situation is managed, the situation will only worsen rapidly.

14

Regulate the private rented sector

Tenancy in the private rented sector (PRS) is the fastest growing form of household habitation in the UK, with as many as 9–10 million people and the number of PRS households doubling since the year 2000.

It seems like an expanded PRS is the likely immediate and medium-term future for housing in the UK, and increasing numbers of British residents will expect to spend their entire lives in PRS. Given this is the case, currently there are startlingly few policy controls, levers and regulations to protect the rights of tenants, or to maintain the condition of properties (or upgrade them to net-zero standards).

Prior to the 1988 Housing Act, the UK's PRS was subject to substantially more regulation than exists today. From 1915 and the introduction of the Rent and Mortgage Interest (War Restrictions) Act, varying degrees of rent controls and limitations on landlords right to evict tenants were embedded in legal statute. From 1945 onwards, these controls were increased, with the 'Protection from Eviction Act' in 1964 establishing universal protection from eviction for all tenants, and the concept of property valuation into the setting of rents, assessing acceptable rent levels on the basis of the state of the property. These protections lasted until the creation of the Assured Shorthold Tenancy under the 1988 Housing Act.

The period from 1964 to 1988 correlated with the period of the greatest improvements in housing standards in recorded history, alongside the period of the most affordable accommodation. From the introduction of the act, no effective regulation over standards, rents or breaches of acceptable conduct have been in place over the PRS, during a period of historic growth for the sector.

Statistically we know that most of the poorest conditions in our housing market are located in the PRS. We also know that the primary cause of homelessness is eviction from PRS accommodation, and that the majority of private tenants are not tenants in PRS as a matter of 'choice', but of circumstance. The relatively new phenomenon of mass, lifelong renting in PRS in the UK contrasts with the long-established renting culture in other parts of the world, where protections for tenants are far more substantial and significant controls are levied on rents, quality and tenure.

If we are to address the ongoing issues of quality of tenure for Britain's increasing population of private tenants, we must engage with the issue of an effectively unregulated sector of the British housing market which is increasingly home to poor conditions and expensive rents.

Licensing and rental sector reform

While social housing holds its share of non-decent homes, as we have previously discussed, the PRS has by far the most homes in a state of non-decency – and is the hardest to legislate for. It is illegal to own certain breeds of dogs without a licence in the UK – yet it is perfectly legal to be an unregistered slum landlord. Without further legislation, protections and an empowered regulator operating in the space of rented accommodation, renters will continue to suffer in unsanitary and unsuitable conditions (as we have discussed, the revitalised Renters' Rights Bill does begin to address many of these issues).

In addition to the quality of homes, renters in PRS also face added pressures of short-term tenancies, uncontrolled rent increases, breaches of contract by landlords and regular malpractice. However, there are some exceptions to this rule: namely, areas in which landlord licensing is imposed by local authorities. Through mandatory licensing of landlords, councils have powers to monitor standards and conditions in PRS properties, and powers to fine and intervene where tenants' health and wellbeing is put under threat by poor practices.

Such licensing areas are hugely effective where they are implemented, and even revenue-generating through the levy of fees and charges against non-compliant landlords. A joint report from the Chartered Institute of Environmental Health and the Chartered Institute of Housing in 2019 noted that selective landlord licensing effectively improve housing conditions in their areas, using regular inspections to identify poor conditions without the need for resident complaints. The report also found that landlords within selective licensed areas were 'more willing' to perform required works on their properties, with general attitudes among landlords in those areas changing to become more socially responsible. Other identified benefits from selective licensing schemes include better knowledge and data on general housing stock and condition, better joint working alongside other public sector partners such as the police to identify criminal behaviour, clear evidence of reductions in anti-social behaviour and an overall improvement in housing conditions.[1]

Yet up until 2024, an arbitrary limit has been placed upon councils as to the extent of the area under which licensing can be issued – 30 per cent of the area of their local authority. To expand beyond this limit, explicit Secretary of State approval has had to be sought alongside an extensive evidence case for the necessity of implementing the scheme. There appears to be little rationale behind the limitation of landlord licensing powers to local authorities, and indeed, given the evidence base, there is a clear argument that such licensing responsibilities should be both universal and statutory obligations.

There are some signs of progress on this front. Through negotiations between the Department for Housing, Levelling Up and Communities and Mayoral Combined Authorities such as Greater Manchester via the

'Trailblazer schemes' of devolved powers, the ability to landlord license universally without Secretary of State approval is being trialled. Amendments to the Renters' Rights Bill as it progresses through Parliament have also expanded the enforcement powers of Local Authorities in general, enabling them to directly levy fines against landlords operating outside the terms of the new legislation.[2] Close attention should be paid to the rollout of universal landlord licensing in Greater Manchester, and should it be successful, a programme of universal licensing for landlords could quickly begin to improve standards across the PRS.

Licensing is potentially the biggest opportunity within the Renters' Rights Bill. As of December 2024, it has no longer been required for English Councils to require approval from the Secretary of State to introduce selective licensing schemes – leading to a surge of 37 new schemes across the country. However, legal guidance still requires Local Authorities to provide data to government on their schemes at the commencement and end of their schemes, evidencing their impact against stated goals. These reforms still assume that selective licensing schemes are to be temporary, in order to address specific issues prior to being resolved. The Renters' Rights Bill falls short of mandatory universal landlord licensing, a missed opportunity to increase the impact of reforms and enable robust enforcement of standards.[3]

Powers to acquire non-compliant properties

In addition to universal landlord licensing, enhanced powers for local government to acquire properties which fail to reach the decency thresholds. As the recent case of Awaab Ishak has shown, the dangers to tenants from occupying houses blighted with damp and mould are substantial – and the UK's ageing housing stock is prone to such issues, particularly given our humid climate. At present, councils do possess Compulsory Purchase Order (CPO) powers, yet these powers are not suited for the acquisitions of poor quality rental properties.

As of 1961, the Land Compensation Act has codified the modern iteration of CPOs, with subsequent reforms in 1965 and 1981 consolidating the powers available to local authorities today. At present, CPOs are considered to be means of 'assembling land needed to help deliver social, environmental and economic change',[4] as a mechanism of last resort, following a breakdown of negotiations with the owner over a required purchase. When undertaking this exercise, a public body is liable to incur legal fees, processing costs (such as staff time and resources), professional fees undertaken by the owner of the compulsorily purchased property in bringing forward their defence, and any costs associated with project delays. Furthermore, subjects of CPOs are also entitled to compensation, covering several categories of damage:

- the value of the land taken;
- disturbance payments;
- loss payments; and
- severance and injurious affection caused by public works.

Until 2022, owners of compulsorily purchased land could also claim for 'hope value' (the projected value of a site once further developed, regenerated or otherwise put to use), 'ransom value' (the value of the land's ability to unlock development potential through providing the only possible access) and 'marriage value' (a calculation of the sites value, in tandem with another site, where owned together, the sites would be worth more than their individual values). The process of a CPO will usually take between 12 and 18 months, not including the time taken to prepare the case for a CPO and conduct the initial negotiations. 'Hope value' is no longer required as a consideration for public bodies utilising CPO powers, since the 2022 Levelling Up and Regeneration Bill.

Several features of this process make the CPO mechanism too clunky for its effective use in monitoring and enforcing housing standards in rental accommodation. In the first instance, the legal burden to evidence the 'greater public good' reflected in the CPO is time-consuming and costly, and the terms of reference for such legal arguments are focused primarily on the function of CPO as a tool to unlock development. Second, the damages and compensation regime around CPO is generous to the recipient of CPO, as well as complex, making it particularly uneconomical for small purchases of individual houses. Lastly, the process can also be time-consuming – with inadequate security on the side of the public body that the CPO order will be accepted by the Secretary of State.

For CPO powers to be modified to have more utility in the enforcement of decent standards in the PRS, a particular legal framework for constructing the case for CPOs should be developed as guidance for local authorities, establishing a clear and low-risk route to CPO in the instance of a rented property which is failing to meet certain benchmarks of standards for human habitation. In addition to a legal framework, alterations to the rules around compensation for slum landlords in instance of a CPO could be incorporated into legislation, on the grounds of public health. In combination with universal landlord licensing, enhanced CPO powers for poor quality rented accommodation would be a powerful tool to increase standards in rented accommodation across both PRS and social rented sectors.

The future for the private rented sector

The growing PRS provides a huge problem for policy makers in housing on several fronts. PRS is the worst offender in tenure quality, as well as the most resistant and difficult to adapt and retrofit. It is a huge contributor to generalised price inflation in housing, competing with prospective owner-occupiers to push up prices. PRS is also a source of great injustice for renters through landlord malpractice, particularly in the UK, where tenancy protections are weak. Long-term PRS tenancy is still a relatively recent cultural phenomenon in the UK, having been rendered almost obsolete under previous eras of rent control and mass social housing provision. Our legal system is still adapting to its rapid growth, and the enormous social consequences it brings. Ultimately, policy makers need to decide what they want PRS to provide for UK residents as a service – and develop appropriate enforcement mechanisms. None of these mechanisms are likely to prove popular with the landlord lobby – yet the continued unchecked growth and importance of this sector can only continue to worsen the housing crisis if left unanswered.

15

Housing standards

Britain's housing stock is the oldest in Europe, and quite possibly the oldest in the world. It is well established now that in many areas, our ageing housing stock is lagging behind comparable nations in quality and energy efficiency.

On energy efficiency, Britain's homes are the least efficient in Europe, with 13.4 per cent of households living in 'fuel poverty' (3.26 million people).[1] Seventeen per cent of Britain's homes are considered to be 'non-decent', with the poorest stock condition in the rapidly growing private rented sector.[2] In respect of issues such as damp and mould, poor housing quality in the UK is estimated to cost health services £1.4 billion a year – and according to the Centre for Ageing Better, an estimated 10 million people in England live at risk due to their home failing to meet basic standards.

Since 2012, most of the prevailing funds and initiatives for bringing our existing housing stock up to a decent standard have been wound down or removed – leaving us with a lost decade of stagnation among our housing stock. Prior to 2012, those schemes which did provide funding and support for improving housing stock, such as Housing Market Renewal, were problematic in many alternative respects, reducing the available housing supply for low-income families and contributing to house price inflation.

The UK's retrofit market has never recovered from the scrapping of insulation grants by the Coalition government in 2010 with the removal of the Warm Front grant scheme, leaving our retrofit economy without a clear skills pipeline or strategic supply network to deliver the scale of change that we need. The condition of our existing housing stock is a huge and ongoing issue, which for the sake of delivering decent quality homes for UK residents is a crucial question.

But there is another side to the story with our ageing housing stock. Much of it is beautiful, spacious and – for its time – well constructed. In environmental terms, the embedded carbon costs of demolition and rebuilding old homes more than outweigh the benefits of more efficient energy and heating systems in new builds, were we to pursue an approach of replacing them.[3] Our old homes provide character and identity to our streets and communities – and they continue to be popular.[4]

Like it or not, we are stuck with much of our existing residential infrastructure and our policy landscape must adapt to the question of renewing and revitalising it. It is tempting to see the process of renovation and retrofit as a gigantic potential cost: however there are also huge opportunities to use the demand for retrofit and renovation in the UK to pump-prime new market sectors – particularly in renewable renovation methods and practices – driving growth and employment in skilled industries.

Maintaining our existing housing stock

Since 2012, most of the prevailing funds and initiatives for bringing our existing housing stock up to a decent standard have been wound down or removed – leaving us with a lost decade of stagnation among our housing stock. Be these explicit urban renewal and regeneration schemes, or retrofit schemes to improve fuel efficiency – as it stands, there is no strategic, nationwide effort to improve the quality of Britain's ageing housing stock.

Historic schemes to upgrade poor housing stock, such as Housing Market Renewal, were clearly flawed: simply demolishing low-value homes, and investing in substantial upgrades of poor quality housing stock cannot solve some of the most substantial elements of our present-day housing crisis, particularly around housing affordability. Yet it should be recognised that Housing Market Renewal was at least a recognition that the natural cycle of housing markets included 'market failure', and of the need for government to intervene to ensure against serious decline.

And in respect of schemes to improve the fuel efficiency of homes, it is hugely regrettable that historic schemes such as Warm Front, which both provided consistent progress against retrofitting homes with modern insulation and heating, and simultaneously sustained a market in retrofit and modern heating installation methods (alongside a skills and training pipeline), were effectively wound up in 2010. The legacy of this decision has been hugely damaging – crippling the sector and leaving us with a gigantic skills gap within the present construction market.

Any future scheme would have to be cognisant of the impact that investment into housing stock may have on affordability – particularly pumping taxpayer money into privately held assets where the gain will disproportionately be received by homeowners and landlords (potentially increasing rents and inflating property prices).

It will also have to overcome the huge skills shortage in retrofit – exacerbated by nearly a decade of inactivity in the field of insulating and carbon retrofitting homes. Providing training opportunities as part of larger state-sponsored work programmes is likely the only measure which can be taken to develop this pipeline of qualified fitters – potentially developed from a national programme of retrofitting public buildings and assets.

In this vein, government could learn from the myriad of local authority initiatives which are presently distributing the limited funding which is available to maximise impact on carbon retrofit. In Greater Manchester, public monies have been invested into a mixture of grant schemes and financing tools to maximise the spread of limited financial resources made available from government. The local authority has also identified 150 public buildings it is targeting for low carbon energy generation, alongside a Retrofit Skills Hub to provide training places for up to 1,140 construction workers to 'upskill' to new green jobs.

Such initiatives are good examples of how to stretch and manage insubstantial budgets – but as the Greater Manchester Combined Authority Retrofit Action Plan notes, these aspirations fall far short of the requirements to hit net zero, or even adequately insulate and heat the city-region's homes.[5] Greater Manchester has over 887,000 homes, 2,700 public buildings and an 'as yet unknown number of commercial buildings' which will require some form of renovation by 2038, if the city region is to reach its target for net zero. To add to this problem, the city region estimates a shortfall of between 7,000 and 8,000 construction workers over the next five years.

And yet, the Greater Manchester Combined Authority sees great potential for economic growth in investing in this sector. The Retrofit Action Plan estimates that over 1,000 apprenticeships can be created through the process of developing a market for retrofitting Greater Manchester's homes, 85,000 construction workers stand to be upskilled, 90,000 new jobs can be created and a Greater Manchester renovation market with an annual value of up to £800 million could be created and sustained.[6]

Greater Manchester is not alone in its ambition. Historic England has conducted its own research into the required skills needed to restore and retrofit Britain's historic buildings, calculating an added value of £570 million of economic output each year for the retrofit of Greater Manchester's ageing buildings, £320 million of annual output for retrofitting Liverpool's ageing housing stock, £360 million annual output for West Yorkshire and a colossal £3.1 billion in economic output for the retrofit and renovation of Greater London's ageing housing stock.[7] Analysis from PricewaterhouseCoopers suggests that as many as 580,000 jobs could be supported annually through a nationwide UK retrofit scheme, cutting fuel bills and improving the country's energy security.[8] Seen through this lens, investment into green retrofit for Britain's homes could act as a huge boost to the broader economy, providing skilled jobs for an entire generation of UK residents. But key to developing a successful programme will be developing a skills and training pipeline to overcome the UK's current shortage of skilled construction workers. Speaking to the research, the UK Consulting Leader for PricewaterhouseCoopers, Nick Forrest, comments:

> The UK has consistently under-invested in developing and transitioning skills to support the green retrofit opportunity. Currently, there are few recognised technical education pathways into the retrofit sector and most training is done on the job as quickly as possible. In addition, the

SMEs and sole traders, who are a lifeblood of the construction industry, require stronger incentives to invest in training as their opportunity cost for taking time out of paid work is greater.[9]

However, as it stands we are moving in the wrong direction. Numbers of workers in construction have been falling, and even without an expansive retrofit programme, we are on track for a severe shortage in this sector in the coming years. According to the Office for National Statistics, there are nearly a quarter of a million fewer workers in the construction sector in 2022 than there were in 2019. The Construction Leadership Council has also warned that 'diminishing labour supply is now of greater concern than product availability in most construction sectors'.[10] Creating new skills pathways into construction, and particularly into trades with the skills required for renovation and retrofit, is clearly a hugely important in the process of upgrading and maintaining our existing housing stock. Nationally, the UK is in dire need of a co-ordinated programme for creating apprenticeship and training opportunities in this sector which will pay dividends over the coming decades.

With a government policy committed to updating Britain's housing stock, and truly grappling with the scale of our net-zero challenges, this process of job creation, upskilling and economic growth could be scaled up massively – starting with a serious and systemic approach to public assets and buildings, including social housing. Britain could yet become a world leader in the retrofit market with forthright workforce planning and serious state investment. But the political will and vision will be required to achieve these tasks.

Fixing the construction sector

Britain's construction and development industry is failing. The industry is plagued by short-termism, a by-product of its disjointed structure. To have developers who don't directly employ a single labourer on site, who operate instead through a chain of intermediaries each taking a fee and squeezing the money passed down to their subsidiaries, is both incredibly wasteful and ineffective … yet this is the model employed by most of the UK's major developers. Such 'contracting' gives each intermediary a short-term focus on driving down costs above all else, which has a negative impact on quality, site management and workforce planning. From a macroeconomic perspective, this system ultimately drives up costs across the board as projects are delayed, riddled with mistakes and a shortage of labourers develops following a lack of adequate training places.

The financial models of developers also trend towards value extraction and rapid sale, a model which discourages long-term investment in quality assets and a wider commitment to 'place'. Increasingly financialised and debt-ridden organisations under pressure to make returns to remote shareholders and creditors tend not to see themselves as partners to a community or government. Nor do they have any true investment in the longevity of their product. These pressures impact every element of construction, from the value-engineering of design through to the repeated delivery of a restricted, 'safe' model of housing.

The UK's large developers should be encouraged to integrate their services, bringing outsourced sectors back in house enabling them to scale up their ambitions. The increasing emphasis from government and some local authorities on vocational qualifications and skills must also be integrated with a dedicated project to reskill the construction sector in general, and plan the workforce we will need to both build our next generation of homes, and successful retrofit and upgrade our existing stock. Construction needs to be recognised as a strategically vital sector, and brought together as part of a national strategy for renewal. The new Labour Government's recent commitments to the development of new towns could be a catalyst for such co-ordination.

Support should also be given to self-build as well small- and medium-sized enterprise builders to develop and build new properties – providing much-needed variety and, crucially, competition to the large volume developers currently crowding out the market.

Revisiting Hackitt

The Hackitt Review of the UK's building regulations, following the disastrous fire at Grenfell Tower, has been a missed opportunity to both simplify the UK's labyrinthine building regulations while also increasing accountability. At its heart, Hackitt's core recommendations centred on the development of holistic and person-centred approaches to assessing fire safety, site visits, clear reporting mechanisms for any incidents or alterations to buildings during their lifecycle, and rights of tenants and residents. What has emerged through the process of implementing Hackitt is a new system of restrictive and stringent design codes for buildings over ten storeys, and startlingly little on anything else.

Hackitt was an opportunity to revisit Britain's failed building regulatory system in its entirety, re-establishing the role and accountability of professional fire safety experts in the design and delivery of new buildings. While there is little doubt that the ten-storey-plus buildings covered through Hackitt will be safer than before, these changes have been achieved in many respects by further complicating the existing regulatory burdens and without reforming the overwrought system of 'guidance' and testing which provides so much ambiguity for developers.

There is still a clear opportunity to embed further changes to the building regulatory system post-Hackitt, particularly opportunities to address both the issues of quality and accountability while reducing administrative burdens for developers.

Future-proofing our housing

The UK's relative underperformance in housing quality is the product of multiple causes, from the age of our housing stock to the removal of initiatives and programmes upgrading and renovating our stock, and the composition of our construction industry and financing. None of these problems have easy or quick fixes – insofar as each of them speak to a vicious circle of long-standing failures. We have failed to build enough new units to generally improve the age of our housing stock. We have failed to train enough labourers and technicians to build the homes we hypothetically might need. We have failed to sustain and develop demand within the industry for novel techniques such as low-carbon retrofit, which in turn has left the sector with less capacity to provide those functions affordably. What's more, we have allowed our construction sector to organise itself into a sequence of tiered functions, contracting and subcontracting downwards, and severing any connection at the strategic level with the process of directly employing and training the labourers of the future.

Fundamentally, the solutions for our issues with the quality of both our existing and future stock of housing lie within the construction sector, fixing our skills and workforce shortages and adopting longer-term and more strategic attachments to developments as assets. To begin to recoup our lost standing against comparable nations in terms of housing quality, nothing short of a decades-long plan for reskilling is required, including strategic investment to pump-prime sectors such as zero-carbon retrofit creating new demand.

Nothing short of this long-term commitment to increasing standards within our housing stock is likely to shift the dial on the most entrenched issues of old, damp and poorly constructed properties in the UK.

Conclusion

This book's central thesis is that the post-war era provided a sustainable series of policies and initiatives which collectively provided quantity, affordability and improved quality of homes. Such a situation was afforded not just through housing policy itself, but a wider coordination and integration of housing as part of a wider vision for an equitable economy. Housing in the post-war era was treated functionally – it was a place to house people, who themselves must take their part in a wider social and economic ecosystem. Not only did this system provide clear and sustainable improvements in housing for the people of this country, but it revolutionised our expectations of housing as a society – creating, for the first time in history, a situation where an average person on an average income could easily access and afford accommodation of a reasonable (and vastly improved) quality.

Since the 1980s, successive governments have however eroded the policies, regulation and legislation which had enabled this new reality in housing to emerge. Generally, the reforms have taken the form of removing the state and other public sector actors from strategic roles in housing delivery and provision, removing or weakening strategic regulatory functions around quality control, and more recently chipping away at the democratic edifice of the post-1947 planning system as initiated in the Town and Country Planning Act. At a national level, measures have been introduced to liberalise investment into housing, creating baked-in house price inflation, and actively pursuing policies towards urban regeneration and renewal which are to a great extent predicated in consciously increasing values in urban areas to induce further inward investment.

Taken in totality, this process has gutted our housing system of coherence – removing the once clear connections between housing policy, industrial strategy and workforce planning, public health and capital controls. What we have instead is a disconnected patchwork of abortive reactions to the symptoms of the emerging disorder – less a 'crisis', in some senses, than a reversion to historical 'type' trailed by a series of ineffective counter-interventions. Somehow, we have come to expect the conditions which defined our housing system in the post-war period to replicate themselves as the default – where in fact they were the exception. In so doing, we have systematically removed almost every major plank of policy, infrastructure and connected thinking which enabled that period to exist, only to appear confused as the fruits of those reforms disappear. Today, in blunt terms, the instruments we rely upon to resolve our housing crisis are almost all worsening its symptoms: the volume developers we rely upon to build our homes have no interest in reducing house prices. The financial system we use to finance the development of our homes is proactively invested in endless house-price inflation. The grants and funding provided to alleviate symptoms of the housing crisis are feeding a spiral of inflation. Not one part of this system is working as it should.

Through the process of my research and interviews for this book, a central recurrent theme has recurred in conversation regarding the wider understanding of housing as part of a functioning society and economy. Charlotte Norman, chief executive officer of social housing provider Mosscare St. Vincent called for 'a national housing strategy that cuts across planning, health and social care, and then is supported by cross-departmental working'. Tim Heatley, founder and chief executive officer of private volume developer Capital and Centric returns to the theme of 'an entire UK-wide strategy, looking at [housing] more as infrastructure' and 'having a delegating authority to central government to say, "No, you're having a new town here. There's gonna be 10,000 homes"'. Salford Mayor Paul Dennett sees housing as a plug-in to a potential future industrial strategy: 'Some of the solutions for me are to be found in work and skills, and industrial strategy' with an aspiration to create 'a highly paid, highly skilled labour market'.

The piecemeal, disjointed picture for UK housing policy today couldn't be further from this unified vision for housing, a vision which sees housing as a component part within a wider and more equitable society. The policies and structures which once enabled our post-war housing system to exist weren't the only things which have been removed in the decades since: so has been the very concept of planning at the scale of the society and economy. Driving such grand vision was a level of aspiration and belief in the potential achievements of conscious and collective action which has been all but erased in contemporary polity. Today, our heads are in the weeds of today's housing crisis, obsessing over the detail of the symptoms while never addressing the causes.

Not every facet of the post-war system should be replicated. Pre-planned towns and overspill estates were often loftily and inhumanely conceived, from the architectural designs to the layout of the built environment. However, these towns were experiments, some of the first of their kind, from which so many valuable lessons have been learned to educate future attempts. The green belt, too, while serving a valuable purpose, is in dire need of reform, and the decentralisation of populations from urban centres under the 1947 Town and Country Planning Act resulted in an over-correction, the dereliction of urban centres creating the conditions for ill-conceived concepts of 'regeneration' from the 1990s.

While there is no perfect housing system, and it has to be said that on the key issues of availability, affordability and improving tenure quality, the fusion of different policies and forces operating within that post-war period provide a clear illustration that the crises we currently face are not inevitable.

The biggest obstacle that we face in tackling the housing crisis today is conceptual: having privatised responsibility for the delivery of and access to homes throughout successive waves of reforms, we now rely on institutions to provide our housing needs for whom housing is not primarily a means to ensure a roof over our heads – but instead as an investment vehicle for capital. So much of the discourse around housing and responding to our housing crisis is strait-jacketed in these terms, restricting itself artificially to means and mechanisms which dance to the interests and requirements of potential housing investors, rather than those expected to live in them.

We may not walk the same path as our ancestors to resolve the problems we face today, although some lessons can clearly be learned (if there is one central mission I would like to impart from this book, it is the central importance of delivering council and social housing – a golden thread which could create so many further positive ramifications across our society, and even help to heal the wider housing market).

But beyond the specifics, what is truly missing from our policy picture is the scale and scope of the design and political vision. What I also hope is apparent from this book is that no 'one neat trick' will be sufficient to return to the norms and standards in housing which the public now expects. We cannot achieve an equitable housing system without an equitable economy and society; and we cannot create an equitable economy and society without an equitable housing system. Any truly successful approach to fixing the UK's broken housing polity must begin from no less place of ambition than the transformation of our society and economy as a whole.

Notes

Introduction

1. Savills UK, A brief history of the UK housing market [2022]. Available from www.savills.co.uk [Accessed 23 May 2024].
2. City Harvest London, Editorial [2023]. Available from www.cityharvest.org.uk/blog [Accessed 23 May 2024].
3. P. Cryer, Rents and incomes, early 20th century [2014]. Available from www.1900s.org.uk [Accessed 24 May 2024].
4. Hansard, Homelessness, vol 361 [1975]. Available from https://api.parliament.uk/ [Accessed 18 June 2025].
5. F. Engels, Condition of the Working Class in England, Otto Wigand [1845].
6. E. Chadwick, Report on the Sanitary Condition of the Labouring Population and on the Means of Its Improvement, HMSO [1842].
7. Ibid.
8. S. Szreter and G. Mooney, Urbanization, mortality, and the standard of living debate: New estimates of the expectation of life at birth in nineteenth-century British cities, *The Economic History Review* [1998].
9. R.J. Davenport, Urbanization and mortality in Britain, c. 1800–50, *Economic History Review* [2020].
10. A. de Tocqueville, *Journeys to England and Ireland*, Yale University Press [1835].
11. B. Disraeli, Speech of the Right Hon. B. Disraeli [1872]. Available from https://archive.org [Accessed 12 June 2025].
12. J. Harrison, The origin, development and decline of back-to-back houses in Leeds, 1787–1937, University of York [2017].
13. A. Mearns, *The Bitter Cry of Outcast London: An Inquiry into the Condition of the Abject Poor*, James Clarke & Co. [1883].
14. Ibid.
15. Historic England, *A Brief Introduction to Garden Cities* [2016]. Available from www.heritagecalling.com
16. G. Livesey, Innovation, the agricultural belt, and the early garden city, *Berkeley Planning Journal* [2016].
17. C. Hird, Building societies: Stakeholding in practice and under threat, *New Left Review* [1996].
18. H.J.G. Bab, The evolution of the British building society, *Economic History Review*, 9(1) [1938].
19. Ibid.
20. P. Scott, *Selling Owner-Occupation to the Working-Classes in 1930s Britain*, University of Reading [2004].
21. Ibid.
22. Ibid.
23. E.J. Cleary, *The Building Society Movement*, Elek Books [1965].
24. Hansard, Building societies [1939]. Available from www.api.parliament.uk [Accessed 18 June 2025].
25. L. Talbot, Keeping bad company: Building societies – a case study, Warwick University [2009].
26. F. Mitra, *Instruments of Monetary Management: Bank-by-Bank Credit Ceilings: Issues and Experiences*, IMF [1997].

27. Bank of England, The development of the building societies sector in the 1980s [1990]. Available from www.bankofengland.co.uk [Accessed 18 June 2025].
28. ONS, *Housing in England 2007–08* [2009]. Available from www.webarchive.nationalarchives.gov.uk [Accessed 18 June 2025].
29. P. Kemp, Private renting in England, *Netherlands Journal of Housing and the Built Environment* [1998].
30. Hansard, Housing stock, vol 970 [1979]. Available from www.hansard.parliament.uk [Accessed 18 June 2025].
31. ONS, *Housing in England 2007–08*.
32. D.K. Fetter, The home front: Rent control and the rapid wartime increase in home ownership, *The Journal of Economic History* [2016].
33. J.T. Walters, *Report of the Committee Appointed to Consider Questions of Building Construction in Connection with the Provision of Dwellings for the Working Classes* [1918]. Available from JSTOR [Accessed 12 June 2025].
34. UK Parliament Research Briefings, Housing supply: Historical statistics for the UK [2003]. Available from www.parliament.uk [Accessed 18 June 2025].
35. Ibid.
36. J. Boughton, *Municipal Dreams*, Verso [2018].
37. ONS, *Housing in England 2007–08*.
38. Hansard, Council house rents [1981]. Available from www.api.parliament.uk [Accessed 18 June 2025].
39. Hansard, Average weekly wage [1983]. Available from www.api.parliament.uk [Accessed 18 June 2025].
40. UK Housing Review, Rents and earnings in England [2006]. Available from www.ukhousingreview.org.uk [Accessed 18 June 2025].
41. ONS, Average weekly earnings in Great Britain: September 2024 [2024]. Available from www.ons.gov.uk [Accessed 18 June 2025].
42. C. Turner, *Homes through the Decades*, National House Building Council [2015].
43. Hansard, Ribbon development [1935]. Available from www.api.parliament.uk [Accessed 18 June 2025].
44. Ibid.
45. *Town Planning Act 1925*. Available from www.legislation.gov.uk [Accessed 12 June 2025].
46. B. Lund, *The Beveridge Report 80 Years On: 'Squalor' and Housing – 'a True Goliath'*, University of Strathclyde [2021].

Chapter 1

1. Statista Research Department, Number of housing units in England from 2001 to 2022 [2024]. Available from www.statista.com [Accessed 24 May 2024].
2. P. Laslett, Size and structure of the household in England over three centuries, *Population Studies* [1969].
3. D. Clark, Average household size in the UK 1996–2022, Statista [2023]. Available from www.statista.com [Accessed 2 May 2024].
4. DLUHC, English housing survey 2022–23 [2023].
5. The Health Foundation, Trends in household overcrowding by tenure [2023]. Available from www.health.org.uk [Accessed 23 May 2024].
6. P. Walker, England has 'twice as many empty homes as families stuck in B&Bs', *The Guardian* [2023].
7. MHCLG, Empty homes reach all time low [2016]. Available from www.gov.uk [Accessed 3 June 2024].

Notes

8. S. Bruce, N. Bowers and T. Wilkins, Housing in England and Wales: 2021 compared with 2011, ONS [2023].
9. C. Rogers and I. Gough, Solving the housing crisis without building new houses, London School of Economics [2024]. Available from www.lse.ac.uk [Accessed 3 June 2024].
10. K. Niemitz, Why Britain needs more empty homes, *The Critic* [2024].
11. Home Builders Federation, Housing horizons: Examining UK housing stock in an international context [2023]. Available from www.hbf.co.uk [Accessed 3 June 2024].
12. Ibid.
13. Ibid.
14. N. Gutteridge, Number of second homes in England soars by more than 50 per cent, *The Telegraph* [2023].
15. ONS, More than 1 in 10 addressed used as holiday homes in some areas of England and Wales [2023].
16. Centre Point, *Ready to Move On: Barriers to Homeless Young People Accessing Longer Term Accommodation* [2023]. Available from www.centrepoint.org.uk [Accessed 23 May 2024].
17. DLUHC, Social housing lettings in England, tenants: April 2022 to March 2023 [2023]. Available from www.gov.uk [Accessed 23 May 2024].
18. Written evidence presented by Shelter to Parliament [2022]. Available from www.committees.parliament.uk [Accessed 23 May 2024].
19. BBC, Asylum-seeker hotels for children 'a supermarket for gangs' [2023]. Available from www.bbc.co.uk/news [Accessed 23 May 2024].
20. DWP and DCLG, Supported accommodation review [2016].
21. J. Murray, UK crime gangs rake in millions through supported housing, say police, *The Guardian* [2023].
22. Centre for Ageing Better, *The State of Ageing 2022* [2022]. Available from www.ageing-better.org.uk [Accessed 23 May 2024].
23. English Housing Survey, 2018.
24. Aspire, Examining lives in adapted and unadapted homes [2016]. Available from www.aspire.org.uk [Accessed 23 May 2024].
25. Age UK, We can't wait for care [2017]. Available from www.ageuk.org.uk [Accessed 23 May 2024].
26. King's Fund, Key facts and figures about social care [2023]. Available from www.kingsfund.org.uk [Accessed 25 May 2024].
27. CSI Market Intelligence 2020 report.
28. K. Woodward, *Social Sciences, the Big Issues*, Routledge [2014].
29. English Housing Survey, 2023–24.
30. National Housing Federation, Conservative voters support building social housing over homes for sale [2023]. Available from www.housing.org.uk [Accessed 25 May 2024].
31. National Housing Federation, The real 'social housing waiting list' is 500,000 more than official figures [2020]. Available from www.housing.org.uk [Accessed 25 May 2024].
32. National Housing Federation, People in housing need: A comprehensive analysis of the scale and shape of housing need in England today [2020]. Available from www.housing.org.uk [Accessed 29 May 2024].
33. Written evidence submitted to Parliament by the Northern Housing Consortium [2022]. Available from www.committees.parliament.uk [Accessed 25 May 2024].

Chapter 2

1. P. Cryer, Rents and incomes, early 20th century [2014]. Available from www.1900s.org.uk [Accessed 25 May 2024].

2. J. Cribb, T. Wernham and X. Xu, *Housing Costs and Income Inequality in the UK*, Institute for Fiscal Studies [2023].
3. ONS, Private rental affordability, England and Wales [2023].
4. English Housing Survey, 2023–2024.
5. ONS, Housing affordability in England and Wales [2021]. Available from www.ons.gov.uk [Accessed 27 May 2024].
6. Schroders, What 175 years of data tell us about house price affordability in the UK [2023]. Available from www.schroders.com [Accessed 27 May 2024].
7. Ibid.
8. Cribb et al, Housing costs and income inequality in the UK.
9. Written evidence submitted to Parliament by the UK Women's Budget Group [2022]. Available from www.committees.parliament.uk [Accessed 27 May 2024].
10. The Equality Trust, *The Scale of Economic Inequality in the UK* [2022]. Available from www.equalitytrust.org.uk [Accessed 27 May 2024].
11. Schroders, What 175 years of data tell us about house price affordability.
12. DEFRA, Housing availability and affordability [2022].
13. D. Chan and M. Thompson, Understanding the growth in private rented housing, Core Cities [2021]. Available from www.corecities.com [Accessed 27 May 2024].
14. V. Romei, UK mortgages in arrears jump to seven-year high, *Financial Times* [2023].
15. J. Kollewe, Britain's housing market may be 'past peak pain' but what will 2024 bring, *The Guardian* [2023].
16. T. Rees, UK lenders see growing mortgage demand even as defaults rise, *Bloomberg* [2024]. Available from www.bloomberg.com [Accessed 27 May 2024].
17. *Reuters*, UK lenders see mortgage default rates rising [2024].
18. English Housing Survey, 2019–2020.
19. Hamptons, Rents to grow more than four times faster than house prices over the next four years [2023]. Available from www.hamptons.co.uk [Accessed 27 May 2024].
20. Hamptons, Rents to grow more than four times faster than house prices over the next four years [2023]. Available from www.hamptons.co.uk [Accessed 27 May 2024].
21. English Housing Survey, 2020–2021.
22. N. Bailey, Poverty and the re-growth of private renting in the UK, 1994–2018, *PLoS One*, 15(2) [2020].
23. Zillow, Birth rates are falling most where homes are appreciating fastest [2018]. Available from www.zillow.mediaroom.com [Accessed 27 May 2024].
24. C.G. Aksoy, The housing bubble baby boom, The Royal Economic Society [2017]. Available from www.res.org.uk [Accessed 27 May 2024].
25. L. Scullion, A. Gibbons and P. Martin, *Precarious lives: Exploring Lived Experiences of the Private Rented Sector in Salford*, University of Salford and Salford Council [2018].
26. I. Hudspeth, Supporting the health needs of those who are experiencing rough sleeping, Local Government Association [2024]. Available from www.local.gov.uk [Accessed 27 May 2024].
27. DLUHC, Rough sleeping snapshot in England: Autumn 2021 [2022]. Available from www.gov.uk [Accessed 27 May 2024].
28. DLUHC, Rough sleeping snapshot in England: Autumn 2023 [2024]. Available from www.gov.uk [Accessed 27 May 2024].
29. Shelter, 116% annual rise in no-fault evictions shows why Renters (Reform) Bill is vital [2023]. Available from www.england.shelter.org.uk [Accessed 27 May 2024].
30. Shelter, Homeless accommodation bill hits £1.7bn [2023]. Available from www.england.shelter.org.uk [Accessed 27 May 2024].
31. English Housing Survey, 2022–2023.

Notes

32. Shelter, Loss of social housing [2023]. Available from www.england.shelter.org.uk [Accessed 27 May 2024].
33. DLUHC, Summary of housing service spend in England 2020–21. Available from www.gov.uk [Accessed 27 May 2024].
34. J. Burn-Murdoch, Why Britain is the world's worst on homelessness, *Financial Times* [2024].

Chapter 3

1. Institute of Health Equity, *Fuel Poverty, Cold Homes and Health Inequalities in the UK* [2022].
2. English Housing Survey, 2022–2023.
3. A. Kulakiewicz, Housing and health: A reading list [2022]. Available from www.commonslibrary.parliament.uk [Accessed 27 May 2024].
4. D. Orr, *The Good Home Inquiry*, Centre for Ageing Better [2021]. Available from www.ageing-better.uk [Accessed 27 May 2024].
5. English Housing Survey, 2022–2023.
6. W. Wilson, C. Barton and H. Carthew, Overcrowded housing (England) [2023]. Available from www.commonslibrary.parliament.uk [Accessed 27 May 2024].
7. L. Scullion, A. Gibbons and P. Martin, *Precarious Lives: Exploring Lived Experiences of the Private Rented Sector in Salford*, University of Salford and Salford Council [2018].
8. L. Scullion, A. Gibbons and P. Martin, *Precarious Lives: Exploring Lived Experiences of the Private Rented Sector in Salford*, University of Salford and Salford Council [2018].
9. H. Garrett, M. Mackay, S. Nicol, J. Piddington and M. Roys, The cost of poor housing in England, *The Building Research Establishment* [2021].
10. Shelter, 'Rigged' housebuilding system means eight in ten families cannot afford new home, says Shelter [2017]. Available from www.england.shelter.org.uk [Accessed 27 May 2024].
11. Home Builders Federation & National House Building Council, *Annual Survey of House Builders 2020–21* [2022].
12. F. Parker, Our new build nightmares, *This Is Money* [2021]. Available from www.thisismoney.co.uk [Accessed 27 May 2024].
13. R. Wearn, Growing complaints about new-build houses, *BBC News* [2019]. Available from www.bbc.co.uk [Accessed 27 May 2024].
14. Environment Agency, *Flooding in England: A National Assessment of Flood Risk* [2021].
15. GBN, Michael Gove stands by 'cartel' comments as he calls for better accessibility into housebuilding market [2022]. Available from https://www.gbnews.com/news/michael-gove-stands-by-cartel-comments-as-he-calls-for-better-accessibility-into-housebuilding-market/325581 [Accessed 18 June 2025].
16. T. Copley, *Slums of the Future*, London Labour Assembly [2019].
17. Local Government Association, 18,000 affordable houses lost in office-to-residential conversions [2022]. Available from www.local.gov.uk [Accessed 27 May 2024].
18. M. Precey, J. Sturdy and L. Cawley, Inside Harlow's office block 'human warehouse' housing, *BBC News* [2019]. Available from www.bbc.co.uk [Accessed 27 May 2024].
19. Raynsford Review of Planning in England, *Planning 2020* [2018]. Available from www.tcpa.org.uk [Accessed 27 May 2024].
20. J. Tilley, Government rejects central London boroughs' bid to block permitted development rights, Planning Resource [2021]. Available from www.planningresource.co.uk [Accessed 27 May 2024].
21. P. Apps, How the products used in Grenfell Tower's cladding system were tested and sold, *Inside Housing* [2021]. Available from www.insidehousing.co.uk [Accessed 27 May 2024].

22. R. Booth, 'A raging inferno': Testimony reveals how deadly cladding ended up on Grenfell Tower, *The Guardian* [2020].
23. BBC News, Grenfell Tower fire: More high-rises fail fire safety tests [2017]. Available from www.bbc.co.uk [Accessed 27 May 2024].
24. R. Booth, Cladding tests after Grenfell Tower fire 'utterly inadequate', *The Guardian* [2018].

Chapter 5

1. R. Landberg, UK house building slows despite record prices as outlook dims, *Bloomberg* [2022]. Available from www.bloomberg.com [Accessed 28 May 2024].
2. Home Builders Federation, Planning delays continue to pose greatest obstacle to UK home builders [2024]. Available from www.hbf.co.uk [Accessed 28 May 2024].
3. R. Burford, Homes must be built on London's green belt to tackle housing crisis, warn business chiefs, *Evening Standard* [2023].
4. Local Government Association, Housing backlog – more than a million homes with planning permission not yet built [2020]. Available from www.local.gov.uk [Accessed 28 May 2024].
5. Ibid.
6. O. Letwin, *Independent Review of Build Out: Final Report* [2018]. Available from www.gov.uk [Accessed 28 May 2024].
7. Competition and Markets Authority, CMA finds fundamental concerns in housebuilding market [2024]. Available from www.gov.uk [Accessed 28 May 2024].
8. T. Archer and I. Cole, The financialisation of housing production: Exploring capital flows and value extraction among major housebuilders in the UK, *Journal of Housing and the Built Environment* [2021].
9. Homes England, Fact sheet 7: Homes and different land types – brownfield, greenfield and Green Belt [2022]. Available from www.gov.uk [Accessed 28 May 2024].
10. National Housing Federation, Briefing: Mapping brownfield land in England [2019]. Available from www.housing.org.uk [Accessed 28 May 2024].
11. The Guardian, UK housing crisis: what does Labour's shake-up of planning rules involve? [December 2024].
12. N. Crafts, How housebuilding helped the economy recover: Britain in the 1930s, *The Guardian* [2013].
13. J. Boughton, *Municipal Dreams*, Verso [2018].
14. Arcadis International, *International Construction Costs 2024* [2024].
15. Network Homes, Why aren't housing associations building more social rented homes? [2019]. Available from www.networkhomes.org.uk [Accessed 28 May 2024].
16. D. Clark, Median annual earnings for full-time employees in the United Kingdom from 1999 to 2023, Statista [2023]. Available from www.statista.com [Accessed 28 May 2024].
17. Building Cost Information Service, A review of the construction industry 2022 [2022]. Available from www.bcis.co.uk [Accessed 28 May 2024].
18. BCIS, Building material cost increases reach 40 year high [2021]. Available from www.bcis.co.uk [Accessed 28 May 2024].
19. D. Thomas and M. Race, War in Ukraine: Russia says it may cut gas supplies if oil ban goes ahead, *BBC News* [2022]. Available from www.bbc.co.uk [Accessed 28 May 2024].
20. V. Caon, How the rise in material costs is damaging the UK's construction industry, *Investment Monitor* [2022]. Available from www.investmentmonitor.ai [Accessed 28 May 2024].
21. J. Newcomb and P. Caplehorn, *Construction Product Availability Statement*, Construction Leadership Council [2022]. Available from www.constructionleadershipcouncil.co.uk [Accessed 28 May 2024].

Notes

22. Construction Industry Training Board, Britain builds bad: Construction will need 216,800 new workers by 2025 to meet demand [2021]. Available from www.citb.co.uk [Accessed 28 May 2024].
23. BCIS, Building material cost increases reach 40 year high [2021]. Available from www.bcis.co.uk [Accessed 28 May 2024].
24. M. Farmer, Five years on from *Modernise or Die*, where are we now? Construction Management [2021]. Available from www.constructionmanagement.co.uk [Accessed 28 May 2024].
25. M. Farmer, *Modernise or Die: The Farmer Review of the UK Construction Labour Model*, Construction Leadership Council [2016].
26. M. Farmer, Five years on from *Modernise or Die*, where are we now? Construction Management [2021]. Available from www.constructionmanagement.co.uk [Accessed 28 May 2024].
27. G. Plimmer, Why the cracks are showing in Britain's construction industry, *Financial Times* [2018].
28. Institute of Civil Engineers, What should be in the National Infrastructure Strategy? [2019].
29. N. Clark and E. Herman, *Unpaid Britain: Wage Default in the British Labour Market*, Middlesex University [2017].
30. C. Slater, S. Robsen, A. Ruski and R. Day, Traffic chaos on Regent Road roadworks as workmen dump diggers in protest at 'not being paid', *Manchester Evening News* [2019].
31. BBC News, Liverpool Travelodge: Digger driver jailed for rampage [2020]. Available from www.bbc.co.uk [Accessed 28 May 2024].
32. T. Lowe, Planning reforms blamed as Lib Dems shock Tories with by-election upset, *Housing Today* [2021]. Available from www.housingtoday.co.uk [Accessed 28 May 2024].
33. B. Christopher, *The New Enclosure: The Appropriation of Public Land in Neoliberal Britain*, Verso [2018].
34. Local Government Association, One public estate: Brownfield Land Release Fund (BLRF2) round 2 – fund details [2023]. Available from www.local.gov.uk [Accessed 28 May 2024].
35. Homes England, Homes England strategic plan 2018 to 2023 (text version) [2022]. Available from www.gov.uk [Accessed 28 May 2024].
36. National Audit Office, Investigation into NHS Property Services Limited [2014]. Available from www.nao.org.uk [Accessed 28 May 2024].
37. NHS Property Services, NHS Property Services creates £200million for the NHS from surplus property sales [2017]. Available from www.property.nhs.uk [Accessed 28 May 2024].
38. National Audit Office, Network Rail's sale of railway arches [2019]. Available from www.nao.org.uk [Accessed 28 May 2024].
39. G. Davies, E. Youle, C. Boutaud and H. Sheffield, Revealed: The thousands of public spaces lost to the council funding crisis, *Huffington Post* [2019].
40. R. Evans, Half of England is owned by less than 1% of the population, *The Guardian* [2019].
41. J. Ryan-Collins, *Why Can't You Afford a Home?* Polity Press [2018].
42. F. Sa, *The Effect of Foreign Investors on Local Housing Market: Evidence from the UK*, KCL [2017].
43. A. Bowen, G. Hoggarth and D. Pain, *The Recent Evolution of the UK Banking Industry and Some Implications for Financial Stability*, Bank for International Settlements [2017].
44. Bank of England, Will there be another financial crisis? [2019]. Available from www.bankofengland.co.uk [Accessed 28 May 2024].

45 Grant Thornton, Half of new homes in London are not being built [2019]. Available from www.grantthornton.co.uk [Accessed 29 May 2024].
46 Parliament, Publications & Records, Land value capture [2019]. Available from www.publications.parliament.uk [Accessed 29 May 2024].
47 Ibid.
48 Ibid.

Chapter 6

1 Joint infrastructure levy letter to DLUHC, June 2023. Available from www.rtpi.org.uk [Accessed 29 May 2024].
2 Planning Advisory Service, Objectively Assessed Need and Housing Targets Technical advice note: Second edition [2015].
3 House of Commons Committee Report, *Seventh Report of Sessions 2022–23: Reforms to National Planning Policy* [2023]. Available from www.publications.parliament.uk [Accessed 29 May 2024].
4 M. Spry, The political economy of planning for housing: Six barriers in the planning system holding back the supply of the homes we need, Lichfields [2023]. Available from www.lichfields.uk [Accessed 29 May 2024].
5 H. Bennett, Your official top 20: The new Standard Method and the cities/urban centres uplift, Lichfields [2021]. Available from www.lichfields.uk [Accessed 29 May 2024].
6 Ibid.
7 Key Cities, Homes England grants – the geographical spread [2018]. Available from www.keycities.uk [Accessed 29 May 2024].
8 O. Knight, Government funding to unlock housing acting as a barrier to the levelling up agenda, Knight Frank [2020]. Available from www.knightfrank.com [Accessed 29 May 2024].
9 G. Hammond and J. Pickard, South of England gets lion's share of housebuilding funds, *Financial Times* [2020].
10 Ibid.
11 J. Williams, How ministers gave Cheadle £25m for 'left behind towns' despite civil service advice – while Swinton and Wigan got nothing, *Manchester Evening News* [2020].
12 C. Hanretty, *The Pork Barrel Politics of the Towns Fund: Funding Decisions Were Driven by Part-Political Considerations, Not by Need*, LSE [2020].
13 J. Walker, No more #Brumcuts: Fury as government hands £300m to Tory councils while Birmingham gets nothing, *Business Live* [2016]. Available from www.business-live.co.uk [Accessed 29 May 2024].
14 P. Walker, Surrey council received boost in budget after 'sweetheart deal' claims, *The Guardian* [2017].

Chapter 7

1 House Condition Survey, England and Wales [1967]. Available from www.gov.uk [Accessed 29 May 2024].
2 W. Wilson, *Housing Market Renewal Pathfinders*, Social Policy Section of the House of Commons Library SN/SP/5953 [2013]. Available from www.parliament.uk [Accessed 29 May 2024].
3 BBC News, Budget 2001: At-a-glance [2001]. Available from www.news.bbc.co.uk [Accessed 29 May 2024].
4 A. Seeley, *Briefing Paper (587): VAT and Construction*, House of Commons Library [2019].
5 Wilson, *Housing Market Renewal Pathfinders*.

Notes

6. B. Nevin and I. Cole, *The Road to Renewal: The Early Development of the Housing Market Renewal Programme in England*, Joseph Rowntree Foundation [2004].
7. Ibid.
8. Ibid.
9. Ibid.
10. P. Hetherington, How Pathfinder lost its way, *The Guardian* [2007].
11. B. Nevin and I. Cole, The Road to Renewal: The Early Development of the Housing Market Renewal Programme in England, Joseph Rowntree Foundation [2004].
12. R. Atkinson, The evidence on the impact of gentrification: New lessons for the urban renaissance? *European Journal of Housing Policy*, 4 [2004].
13. O. Hatherley, Pathfinder was slum clearances without the socialism, *The Guardian* [2010].
14. Ibid.
15. C. Chope, Home Energy Efficiency Scheme, *Hansard*, vol 364 [2001]. Available from www.hansard.parliament.uk [Accessed 29 May 2024].
16. DECC, Process evaluation of the Warm Front Scheme [2014]. Available from www.gov.uk [Accessed 29 May 2024].
17. B. Nevin and I. Cole, The Road to Renewal: The Early Development of the Housing Market Renewal Programme in England, Joseph Rowntree Foundation [2004].
18. S. Cran-McGreehin, Insulation and gas prices: Households are paying the price for slow progress on insulating homes, Energy and Climate Intelligence Unit [2022]. Available from www.eciu.net [Accessed 29 May 2024].
19. Insulate Britain list of demands: 'That the UK government immediately promises to produce within four months a legally binding national plan to fully fund and take responsibility for the full low-energy and low-carbon whole-house retrofit, with no externalised costs, of all homes in Britain by 2030 as part of a just transition to full decarbonisation of all parts of society and the economy.' [2021]. Available from www.insulatebritain.com [Accessed 29 May 2024].
20. DESNZ, *Summary of the Great British Insulation Scheme: January 2024*, Official Statistics [2024]. Available from www.gov.uk [Accessed 29 May 2024].
21. Propertymark, Evaluation of rent smart Wales [2024]. Available from www.propertymark.co.uk.
22. J. Scott, Renters' Reform Bill gets sign off from MPs – but indefinite delay to no-ult evictions ban remains, *Sky News* [2024].
23. W. Wilson, Selective licensing of private rented housing in England and Wales, House of Commons Library Research Briefing (Number CBP04634) [2023].
24. House of Commons, *Renters (Reform) Bill, as Amended (Amendment Paper) 22/04/24* [2024].
25. H. Ulaeto, Will selective licensing schemes survive the Renters (Reform) Bill? Home Safe [2024]. Available from www.home-safe.org.uk [Accessed 31 May 2024].
26. S. Woods, D. Ormandy and J. Harrison, Comparing the rights of private sector tenants in England with those in other jurisdictions, Warwick University [2018]. Available from www.warwick.ac.uk [Accessed 31 May 2024].
27. DLUHC, Social housing lettings in England, tenancies: April 2021 to March 2022 [2024]. Available from www.gov.uk [Accessed 31 May 2024].

Chapter 8

1. Shelter, Loss of social housing [2021]. Available from www.england.shelter.org.uk [Accessed 29 May 2024].
2. L. Goodall, Britain's hidden homeless children, *The News Agents Investigates* [Podcast] [2024]. Available from www.podcasts.apple.com [Accessed 29 May 2024].
3. Ibid.

4 Ibid.
5 J. Williams, The hidden 'Manchester slums': Squalor, danger and death in our city's grim private guesthouses, *Manchester Evening News* [2019].
6 Greater Manchester Combined Authority, *Temporary Accomodation in Greater Manchester* [2024]. Available from www.democracy.greatermanchester-ca.gov.uk [Accessed 29 May 2024].
7 DLUHC, General fund revenue account outturn R04: Housing services 2020–21 [2021]. Available from www.gov.uk [Accessed 29 May 2024].
8 P. Butler, Two-thirds of councils say they can't afford to comply with homelessness law, *The Guardian* [2019].
9 National Housing Federation, People in housing need: A comprehensive analysis of the scale and shape of housing need in England today [2020]. Available from www.housing.org.uk [Accessed 29 May 2024].
10 MHCLG, Evaluation of the implementation of the Homelessness Reduction Act: Final report [2020]. Available from www.gov.uk [Accessed 29 May 2024].
11 Ibid., author's emphasis.
12 S. Moffatt, S. Lawson, R. Patterson, E. Holding, A. Dennison, S. Snowden, et al, A qualitative study of the impact of the UK 'bedroom tax', *Journal of Public Health*, 38 [2016].
13 S. Wright, D.R. Fletcher and A.B.R. Stewart, Punitive sanctions, welfare conditionality, and the social abuse of unemployed people in Britain: Transforming claimants into offenders? *Social Policy & Administration*, 54 [2020].
14 Ibid.
15 Ibid.
16 Ibid.
17 Crisis, *The Homelessness Monitor: England 2019* [2019]. Available from www.crisis.org.uk [Accessed 29 May 2024].
18 Greater London Authority, The impact of welfare reform on homelessness in London [2019]. Available from www.london.gov.uk [Accessed 29 May 2024].
19 D. Hewitt, Landlords to be banned from discriminating against benefit claimants and families with children, *ITV News* [2023].
20 The Centre for Social Justice, Close to home: Delivering a national Housing First programme in England [2021].
21 DLUHC, Evaluation of the Housing First Pilots, report on clients' outcomes twelve months after entering Housing First [2024]. Available from www.gov.uk [Accessed 29 May 2024].
22 Ibid.
23 MHCLG, Evaluation of the Housing First pilots: Second process evaluation report [2021]. Available from www.gov.uk [Accessed 29 May 2024].
24 Homeless Link, *Housing First in England, Frequently Asked Questions* [2023]. Available from www.homeless.org.uk [Accessed 29 May 2024].
25 J. Williams, 'The numbers on the streets are going to rocket': Homeless people put up in hotels amid pandemic to be kicked out as government quietly scraps scheme, *Manchester Evening News* [2020].
26 Shelter, Everyone In: Where are they now? The need for a roadmap out of street homelessness in England [2021]. Available from www.england.shetler.org.uk [Accessed 29 May 2024].
27 Ibid.

Chapter 9

1 P. Neate, Right to Buy has already torn a massive hole in our social housing stock as less than 5% of the homes sold off have ever been replaced. Press release: Shelter comments

on government's 'hare-brained' idea to extend Right-to-Buy to housing association homes [2022]. Available from www.england.shelter.org.uk [Accessed 28 May 2024].
2. A. Diner and H. Wright, *Reforming Right to Buy: Options for Preserving and Delivering New Council Homes for the Twenty-First Century*, New Economics Foundation [2024].
3. M. Lloyd, Scotland's housebuilding boom: can English councils emulate it? *Inside Housing* [2019]. Available from www.insidehousing.co.uk [Accessed 28 May 2024].
4. H. Pawson, E. Davidson, J. Morgan, R. Smith and R. Edwards, *The Impacts of Housing Stock Transfer in Urban Britain*, Joseph Rowntree Foundation [2009].
5. National Housing Federation, About social housing [2020]. Available from www.housing.org.uk [Accessed 28 May 2024].
6. DLUHC, MHCLG and Regulator of Social Housing, Policy statement on rents for social housing [2022]. Available from www.gov.uk [Accessed 28 May 2024].
7. Office for Budget Responsibility, Housing associations, classification changes and fiscal risks, Fiscal Risks Report [2019].
8. S. Adam, D. Chandler, A. Wood and R. Joyce, *Cuts to Social Rents Will Benefit Exchequer More than Tenants, but Will Strengthen Work Incentives*, Institute for Fiscal Studies [2015].
9. Network Homes, Why aren't housing associations building more social rented homes? [2018]. Available from www.thinkhouse.org.uk [Accessed 12 June 2025].
10. J. Oliver, Housing associations in England warn 'we can't build houses', *Financial Times* [2024].
11. *Inside Housing*, Right to Buy for housing associations: The main challenges behind extending the policy [2022]. Available from www.insidehousing.co.uk [Accessed 28 May 2024].
12. Local Government Association, Right to Buy position statement [2024]. Available from www.local.gov.uk [Accessed 29 May 2024].
13. N. Pickles, What do the Affordable Homes Programme 21–26 strategic partnership grant allocations tell us?, National Housing Federation [2021]. Available from www.housing.org.uk [Accessed 29 May 2024].
14. M. Pennycook, *written statement to Parliament*, MHCLG (2025).

Chapter 10

1. G. Shapps, 1st Dec 2010, Hansard Column 831W [2010]. Available from www.parliament.uk [Accessed 29 May 2024].
2. Built Environment Committee, Meeting housing demand, 1st report of Session 2021–22, HL Paper 132 [2022]. Available from www.parliament.uk [Accessed 12 June 2025].
3. W. Wilson, Extending home ownership: Government initiatives, House of Commons Library Number 03668 [2021]. Available from www.parliament.uk [Accessed 29 May 2024].
4. Built Environment Committee, Meeting housing demand, 1st report of Session 2021–22, HL Paper 132 [2022].
5. Ibid.
6. Ibid.
7. L. Macfarlane, *Opinion: Extending Help-to-Buy Will Only Make the Housing Crisis Worse*, University College London [2020].
8. The Property Institute, *Spending Review 2025: Record Investment to Drive Housing Growth and Regeneration* (2025). Available from www.tpi.org.uk [Accessed 7 July 2025].
9. A. Cocola-Gant, Holiday rentals: The new gentrification battlefront, *Sociological Research Online*, 21(3) [2016].
10. J. Bivens, The economic costs and benefits of Airbnb, Economic Policy Institute [2019]. Available from www.epi.org [Accessed 31 May 2024].
11. *ITV News*, The number of Airbnbs in Cornwall compared to long-term rentals [2022]. Available from www.itv.com [Accessed 31 May 2024].
12. Ibid.

13. T. Woodman, Holiday lets are houses not homes; they are zombie houses that are hollowing out our communities, Chartered Institute of Housing [2022]. Available from www.cih.org [Accessed 31 May 2024].
14. ONS, English Housing Survey 2018–2019: Second homes – fact sheet [2020].
15. F. Sa, *The Effect of Foreign Investors on Local Housing Markets: Evidence from the UK*, KCL [2017].
16. The Centre for Public Data, New data on property in England & Wales owned by overseas individuals [2023]. Available from www.centreforpublicdata.org [Accessed 31 May 2024].
17. J. Siebrits, Should we restrict overseas buyers?, CBRE [2024]. Available from www.cbre.co.uk [Accessed 31 May 2024].
18. K. Scanlon, C. Whitehead, F. Blanc and U. Moreno-Tabarez, The role of overseas investors in the London new-build residential market: Final report for Homes for London, London Schools of Economics [2017]. Available from www.lse.ac.uk [Accessed 31 May 2024].
19. A. Cocola-Gant and A. Gago, Airbnb, buy-to-let investment and tourism-driven displacement: A case study in Lisbon, *Economy and Space*, 53(7) [2019].
20. Ibid.
21. Department of Finance Canada, Government announces two-year extension to ban on foreign ownership of Canadian housing [2024]. Available from www.canada.ca [Accessed 31 May 2024].
22. P. Mukherjee and N. Balu, Canada's extension of ban on foreign real estate buyers labelled political, not practical, *Reuters* [2024].

Chapter 11

1. PwC, 2021 UK and global economic outlook [2021]. Available from www.pwc.co.uk [Accessed 25 May 2024].
2. *BBC News*, Most mortgages go to first-time buyers, Halifax research shows [2019]. Available from www.bbc.co.uk [Accessed 27 May 2024].
3. UK Land Registry, UK House Price Index. Available from www.landregistry.data.gov.uk.
4. T. Gasparyan, *Gentrification in London: A Multi-Method Study of Unequal Growth*, Uppsala University [2020].
5. Ibid.
6. Ibid.
7. D. Orr, A blueprint for the rich, *The Independent* [1999].
8. N. Barker, Exclusive: 7% rise in former Right to Buy homes now rented privately, *Inside Housing* [2017]. Available from www.insidehousing.co.uk [Accessed 27 May 2024].
9. M. Engel, The bubble that turned into a tide: how London got hooked on gentrification, *The Guardian* [2016].
10. Ibid.
11. S. Begum, 2025 vision for the city is revealed, *Manchester Evening News* [2015]. Available from www.manchestereveningews.co.uk [Accessed 27 May 2024].
12. J. Houston, From bomb site to style capital, *BBC News* [2006]. Available from www.news.bbc.co.uk [Accessed 27 May 2024].
13. J. Williams, Who is really benefitting from the Manchester City Centre housing boom? *Manchester Evening News* [2017].
14. Ibid.
15. J. Froud, S. Johal, J. Tomaney and K. Williams, Manchester's transformation over the past 25 years: Why we need a reset of city region policy, LSE [2017]. Available from www.blogs.lse.ac.uk [Accessed 28 May 2024].
16. Ibid.
17. Ibid.

18. T. Buffel and C. Phillipson, *Ageing in a Gentrifying Neighbourhood: Experiences of Community Change in Later Life*, British Sociological Association [2019].
19. Ibid.
20. Ibid.
21. Contribution of Lord Leatherland to a debate on 'The Housing Situation', *Hansard*, vol 336, cc714–804 [1972].
22. DLUHC, Supplementary estimates memorandum 2022–23 [2023]. Available from www.gov.uk [Accessed 29 May 2024].
23. Key Cities, Homes England grants – the geographical spread [2018]. Available from www.keycities.uk [Accessed 29 May 2024].
24. Greater Manchester Combined Authority, Housing investment skewed in favour of South of England, new report finds [2018]. Available from www.greatermanchester-ca.gov.uk [Accessed 29 May 2024].
25. F. Buchan, statement made to Parliament on 28th February 2024 [2024]. Available from www.parliament.uk [Accessed 29 May 2024].
26. A. Fitri, The UK now spends more on housing benefit than on most government departments, *The New Statesman* [2022].
27. A.G. Haldane, Whose recovery? [Speech], Bank of England [2016]. Available from www.bankofengland.co.uk [Accessed 29 May 2024].
28. Ibid.
29. S. Clarke and P. Gregg, *Count the Pennies: Explaining a Decade of Lost Pay Growth*, Resolution Foundation [2018].

Part III
1. United Nations, Affordable housing, inclusive economic policies key to ending homelessness, speakers sat as social development commission begins annual session [2020]. Available from www.press.un.org [Accessed 29 May 2024].
2. B. Rajagopal, Report of the Special Rapporteur on adequate housing as a component of the right to an adequate standard of living, and on the right to non-discrimination in this context, item 73b of the provisional agenda to the 78th session of the UN General Assembly [2023].

Chapter 12
1. DLUHC, Social housing lettings in England, tenants: April 2022 to March 2023 [2023]. Available from www.gov.uk [Accessed 30 May 2024].
2. MHCLG, *Reforming the Right to Buy* [2024]. Available from www.gov.uk [Accessed 12 June 2025].
3. C. Barton and W. Wilson, What is affordable housing? House of Commons Library research briefing [2023]. Available from www.parliament.uk [Accessed 30 May 2024].
4. K. Wareing, *An Alternative Model for Funding Asylum and Temporary Housing*, SOHA Housing [2024].
5. Shelter, NHF and CEBR, The economic impact of building social housing [2024].
6. Sage Homes, Sparrow shared ownership launches as USS acquires 3,000 shared ownership homes from Blackstone and Regis Group plc [2024]. Available from www.sagehomes.co.uk [Accessed 12 June 2025].

Chapter 13
1. British Property Federation, About real estate [2024]. Available from www.bpf.org.uk [Accessed 30 May 2024].

2. T. Nguyen and K. Johannsson, Improving estimates of land underlying dwellings in the national balance sheet, UK: 2022, ONS [2022]. Available from www.ons.gov.uk [Accessed 31 May 2024].
3. M. Keep, Regional house price: Affordability and income ratios, House of Commons Library, Standard Note SN/SG/1922 [2012]. Available from www.parliament.uk [Accessed 30 May 2024].
4. R. Owen, The influence of buy-to-let on UK housing, *Mortgage Finance Gazette* [2017].
5. G. Zemaityte, E. Hughes and K. Blood, The buy-to-let sector and financial stability, *Bank of England Quarterly Bulletin 2023* [2023]. Available from www.bankofengland.co.uk [Accessed 31 May 2024].
6. D. Chan and M. Thompson, Understanding the growth in private rented housing, Core Cities [2020].
7. D. Rhodes and J. Rugg, Vulnerability amongst low-income households in the private rented sector in England, Nationwide Foundation [2018]. Available from www.nationwidefoundation.org.uk [Accessed 31 May 2024].
8. Ibid.
9. OECD, *Housing Sector Country Snapshot: United Kingdom* [2023]. Available from www.oecd.org [Accessed 31 May 2024].
10. J. Ryan-Collins, *The Demand for Housing as an Investment*, IIPP (UCL) [2024].
11. DCLG, Land value estimates for policy appraisal [2019]. Available from www.gov.uk [Accessed 31 May 2024].
12. R. Turvey, Development charges and the compensation-betterment problem, *The Economic Journal*, 63(250) [1953].
13. Office of the Deputy Prime Minister, ODPM circular 05/2005: Planning obligations [2005]. Available from www.gov.uk [Accessed 31 May 2024].
14. MHCLG, National Planning Policy Framework [2012]. Available from www.nationalarchives.gov.uk [Accessed 31 May 2024].
15. V. Masterson, What is land value tax and could it fox the housing crisis? World Economic Forum [2022]. Available from www.weforum.org [Accessed 31 May 2024].

Chapter 14

1. Chartered Institute of Housing and Chartered Institute of Environmental Health, A licence to rent [2019]. Available from www.cieh.org [Accessed 31 May 2024].
2. M. Sandford, Trailblazer devolution deals (Research Briefing Number 9901), House of Commons Library [2023]. Available from www.parliament.uk [Accessed 31 May 2024].
3. Fraser Bond, *UK landlord licensing schemes in 2025: Key changes and implications* [2025]. Available from www.fraserbond.com [Accessed 12 June 2024].
4. DLUHC, Compulsory purchase – compensation reforms: Consultation [2023]. Available from www.gov.uk [Accessed 31 May 2024].

Chapter 15

1. DESNZ, Annual fuel poverty statistics in England, 2023 (2022 data) [2023]. Available from www.gov.uk [Accessed 31 May 2024].
2. English Housing Survey, 2023.
3. A. Chalkias, Rebuild or retrofit: The environmental case, Savills [2022]. Available from www.savills.com [Accessed 31 May 2024].
4. M. Griffiths, Britain has spoken – old homes are better than new builds, *Realhomes*. Available from www.realhomes.com [Accessed 31 May 2024].

Notes

5. Greater Manchester Combined Authority, *RetrofitGM: Accelerating the Renovation of Greater Manchester's Buildings* [2022].
6. Ibid.
7. Historic England, *Delivering Net Zero for England's Historic Buildings: Local Data on the Demand for Retrofitting Skills and Economic Growth* [2023]. Available from www.historicengland.org.uk [Accessed 31 May 2024].
8. PwC, Making homes more energy efficient could sustain 500,000 jobs [2022]. Available from www.pwc.co.uk [Accessed 31 May 2024].
9. Ibid.
10. J. Newcomb and P. Caplehorn, *Construction Product Availability Statement*, Construction Leadership Council [2022]. Available from www.constructionleadershipcouncil.co.uk [Accessed 28 May 2024].

References

Adam, S., Chandler, D., Wood, A. and Joyce, R., *Cuts to Social Rents Will Benefit Exchequer More than Tenants, but Will Strengthen Work Incentives*, Institute for Fiscal Studies [2015].

Age UK, We can't wait for care [2017]. Available from www.ageuk.org.uk [Accessed 23 May 2024].

Aksoy, C.G., The housing bubble baby boom, The Royal Economic Society [2017]. Available from www.res.org.uk [Accessed 27 May 2024].

Apps, P., How the products used in Grenfell Tower's cladding system were tested and sold, *Inside Housing* [2021]. Available from www.insidehousing.co.uk [Accessed 27 May 2024].

Arcadis International, *International Construction Costs 2024* [2024].

Archer, T. and Cole, I., The financialisation of housing production: Exploring capital flows and value extraction among major housebuilders in the UK, *Journal of Housing and the Built Environment* [2021].

Aspire, Examining lives in adapted and unadapted homes [2016]. Available from www.aspire.org.uk [Accessed 23 May 2024].

Atkinson, R., The evidence on the impact of gentrification: new lessons for the urban renaissance? *European Journal of Housing Policy*, 4 [2004].

Bab, H.J.G., The evolution of the British building society, *Economic History Review*, 9(1) [1938].

Bailey, N., Poverty and the re-growth of private renting in the UK, 1994–2018, *PLoS One*, 15(2) [2020].

Bank of England, The development of the building societies sector in the 1980s [1990]. Available from www.bankofengland.co.uk [Accessed 28 May 2024].

Bank of England, Will there be another financial crisis? [2019]. Available from www.bankofengland.co.uk [Accessed 28 May 2024].

Barker, N., Exclusive: 7% rise in former Right to Buy homes now rented privately, *Inside Housing* [2017]. Available from www.insidehousing.co.uk [Accessed 27 May 2024].

Barton, C. and Wilson, W., What is affordable housing? House of Commons Library Research Briefing [2023]. Available from www.parliament.uk [Accessed 30 May 2024].

BBC, Asylum-seeker hotels for children 'a supermarket for gangs' [2023]. Available from www.bbc.co.uk/news [Accessed 23 May 2024].

BBC News, Budget 2001: At-a-glance [2001]. Available from www.news.bbc.co.uk [Accessed 29 May 2024].

BBC News, Grenfell Tower fire: More high-rises fail fire safety tests [2017]. Available from www.bbc.co.uk [Accessed 27 May 2024].

References

BBC News, Liverpool Travelodge: Digger driver jailed for rampage [2020]. Available from www.bbc.co.uk [Accessed 28 May 2024].

BBC News, Most mortgages go to first-time buyers, Halifax research shows [2019]. Available from www.bbc.co.uk [Accessed 27 May 2024].

BCIS, Building material cost increases reach 40 year high [2021]. Available from www.bcis.co.uk [Accessed 28 May 2024].

Begum, S., 2025 vision for the city is revealed, *Manchester Evening News* [2015]. Available from www.manchestereveningews.co.uk [Accessed 27 May 2024].

Bennett, H., Your official top 20: The new Standard Method and the cities/urban centres uplift, Lichfields [2021]. Available from www.lichfields.uk [Accessed 29 May 2024].

Bivens, J., The economic costs and benefits of Airbnb, Economic Policy Institute [2019]. Available from www.epi.org [Accessed 31 May 2024].

Booth, R., Cladding tests after Grenfell Tower fire 'utterly inadequate', *The Guardian* [2018].

Booth, R., 'A raging inferno': Testimony reveals how deadly cladding ended up on Grenfell Tower, *The Guardian* [2020].

Boughton, J., *Municipal Dreams*, Verso [2018].

Bowen, A., Hoggarth, G. and Pain, D., *The Recent Evolution of the UK Banking Industry and Some Implications for Financial Stability*, Bank for International Settlements [2017].

British Property Federation, About real estate [2024]. Available from www.bpf.org.uk [Accessed 30 May 2024].

Bruce, S., Bowers, N. and Wilkins, T., Housing in England and Wales: 2021 compared with 2011, ONS [2023].

Buchan, F., Statement made to Parliament on 28th February 2024 [2024]. Available from www.parliament.uk [Accessed 29 May 2024].

Buffel, T. and Phillipson, C., *Ageing in a Gentrifying Neighbourhood: Experiences of Community Change in Later Life*, British Sociological Association [2019].

Building Cost Information Service, A review of the construction industry 2022 [2022]. Available from www.bcis.co.uk [Accessed 28 May 2024].

Built Environment Committee, Meeting housing demand, 1st report of Session 2021–22, HL Paper 132 [2022].

Burford, R., Homes must be built on London's green belt to tackle housing crisis, warn business chiefs, *Evening Standard* [2023].

Burn-Murdoch, J., Why Britain is the world's worst on homelessness, *Financial Times* [2024].

Butler, P., Two-thirds of councils say they can't afford to comply with homelessness law, *The Guardian* [2019].

Caon, V., How the rise in material costs is damaging the UK's construction industry, *Investment Monitor* [2022]. Available from www.investmentmonitor.ai [Accessed 28 May 2024].

Centre for Ageing Better, *The State of Ageing 2022* [2022]. Available from www.ageing-better.org.uk [Accessed 23 May 2024].

Centre Point, *Ready to Move On: Barriers to Homeless Young People Accessing Longer Term Accommodation* [2023]. Available from www.centrepoint.org.uk [Accessed 23 May 2024].

The Centre for Public Data, New data on property in England & Wales owned by overseas individuals [2023]. Available from www.centreforpublicdata.org [Accessed 31 May 2024].

The Centre for Social Justice, Close to home: Delivering a national Housing First programme in England [2021].

Chadwick, E., *Report on the Sanitary Condition of the Labouring Population and on the Means of Its Improvement*, HMSO [1842].

Chalkias, A., Rebuild or retrofit: The environmental case, Savills [2022]. Available from www.savills.com [Accessed 31 May 2024].

Chan, D. and Thompson, M., Understanding the growth in private rented housing, Core Cities [2021]. Available from www.corecities.com [Accessed 27 May 2024].

Chartered Institute of Housing and Chartered Institute of Environmental Health, A licence to rent [2019]. Available from www.cieh.org [Accessed 31 May 2024].

Chope, C., Home Energy Efficiency Scheme, *Hansard*, vol 364 [2001]. Available from www.hansard.parliament.uk [Accessed 29 May 2024].

Christopher, B., *The New Enclosure: The Appropriation of Public Land in Neoliberal Britain*, Verso [2018].

City Harvest London, Editorial [2023]. Available from www.cityharvest.org.uk/blog [Accessed 23 May 2024].

Clark, D., Average household size in the UK 1996–2022, Statista [2023]. Available from www.statista.com [Accessed 2 May 2024].

Clark, D., Median annual earnings for full-time employees in the United Kingdom from 1999 to 2023, Statista [2023]. Available from www.statista.com [Accessed 28 May 2024].

Clark, N. and Herman, E., *Unpaid Britain: Wage Default in the British Labour Market*, Middlesex University [2017].

Clarke, S. and Gregg, P., *Count the Pennies: Explaining a Decade of Lost Pay Growth*, Resolution Foundation [2018].

Cleary, E.J., *The Building Society Movement*, Elek Books [1965].

Cocola-Gant, A., Holiday rentals: The new gentrification battlefront, *Sociological Research Online*, 21(3) [2016].

Cocola-Gant, A. and Gago, A., Airbnb, buy-to-let investment and tourism-driven displacement: A case study in Lisbon, *Economy and Space*, 53(7) [2019].

Competition and Markets Authority, CMA finds fundamental concerns in housebuilding market [2024]. Available from www.gov.uk [Accessed 28 May 2024].

References

Construction Industry Training Board, Britain builds bad: Construction will need 216,800 new workers by 2025 to meet demand [2021]. Available from www.citb.co.uk [Accessed 28 May 2024].

Contribution of Lord Leatherland to a debate on 'The Housing Situation', *Hansard*, vol 336, cc714–804 [1972].

Copley, T., *Slums of the Future*, London Labour Assembly [2019].

Crafts, N., How housebuilding helped the economy recover: Britain in the 1930s, *The Guardian* [2013].

Cran-McGreehin, S., Insulation and gas prices: Households are paying the price for slow progress on insulating homes, Energy and Climate Intelligence Unit [2022]. Available from www.eciu.net [Accessed 29 May 2024].

Cribb, J., Wernham, T. and Xu, X., *Housing Costs and Income Inequality in the UK*, Institute for Fiscal Studies [2023].

Crisis, *The Homelessness Monitor: England 2019* [2019]. Available from www.crisis.org.uk [Accessed 29 May 2024].

Cryer, P., Rents and incomes, early 20th century [2014]. Available from www.1900s.org.uk [Accessed 24 May 2024].

CSI Market Intelligence 2020 report.

Davenport, R.J., Urbanization and mortality in Britain, c. 1800–50, *Economic History Review* [2020].

Davies, G., Youle, E., Boutaud, C. and Sheffield, H., Revealed: The thousands of public spaces lost to the council funding crisis, *Huffington Post* [2019].

DCLG, Land value estimates for policy appraisal [2019]. Available from www.gov.uk [Accessed 31 May 2024].

DECC, Process evaluation of the Warm Front Scheme [2014]. Available from www.gov.uk [Accessed 29 May 2024].

DEFRA, Housing availability and affordability [2022].

Department of Finance Canada, Government announces two-year extension to ban on foreign ownership of Canadian housing [2024]. Available from www.canada.ca [Accessed 31 May 2024].

DESNZ, Annual fuel poverty statistics in England, 2023 (2022 data) [2023]. Available from www.gov.uk [Accessed 31 May 2024].

DESNZ, *Summary of the Great British Insulation Scheme: January 2024*, Official Statistics [2024]. Available from www.gov.uk [Accessed 29 May 2024].

Diner, A. and Wright, H., *Reforming Right to Buy: Options for Preserving and Delivering New Council Homes for the Twenty-First Century*, New Economics Foundation [2024].

Disraeli, B., Speech of the Right Hon. B. Disraeli [1872]. Available from https://archive.org [Accessed 12 June 2025].

DLUHC, General fund revenue account outturn R04: Housing services 2020–21 [2021]. Available from www.gov.uk [Accessed 29 May 2024].

DLUHC, Rough sleeping snapshot in England: Autumn 2021 [2022]. Available from www.gov.uk [Accessed 27 May 2024].

DLUHC, Summary of housing service spend in England 2020–21 [2022]. Available from www.gov.uk [Accessed 27 May 2024].

DLUHC, Compulsory purchase – compensation reforms: Consultation [2023]. Available from www.gov.uk [Accessed 31 May 2024].

DLUHC, English housing survey 2022–23 [2023].

DLUHC, Social housing lettings in England, tenants: April 2022 to March 2023 [2023]. Available from www.gov.uk [Accessed 23 May 2024].

DLUHC, Supplementary estimates memorandum 2022–23 [2023]. Available from www.gov.uk [Accessed 29 May 2024].

DLUHC, Evaluation of the Housing First Pilots, report on clients' outcomes twelve months after entering Housing First [2024]. Available from www.gov.uk [Accessed 29 May 2024].

DLUHC, Rough sleeping snapshot in England: Autumn 2023 [2024]. Available from www.gov.uk [Accessed 27 May 2024].

DLUHC, Social housing lettings in England, tenancies: April 2021 to March 2022 [2024]. Available from www.gov.uk [Accessed 31 May 2024].

DLUHC, MHCLG and Regulator of Social Housing, Policy statement on rents for social housing [2022]. Available from www.gov.uk [Accessed 28 May 2024].

DWP and DCLG, Supported accommodation review [2016].

Engel, M., The bubble that turned into a tide: How London got hooked on gentrification, *The Guardian* [2016].

Engels, F., *Condition of the Working Class in England*, Otto Wigand [1845].

English Housing Survey (EHS) 2023–24.

Environment Agency, *Flooding in England: A National Assessment of Flood Risk* [2021].

The Equality Trust, *The Scale of Economic Inequality in the UK* [2022]. Available from www.equalitytrust.org.uk [Accessed 27 May 2024].

Evans, R., Half of England is owned by less than 1% of the population, *The Guardian* [2019].

Farmer, M., *Modernise or Die: The Farmer Review of the UK Construction Labour Model*, Construction Leadership Council [2016].

Farmer, M., Five years on from *Modernise or Die*, where are we now? Construction Management [2021]. Available from www.constructionmanagement.co.uk [Accessed 28 May 2024].

Fetter, D.K., The home front: Rent control and the rapid wartime increase in home ownership, *The Journal of Economic History* [2016].

Fitri, A., The UK now spends more on housing benefit than on most government departments, *The New Statesman* [2022].

Froud, J., Johal, S., Tomaney, J. and Williams, K., Manchester's transformation over the past 25 years: Why we need a reset of city region policy, LSE [2017]. Available from www.blogs.lse.ac.uk [Accessed 28 May 2024].

Garrett, H., Mackay, M., Nicol, S., Piddington, J. and Roys, M., The cost of poor housing in England, *The Building Research Establishment* [2021].

Gasparyan, T., *Gentrification in London: A Multi-Method Study of Unequal Growth*, Uppsala University [2020].

GBN, Michael Gove stands by 'cartel' comments as he calls for better accessibility into housebuilding market [2022]. Available from https://www.gbnews.com/news/michael-gove-stands-by-cartel-comments-as-he-calls-for-better-accessibility-into-housebuilding-market/325581 [Accessed 18 June 2025].

Goodall, L., Britain's hidden homeless children, *The News Agents Investigates* [Podcast] [2024]. Available from www.podcasts.apple.com [Accessed 29 May 2024].

Grant Thornton, Half of new homes in London are not being built [2019]. Available from www.grantthornton.co.uk [Accessed 29 May 2024].

Greater London Authority, The impact of welfare reform on homelessness in London [2019]. Available from www.london.gov.uk [Accessed 29 May 2024].

Greater Manchester Combined Authority, Housing investment skewed in favour of South of England, new report finds [2018]. Available from www.greatermanchester-ca.gov.uk [Accessed 29 May 2024].

Greater Manchester Combined Authority, *RetrofitGM: Accelerating the Renovation of Greater Manchester's Buildings* [2022].

Greater Manchester Combined Authority, *Temporary Accomodation in Greater Manchester* [2024]. Available from www.democracy.greatermanchester-ca.gov.uk [Accessed 29 May 2024].

Griffiths, M., Britain has spoken – old homes are better than new builds, *Realhomes*. Available from www.realhomes.com [Accessed 31 May 2024].

Gutteridge, N., Number of second homes in England soars by more than 50 per cent, *The Telegraph* [2023].

Haldane, A.G., Whose recovery? [Speech], Bank of England [2016]. Available from www.bankofengland.co.uk [Accessed 29 May 2024].

Hammond, G. and Pickard, J., South of England gets lion's share of housebuilding funds, *Financial Times* [2020].

Hamptons, Rents to grow more than four times faster than house prices over the next four years [2023]. Available from www.hamptons.co.uk [Accessed 27 May 2024].

Hanretty, C., *The Pork Barrel Politics of the Towns Fund: Funding Decisions Were Driven by Part-Political Considerations, Not by Need*, LSE [2020].

Hansard, Ribbon development [1935]. Available from www.api.parliament.uk [Accessed 27 May 2024].

Hansard, Building societies [1939]. Available from www.api.parliament.uk [Accessed 27 May 2024].

Hansard, Homelessness, vol 361 [1975]. Available from: https://api.parliament.uk/ [Accessed 27 May 2024].

Hansard, Housing stock, vol 970 [1979]. Available from www.hansard.parliament.uk [Accessed 27 May 2024].

Hansard, Council house rents [1981]. Available from www.api.parliament.uk [Accessed 27 May 2024].

Hansard, Average weekly wage [1983]. Available from www.api.parliament.uk [Accessed 27 May 2024].

Harrison, J., The origin, development and decline of back-to-back houses in Leeds, 1787–1937, University of York [2017].

Hatherley, O., Pathfinder was slum clearances without the socialism, *The Guardian* [2010].

The Health Foundation, Trends in household overcrowding by tenure [2023]. Available from www.health.org.uk [Accessed 23 May 2024].

Hetherington, P., How Pathfinder lost its way, *The Guardian* [2007].

Hewitt, D., Landlords to be banned from discriminating against benefit claimants and families with children, *ITV News* [2023].

Hird, C., Building societies: Stakeholding in practice and under threat, *New Left Review* [1996].

Historic England, *A Brief Introduction to Garden Cities* [2016]. Available from www.heritagecalling.com [Accessed 27 May 2024].

Historic England, *Delivering Net Zero for England's Historic Buildings: Local Data on the Demand for Retrofitting Skills and Economic Growth* [2023]. Available from www.historicengland.org.uk [Accessed 31 May 2024].

Home Builders Federation, Housing horizons: Examining UK housing stock in an international context [2023]. Available from www.hbf.co.uk [Accessed 3 June 2024].

Home Builders Federation, Planning delays continue to pose greatest obstacle to UK home builders [2024]. Available from www.hbf.co.uk [Accessed 28 May 2024].

Home Builders Federation and National House Building Council, *Annual Survey of House Builders 2020–21* [2022].

Homeless Link, *Housing First in England, Frequently Asked Questions* [2023]. Available from www.homeless.org.uk [Accessed 29 May 2024].

Homes England, Fact sheet 7: Homes and different land types – brownfield, greenfield and Green Belt [2022]. Available from www.gov.uk [Accessed 28 May 2024].

Homes England, Homes England strategic plan 2018 to 2023 [Text version] [2022]. Available from www.gov.uk [Accessed 28 May 2024].

House of Commons, *Renters (Reform) Bill, as Amended (Amendment Paper) 22/04/24* [2024].

House of Commons Committee Report, *Seventh Report of Sessions 2022–23: Reforms to National Planning Policy* [2023]. Available from www.publications.parliament.uk [Accessed 29 May 2024].

House Condition Survey, England and Wales [1967]. Available from www.gov.uk [Accessed 29 May 2024].

Houston, J., From bomb site to style capital, *BBC News* [2006]. Available from www.news.bbc.co.uk [Accessed 27 May 2024].

Hudspeth, I., Supporting the health needs of those who are experiencing rough sleeping, Local Government Association [2024]. Available from www.local.gov.uk [Accessed 27 May 2024].

Inside Housing, Right to Buy for housing associations: The main challenges behind extending the policy [2022]. Available from www.insidehousing.co.uk [Accessed 28 May 2024].

Institute of Civil Engineers, What should be in the National Infrastructure Strategy? [2019].

Institute of Health Equity, *Fuel Poverty, Cold Homes and Health Inequalities in the UK* [2022].

ITV News, The number of Airbnbs in Cornwall compared to long-term rentals [2022]. Available from www.itv.com [Accessed 31 May 2024].

Joint infrastructure levy letter to DLUHC, June 2023. Available from www.rtpi.org.uk [Accessed 29 May 2024].

Keep, M., Regional house price: Affordability and income ratios, House of Commons Library, Standard Note SN/SG/1922 [2012]. Available from www.parliament.uk [Accessed 30 May 2024].

Kemp, P., Private renting in England, *Netherlands Journal of Housing and the Built Environment* [1998].

Key Cities, Homes England grants – the geographical spread [2018]. Available from www.keycities.uk [Accessed 29 May 2024].

King's Fund, Key facts and figures about social care [2023]. Available from www.kingsfund.org.uk [Accessed 25 May 2024].

Knight, O., Government funding to unlock housing acting as a barrier to the levelling up agenda, Knight Frank [2020]. Available from www.knightfrank.com [Accessed 29 May 2024].

Kollewe, J., Britain's housing market may be 'past peak pain' but what will 2024 bring, *The Guardian* [2023].

Kulakiewicz, A., Housing and health: A reading list [2022]. Available from www.commonslibrary.parliament.uk [Accessed 27 May 2024].

Landberg, R., UK house building slows despite record prices as outlook dims, *Bloomberg* [2022]. Available from www.bloomberg.com [Accessed 28 May 2024].

Laslett, P., Size and structure of the household in England over three centuries. *Population Studies* [1969].

Letwin, O., *Independent Review of Build Out: Final Report* [2018]. Available from www.gov.uk [Accessed 28 May 2024].

Livesey, G., Innovation, the agricultural belt, and the early garden city, *Berkeley Planning Journal* [2016].

Lloyd, M., Scotland's housebuilding boom: Can English councils emulate it? *Inside Housing* [2019]. Available from www.insidehousing.co.uk [Accessed 28 May 2024].

Local Government Association, Housing backlog – more than a million homes with planning permission not yet built [2020]. Available from www.local.gov.uk [Accessed 28 May 2024].

Local Government Association, 18,000 affordable houses lost in office-to-residential conversions [2022]. Available from www.local.gov.uk [Accessed 27 May 2024].

Local Government Association, One public estate: Brownfield Land Release Fund (BLRF2) round 2 – fund details [2023]. Available from www.local.gov.uk [Accessed 28 May 2024].

Local Government Association, Right to Buy position statement [2024]. Available from www.local.gov.uk [Accessed 29 May 2024].

Lowe, T., Planning reforms blamed as Lib Dems shock Tories with by-election upset, *Housing Today* [2021]. Available from www.housingtoday.co.uk [Accessed 28 May 2024].

Lund, B., *The Beveridge Report 80 Years On: 'Squalor' and Housing – 'a True Goliath'*, University of Strathclyde [2021].

Macfarlane, L., *Opinion: Extending Help-to-Buy Will Only Make the Housing Crisis Worse*, University College London [2020].

Masterson, V., What is land value tax and could it fox the housing crisis? World Economic Forum [2022]. Available from www.weforum.org [Accessed 31 May 2024].

Mearns, A., *The Bitter Cry of Outcast London: An Inquiry into the Condition of the Abject Poor*, James Clarke & Co. [1883].

MHCLG, National Planning Policy Framework [2012]. Available from www.nationalarchives.gov.uk [Accessed 31 May 2024].

MHCLG, Empty homes reach all time low [2016]. Available from www.gov.uk [Accessed 3 June 2024].

MHCLG, Evaluation of the implementation of the Homelessness Reduction Act: Final report [2020]. Available from www.gov.uk [Accessed 29 May 2024].

MHCLG, Evaluation of the Housing First pilots: Second process evaluation report [2021]. Available from www.gov.uk [Accessed 29 May 2024].

Mitra, F., *Instruments of Monetary Management: Bank-by-Bank Credit Ceilings: Issues and Experiences*, IMF [1997].

Moffatt, S., Lawson, S., Patterson, R., Holding, E., Dennison, A., Snowden, S., et al, A qualitative study of the impact of the UK 'bedroom tax', *Journal of Public Health*, 38 [2016].

Mukherjee, P. and Balu, N., Canada's extension of ban on foreign real estate buyers labelled political, not practical, *Reuters* [2024].

Murray, J. UK crime gangs rake in millions through supported housing, say police, *The Guardian* [2023].

National Audit Office, Investigation into NHS Property Services Limited [2014]. Available from www.nao.org.uk [Accessed 28 May 2024].

National Audit Office, Network Rail's sale of railway arches [2019]. Available from www.nao.org.uk [Accessed 28 May 2024].

National Housing Federation, Briefing: Mapping brownfield land in England [2019]. Available from www.housing.org.uk [Accessed 28 May 2024].

National Housing Federation, About social housing [2020]. Available from www.housing.org.uk [Accessed 28 May 2024].

National Housing Federation, People in housing need: A comprehensive analysis of the scale and shape of housing need in England today [2020]. Available from www.housing.org.uk [Accessed 29 May 2024].

National Housing Federation, The real 'social housing waiting list' is 500,000 more than official figures [2020]. Available from www.housing.org.uk [Accessed 25 May 2024].

National Housing Federation, Conservative voters support building social housing over homes for sale [2023]. Available from www.housing.org.uk [Accessed 25 May 2024].

Neate, P., Right to Buy has already torn a massive hole in our social housing stock as less than 5% of the homes sold off have ever been replaced. Press release: Shelter comments on government's 'hare-brained' idea to extend Right-to-Buy to housing association homes [2022]. Available from www.england.shelter.org.uk [Accessed 29 May 2024].

Network Homes, Why aren't housing associations building more social rented homes? [2019]. Available from www.networkhomes.org.uk [Accessed 28 May 2024].

Nevin, B. and Cole, I., *The Road to Renewal: The Early Development of the Housing Market Renewal Programme in England*, Joseph Rowntree Foundation [2004].

Newcomb, J. and Caplehorn, P., *Construction Product Availability Statement*, Construction Leadership Council [2022]. Available from www.constructionleadershipcouncil.co.uk [Accessed 28 May 2024].

Nguyen, T. and Johannsson, K., Improving estimates of land underlying dwellings in the national balance sheet, UK: 2022, ONS [2022]. Available from www.ons.gov.uk [Accessed 31 May 2024].

NHS Property Services, NHS Property Services creates £200million for the NHS from surplus property sales [2017]. Available from www.property.nhs.uk [Accessed 28 May 2024].

Niemitz, K., Why Britain needs more empty homes, *The Critic* [2024].

OECD, *Housing Sector Country Snapshot: United Kingdom* [2023]. Available from www.oecd.org [Accessed 31 May 2024].

Office for Budget Responsibility, Housing associations, classification changes and fiscal risks, Fiscal Risks Report [2019].

Office of the Deputy Prime Minister, ODPM circular 05/2005: Planning obligations [2005]. Available from www.gov.uk [Accessed 31 May 2024].

Oliver, J., Housing associations in England warn 'we can't build houses', *Financial Times* [2024].

ONS, *Housing in England 2007–08* [2009]. Available from www.webarchive.nationalarchives.gov.uk [Accessed 27 May 2024].

ONS, English Housing Survey 2018–2019: Second homes – fact sheet [2020].

ONS, Housing affordability in England and Wales [2021]. Available from www.ons.gov.uk [Accessed 27 May 2024].

ONS, More than 1 in 10 addressed used as holiday homes in some areas of England and Wales [2023].

ONS, Private rental affordability, England & Wales [2023].

ONS, Average weekly earnings in Great Britain: September 2024 [2024]. Available from www.ons.gov.uk.

Orr, D., A blueprint for the rich, *The Independent* [1999].

Orr, D., *The Good Home Inquiry*, Centre for Ageing Better [2021]. Available from www.ageing-better.uk [Accessed 27 May 2024].

Owen, R., The influence of buy-to-let on UK housing, *Mortgage Finance Gazette* [2017].

Parker, F., Our new build nightmares, *This Is Money* [2021]. Available from www.thisismoney.co.uk [Accessed 27 May 2024].

Parliament, Publications & Records, Land value capture [2019]. Available from www.publications.parliament.uk [Accessed 29 May 2024].

Pawson, H., Davidson, E., Morgan, J., Smith, R. and Edwards, R., *The Impacts of Housing Stock Transfer in Urban Britain*, Joseph Rowntree Foundation [2009].

Pickles, N., What do the Affordable Homes Programme 21–26 strategic partnership grant allocations tell us?, National Housing Federation [2021]. Available from www.housing.org.uk [Accessed 29 May 2024].

Planning Advisory Service, Objectively Assessed Need and Housing Targets Technical advice note: Second edition [2015].

Plimmer, G., Why the cracks are showing in Britain's construction industry, *Financial Times* [2018].

References

Precey, M., Sturdy, J. and Cawley, L., Inside Harlow's office block 'human warehouse' housing, *BBC News* [2019]. Available from www.bbc.co.uk [Accessed 27 May 2024].

Propertymark, Evaluation of rent smart Wales [2024]. Available from www.propertymark.co.uk [Accessed 27 May 2024].

PwC, 2021 UK and global economic outlook [2021]. Available from www.pwc.co.uk [Accessed 25 May 2024].

PwC, Making homes more energy efficient could sustain 500,000 jobs [2022]. Available from www.pwc.co.uk [Accessed 31 May 2024].

Rajagopal, B., Report of the Special Rapporteur on adequate housing as a component of the right to an adequate standard of living, and on the right to non-discrimination in this context, item 73b of the provisional agenda to the 78th session of the UN General Assembly [2023].

Raynsford Review of Planning in England, *Planning 2020* [2018]. Available from www.tcpa.org.uk [Accessed 27 May 2024].

Rees, T., UK lenders see growing mortgage demand even as defaults rise, *Bloomberg* [2024]. Available from www.bloomberg.com [Accessed 27 May 2024].

Reuters, UK lenders see mortgage default rates rising [2024].

Rhodes, D. and Rugg, J., Vulnerability amongst low-income households in the private rented sector in England, Nationwide Foundation [2018]. Available from www.nationwidefoundation.org.uk [Accessed 31 May 2024].

Rogers, C. and Gough, I., Solving the housing crisis without building new houses, London School of Economics [2024]. Available from www.lse.ac.uk [Accessed 3 June 2024].

Romei, V., UK mortgages in arrears jump to seven-year high, *Financial Times* [2023].

Ryan-Collins, J., *The Demand for Housing as an Investment*, IIPP (UCL) [2024].

Ryan-Collins, J., *Why Can't You Afford a Home?* Polity Press [2018].

Sa, F., *The Effect of Foreign Investors on Local Housing Market: Evidence from the UK*, KCL [2017].

Sage Homes, Sparrow shared ownership launches as USS acquires 3,000 shared ownership homes from Blackstone and Regis Group plc [2024]. Available from www.sagehomes.co.uk [Accessed 12 June 2025].

Sandford, M., Trailblazer devolution deals (Research Briefing Number 9901), House of Commons Library [2023]. Available from www.parliament.uk [Accessed 31 May 2024].

Savills UK, A brief history of the UK housing market [2022]. Available from: www.savills.co.uk [Accessed 23 May 2024].

Scanlon, K., Whitehead, C., Blanc, F. and Moreno-Tabarez, U., The role of overseas investors in the London new-build residential market, Final report for Homes for London, London Schools of Economics [2017]. Available from www.lse.ac.uk [Accessed 31 May 2024].

Schroders, What 175 years of data tell us about house price affordability in the UK [2023]. Available from www.schroders.com [Accessed 27 May 2024].

Scott, J., Renters' Reform Bill gets sign off from MPs – but indefinite delay to no-ult evictions ban remains, *Sky News* [2024].

Scott, P., *Selling Owner-Occupation to the Working-Classes in 1930s Britain*, University of Reading [2004].

Scullion, L., Gibbons, A. and Martin, P., *Precarious lives: Exploring Lived Experiences of the Private Rented Sector in Salford*, University of Salford and Salford Council [2018].

Seeley, A., *Briefing Paper (587): VAT and Construction*, House of Commons Library [2019].

Shapps, G., 1st Dec 2010, Hansard Column 831W [2010]. Available from www.parliament.uk [Accessed 29 May 2024].

Shelter, 'Rigged' housebuilding system means eight in ten families cannot afford new home, says Shelter [2017]. Available from www.england.shelter.org.uk [Accessed 27 May 2024].

Shelter, Everyone In: Where are they now? The need for a roadmap out of street homelessness in England [2021]. Available from www.england.shetler.org.uk [Accessed 29 May 2024].

Shelter, 116% annual rise in no-fault evictions shows why Renters (Reform) Bill is vital [2023]. Available from www.england.shelter.org.uk [Accessed 27 May 2024].

Shelter, Homeless accommodation bill hits £1.7bn [2023]. Available from www.england.shelter.org.uk [Accessed 27 May 2024].

Shelter, Loss of social housing [2023]. Available from www.england.shelter.org.uk [Accessed 27 May 2024].

Shelter, NHF and CEBR, The economic impact of building social housing [2024].

Siebrits, J., Should we restrict overseas buyers? CBRE [2024]. Available from www.cbre.co.uk [Accessed 31 May 2024].

Slater, C., Robsen, S., Ruski, A. and Day, R., Traffic chaos on Regent Road roadworks as workmen dump diggers in protest at 'not being paid', *Manchester Evening News* [2019].

Spry, M., The political economy of planning for housing: Six barriers in the planning system holding back the supply of the homes we need, Lichfields [2023]. Available from www.lichfields.uk [Accessed 29 May 2024].

Statista Research Department, Number of housing units in England from 2001 to 2022 [2024]. Available from www.statista.com [Accessed 24 May 2024].

Szreter, S. and Mooney, G., Urbanization, mortality, and the standard of living debate: New estimates of the expectation of life at birth in nineteenth-century British cities, *The Economic History Review* [1998].

Talbot, L., Keeping bad company: Building societies – a case study, Warwick University [2009].

Thomas, D. and Race, M., War in Ukraine: Russia says it may cut gas supplies if oil ban goes ahead, *BBC News* [2022]. Available from www.bbc.co.uk [Accessed 28 May 2024].

Tilley, J., Government rejects central London boroughs' bid to block permitted development rights, Planning Resource [2021]. Available from www.planningresource.co.uk [Accessed 27 May 2024].

Tocqueville, A. de, *Journeys to England and Ireland*, Yale University Press [1835].

Town Planning Act 1925. Available from www.legislation.gov.uk [Accessed 12 June 2025].

Turner, C., *Homes through the Decades*, National House Building Council [2015].

Turvey, R., Development charges and the compensation-betterment problem, *The Economic Journal*, 63(250) [1953].

UK Housing Review, Rents and earnings in England [2006]. Available from www.ukhousingreview.org.uk [Accessed 27 May 2024].

UK Land Registry, UK House Price Index. Available from www.landregistry.data.gov.uk [Accessed 27 May 2024].

UK Parliament Research Briefings, Housing supply: Historical statistics for the UK [2003]. Available from www.parliament.uk [Accessed 27 May 2024].

Ulaeto, H., Will selective licensing schemes survive the Renters (Reform) Bill? Home Safe [2024]. Available from www.home-safe.org.uk [Accessed 31 May 2024].

United Nations, Affordable housing, inclusive economic policies key to ending homelessness, speakers sat as social development commission begins annual session [2020]. Available from www.press.un.org [Accessed 29 May 2024].

Wareing, K., *An Alternative Model for Funding Asylum and Temporary Housing*, SOHA Housing [2024].

Walker, J., No more #Brumcuts: Fury as government hands £300m to Tory councils while Birmingham gets nothing, *Business Live* [2016]. Available from www.business-live.co.uk [Accessed 29 May 2024].

Walker, P., Surrey council received boost in budget after 'sweetheart deal' claims, *The Guardian* [2017].

Walker, P., England has 'twice as many empty homes as families stuck in B&Bs', *The Guardian* [2023].

Walters, J.T., *Report of the Committee Appointed to Consider Questions of Building Construction in Connection with the Provision of Dwellings for the Working Classes* [1918]. Available from JSTOR [Accessed 12 June 2025].

Wareing, K., An alternative model for funding asylum and temporary housing [2024].

Wearn, R., Growing complaints about new-build houses, *BBC News* [2019]. Available from www.bbc.co.uk [Accessed 27 May 2024].

Williams, J., Who is really benefitting from the Manchester City Centre housing boom? *Manchester Evening News* [2017].

Williams, J., The hidden 'Manchester slums': Squalor, danger and death in our city's grim private guesthouses, *Manchester Evening News* [2019].

Williams, J., How ministers gave Cheadle £25m for 'left behind towns' despite civil service advice – while Swinton and Wigan got nothing, *Manchester Evening News* [2020].

Williams, J., 'The numbers on the streets are going to rocket': Homeless people put up in hotels amid pandemic to be kicked out as government quietly scraps scheme, *Manchester Evening News* [2020].

Wilson, W., *Housing Market Renewal Pathfinders*, Social Policy Section of the House of Commons Library SN/SP/5953 [2013]. Available from www.parliament.uk [Accessed 29 May 2024].

Wilson, W., Extending home ownership: Government initiatives, House of Commons Library Number 03668 [2021]. Available from www.parliament.uk [Accessed 29 May 2024].

Wilson, W., Selective licensing of private rented housing in England and Wales, House of Commons Library Research Briefing (Number CBP04634) [2023].

Wilson, W., Barton, C. and Carthew, H., Overcrowded housing (England) [2023]. Available from www.commonslibrary.parliament.uk [Accessed 27 May 2024].

Woodman, T., Holiday lets are houses not homes; they are zombie houses that are hollowing out our communities, Chartered Institute of Housing [2022]. Available from www.cih.org [Accessed 31 May 2024].

Woods, S., Ormandy, D. and Harrison, J., Comparing the rights of private sector tenants in England with those in other jurisdictions, Warwick University [2018]. Available from www.warwick.ac.uk [Accessed 31 May 2024].

Woodward, K., *Social Sciences, the Big Issues*, Routledge [2014].

Wright, S., Fletcher, D.R. and Stewart, A.B.R., Punitive sanctions, welfare conditionality, and the social abuse of unemployed people in Britain: Transforming claimants into offenders? *Social Policy & Administration*, 54 [2020].

Written evidence submitted to Parliament by the Northern Housing Consortium [2022]. Available from www.committees.parliament.uk [Accessed 25 May 2024].

Written evidence submitted to Parliament by the UK Women's Budget Group [2022]. Available from www.committees.parliament.uk [Accessed 27 May 2024].

References

Written evidence presented by Shelter to Parliament [2022]. Available from www.committees.parliament.uk [Accessed 23 May 2024].

Zemaityte, G., Hughes, E. and Blood, K., The buy-to-let sector and financial stability, *Bank of England Quarterly Bulletin 2023* [2023]. Available from www.bankofengland.co.uk [Accessed 31 May 2024].

Zillow, Birth rates are falling most where homes are appreciating fastest [2018]. Available from www.zillow.mediaroom.com [Accessed 27 May 2024].

Index

80:20 ratio, funding schemes 95–96

A

absorption rate 66, 84
Abu Dhabi United Group 149
ACM (Aluminium Composite Material) cladding, fire safety and building regulations 48–55
Act for Friendly Societies 1793 9
adapted accommodation 23–24, 32
Addison Act (Housing and Town Planning Act) 1919 16
affordability of housing 1, 24, 28, 35–37, 58, 59, 60, 66–67, 137, 162–163, 164
　Capital and Centric commercial development model 75–79
　homelessness and rough sleeping 39–41
　homeownership 35–37
　international comparisons 29
　post-war period 2, 21, 59
　private rented sector (PRS) 35, 37–39
　regional variations 36
　see also house price inflation
Affordable Homes Programme 96, 176
　Greater Manchester 174–175
affordable housing
　affordable housing need assessment 92–93
　government investment and funding 170–173
　loss of to conversions 47
　urban regeneration 153–157, 162–163
Affordable Housing Commission 137
Affordable Rent 130
AgeUK 33
'agricultural belts' 8
Airbnb 57, 138–140, 141
　see also short-term rentals
Aluglaze window panels 49
Annual Tax on Enveloped Dwellings 142
Arcadis International, 'Construction Costs 2024' 71
Arconic 48, 49
Ardern, Jacinda 142
Arnott, Dr. 3–4
Artisans' and Labourers' Dwellings Act 1875 6
Arts and Crafts movement 7, 69
Aspire 32
Association of British Insurers 50
Assured Shorthold Tenancies 13, 106, 177, 185
Atkinson, Rowland 101
Australia 106–107, 182

B

Balfour, Jabez 10
Bank of England 12, 37, 38, 72, 127, 161
banking system deregulation, UK 83–84, 143–144, 146, 164
Barber, Anthony 159
Barcelona, Spain 138–139
Barlow Commission, 1940 17, 19, 70
Bazalgette, Joseph 5
BCIS (Building Cost Information Service) 73
　Materials Cost Index 71
'beauty standards' in design 46–47
bed-blocking 31–32, 33
'Bedroom Standard' 27
'bedroom tax' (spare room subsidy) 110, 112–113
　Manchester 153–154
benefit sanctions 112–113
Bernstein, Howard 154
Beveridge, Aneisha 38
Beveridge Report, 1942 19–20, 42, 70
Birmingham 2, 5
　construction costs 71
'Birmingham Society, The' 9
birth rates, decline in 38–39
Bishop, Molly 119–121
Blackstone 172–173
Blake, Judith 160
Blake, William 4
Boundary Street scheme, London 6–7, 16
Bournville (Cadbury) 7
Bristol 71
brownfield sites 63, 64, 67, 159
Brutalist architecture 17, 42
Buffel, T. 151–152
'Builder's Pool Arrangements' 11
Building Act 1984 42
building control system 58
　cutbacks and privatisation 42
　fire safety 48–55
　policies to improve 194–195
Building Research Establishment 45
building societies 9–13
Building Societies Act 1874 9
Building Societies Act 1894 10
Building Societies Act 1939 11
Building Societies Association (BSA) 11–12
Building Societies Protection Association 10
BuildScan 46
Bureau of Investigative Journalism 82
Burnham, Andy 53, 153, 155, 173–174

Index

Burn-Murdoch, John 41
Business LDN 63
Business Rates 86
buy-to-let properties 177–178, 180, 182
  see also PRS (private rented sector)

C

Cameron, David 61, 103, 136
'Can of Ham' construction site, London 74–75
Canada 142
Canary Wharf, London 144–145
Capital and Centric 66, 197
  commercial development model 75–79
Capital Gains Tax 86
Cardiff 71
Care Quality Commission 33
Carillion 75
Celotex RS5000 boards 49
Central Manchester Development Corporation 148
Centre for Ageing Better 43, 190
Centre for Economics and Business Research 172
Centre for Housing Policy 178
Centre for Progressive Capitalism 86
Centre for Public Data 140–141
Centre for Social Justice 114–115
Centrepoint 30–31
Chadwick, Edwin 3, 4–5
Charities Aid Foundation Bank 172
Chartered Institute of Environmental Health 186
Chartered Institute of Housing 91, 140, 186
Chesham and Amersham by-election, 2021 68, 80, 94
Child Tax Credit 112
children
  child poverty, Greater Manchester 130
  living in conversions 48
  living in temporary accommodation 41, 109–110
Chimney Pot Park, Salford 102
Chorlton, Manchester 151–152
Christopher, Brett 81
CIL (Community Infrastructure Levy) 86, 90–91, 181–182
cladding, fire safety and building regulations 48–55
Clay, Ben 154, 155, 156–157
'Clusters of Empty Homes Programme' 29
Coalition government 99, 129, 136, 190
Cocola-Gant, A. 141
Cole, Ian 99–101
Commonwealth Games 2002 148
Community Accommodation programme 119

Community Infrastructure Levy (CIL) 86, 90–91, 181–182
Community Land Act 1975 181
Competition and Credit Control, 1971 12, 83
Competition and Markets Authority, 2024 investigation 66, 67
Comprehensive Spending Review 2025 130, 138, 171, 173
Conservative governments 61, 69, 80–81, 102, 103–104, 112, 126, 127–128, 130, 136, 159, 181
construction costs 71, 79, 88
  construction industry structure 74–79, 88
  finance 72
  land 79–87, 88, 180
  materials 71–72
  skills shortage 72–74, 193
construction industry
  construction costs 74–79, 88
  policies to improve 193–194
Construction Industry Council 42
Construction Industry Training Board 73
Construction Leadership Council 72–73, 193
Construction Products Association 75
contract labour, in the construction industry 73, 75
conversions 47–48
cooperative organisations 9
Core Cities 160, 178
Cornerstone 140
Cornwall, short-term lets 139–140
Corporation Tax 86
council housing *see* social rented housing
'Council of Housebuilding Skills and Capacity Fund' 170
Council of Mortgage Lenders 177
Council for the Preservation of Rural England 19
Council Tax 86
  second home surcharges 140
courts (slum housing, early industrial period) 3–4, 5, 6
COVID-19 pandemic 72, 73
  'Everyone In' programme 116–117, 118, 119
  impact on care sector capacity 33
CPO (compulsory purchase order) powers, PRS (private rented sector) 187–188
Craig, Bev 157
credit controls 12, 13
criminal gangs 31
Crisis 40
  2019 Homelessness Monitor 113

D

damp/mould issues 43, 44, 45, 187, 190
  see also housing quality

Davey, Ed 80–81
Debord, Guy 131
defects, new build properties 46
delivery, of new homes 61
  Capital and Centric commercial development model 75–79
  construction costs 71, 79, 88
  construction industry structure 74–79, 88
  finance 72
  land 79–87, 88
  materials 71–72
  skills shortage 72–74
  government investment, subsidy and spending 85–87
  green belt 63, 64, 65, 67–68
  local government developers loss 70–71, 87
  NPPF (National Planning Policy Framework), 2012 61–62, 63, 64–65, 68, 80, 90, 92, 181
  planning system 61–62, 65–67, 87
  planning reform 64–65, 68–69, 80–81
  planning restrictions 69–70
  policy failure 87–88
  see also house building
Dennett, Paul 51–52, 53, 54, 55, 131, 133, 134–135, 153, 155–156, 197
Department for Culture, Media and Sport 139
Department for Health and Social Care 42
Department for Housing, Levelling Up and Communities 187
Department for Work and Pensions 176
Department of Communities and Local Government 92
deposit size, homeownership 137, 143
Derivé, Salford 131–135
Development Land Tax Act 1976 181
Devon, short-term lets 139
disability, people with
  adapted accommodation crisis 23–24
  Homeownership for People with Long-term Disabilities 130
Disraeli, Benjamin 5
District Councils Network 91

E

Economic Policy Institute 139
Edinburgh 3–4, 71
elderly people
  lack of appropriate housing 32
  residential care shortage 24, 30, 32–33
  single-person households 23
Employment and Support Allowance 112
'Empty Homes Programme' 29
empty properties 28–30

energy efficiency 43, 44, 190
  removal of insulation grants 102–104
Engel, Matthew 146–147
Engels, Friedrich 3
England
  empty homes 29
  holiday homes 30
English Homes Survey 40
English Housing Survey 38, 39, 44
Environment Agency, new builds flood risk 46
Equality Trust 36
Etihad Stadium, Manchester 149–150
EU (European Union), housing affordability 29
Europe, PRS (private rented sector) 15, 106–107
'Everyone In' programme 116–117, 118, 119
Exchange Controls Act 1939 12

F

Far East Consortium 149–150
Farmer, Mark 73–74
Fife Council 125
finance
  construction costs 72
Finance Act 1965 181
financial crash 2008 84, 85, 162, 179
financial sector, London 143–145
Financial Times 74–75, 127
fire safety and building regulations 48–55
First Homes Scheme 171
first-time buyers, Help to Buy scheme 85, 136, 137–138, 159, 161, 167
Fiske, James 71
Fletcher, Del Roy 112–113
flood risk, new builds 46
Forrest, Nick 192–193
Francis, Noble 75
Froud, J. 151
fuel poverty 43
funding, regional iniquities in 94–97
  80:20 ratio 95–96

G

Gago, A. 141
Garden City movement 7–9, 16, 18, 69
Gasparan, Thea 144–145
GDV (Gross Development Value) 66, 80
gentrification 28, 56–57, 144–147
  and community 56–57
  Housing Market Renewal (Pathfinder) schemes 101, 102
  London 144–147
  Manchester 56, 151–152
  see also urban regeneration
Glasgow 71
  rent strikes, 1915–16 13

Glasgow Women's Housing Association 13
G-Mex, Manchester 148
GMHP (Greater Manchester Housing
  Providers) 173, 174
Goldfarb, Micheal 147
Gough, Ian 29
Gove, Michael 46, 65, 81, 105
Great British Insulation Scheme 104
'Great Resignation' 73
Great Stink, London 5
Greater London
  gentrification 56
  housing quality 192
  regional iniquities in policy-making 89, 90
  see also London
Greater London Authority 113
Greater London Regional
  Planning Committee 8
Greater Manchester
  child poverty 130
  gentrification 56
  homelessness and rough sleeping
    services 115, 117
  Housing First 115
  housing quality policies 191–192
  landlord licensing 187
  regional iniquities in
    policy-making 93–94
  temporary accommodation 110
  urban regeneration 147–152, 158
    affordable housing 148, 153–157,
      173–175
  see also Manchester
Greater Manchester Combined
  Authority 149, 173–174
  Retrofit Action Plans 192
Greater Manchester Housing Providers
  (GMHP) 173, 174
Greater Manchester Pension Fund 173
green belts 8, 63, 64, 65, 67–68
  Chesham and Amersham by-election
    issue, 2021 68, 80, 94
Green Deal home efficiency
  programme 103
Green Homes Grant 103–104
Grenfell Tower fire 48, 49, 50, 52, 55,
  58, 194
'grey belt' sites 68
Gross Development Value (GDV) 66, 80
Guardian 82, 101, 146–147

H

Hackett, Paul 127, 194–195
Hackitt, Judith 50
Haldane, Andy 161
Hampstead Garden Suburb 8
Hamptons 38
Hanretty, Chris 97

Harbour Housing 139
Harris Academy 109–110
Harrisburg, Pennsylvania, US 182
Hatherley, Owen 102
Heath, Edward 159
Heatley, Tim 66, 75–79, 197
Help to Buy 85, 136, 137–138, 159,
  161, 167
Hetherington, Peter 101
Hewitt, Daniel 44, 109
Higham, James 10
high-rise tower blocks 17
Hilber, Christian 137–138
Historic England 192
holiday homes 30, 56, 57
  see also Airbnb; second homes;
    short-term rentals
Hollinrake, Kevin 96
Home Builders Federation 29, 46
Home Building Fund 96
Home Counties, regional iniquities in
  policy-making 94
Home Energy Efficiency Scheme 102
homelessness and rough sleeping 1, 58, 59,
  109–110, 122, 164–165
  affordability of housing 39–41
  expenditure on 160
  Homelessness Reduction Act 2017
    110–112, 120
  lack of long-term commitment and
    strategy 118–121
  Manchester 148, 153, 155, 158
  'move-on' accommodation shortage 24,
    30–32, 113
  post-war period 2
  schemes and initiatives 114, 117–118
    'Everyone In' 116–117, 118, 119
    Housing First 114–116, 117–118, 174
  welfare reform impact 110, 112–
    114, 118
Homelessness Prevention Grants 111
Homelessness Reduction Act 2017 40,
  110–112, 120
Homeowners Alliance 46
Homeownership for People with
  Long-term Disabilities 130
homeownership/owner occupation 1,
  10, 13, 15, 35–37, 38, 59, 60,
  136–138, 164
  deposit size 137, 143
  Help to Buy 85, 136, 137–138, 159,
    161, 167
  impact of rent controls on 15
  post-war period 15
  postwar period 59
  quality of housing stock 40, 44
  see also affordability of housing; building
    societies; house price inflation

Homes and Communities Agency 126
Homes England 82, 95, 126
'Homes fit for Heroes' 16, 18
House Builders Federation 62
house building 58
  absorption rate 66, 84
  inter-war years 10, 42, 69
  post-war period 16–17, 59, 69
  'ribbon developments' 18–19, 70
  see also delivery, of new homes
House of Lords 136–137
  Built Environment Committee 137, 161
house price inflation 37, 57, 63, 67, 137–138, 162–163, 164, 167
  impact of government policies 159–161
  international investment properties 140–142, 182–183
  policies to remedy 177, 184
    council and social housing 177–178
    financial speculation 178–184
    grant-based projects 178–179
  second homes and short-term lets 138–140
  see also affordability of housing; homeownership
house prices 1, 35–36
household composition 27–28
household projections see OAHN (Objectively Assessed Housing Need) figures
houses of multiple occupancy 14, 25, 44, 58, 99
Housing Act 1930 16
Housing Act 1964 126
Housing Act 1969 14
Housing Act 1980 42, 123
Housing Act 1985 125
Housing Act 1988 13, 107, 125, 126, 177, 185
Housing Act 1996 110, 127
Housing Act 2004 105
Housing and Planning Bill 2016 123
Housing and Regeneration Act 2008 126
Housing and Town Planning Act 1909 8, 18
Housing and Town Planning Act (Addison Act) 1919 18
housing associations 125–128
  adapted/accessible homes 32
  quality of housing stock 44
  Right to Acquire 123, 127–128, 132
  see also social rented housing
housing availability/supply 23–24, 27
  empty properties 28–30
  household composition 27–28
Housing Benefit 31, 85, 112, 113, 127, 159, 176
  expenditure on 160–161, 178, 179
Housing Corporation 126
housing crisis 58
  defining characteristics of 23–26
housing distribution 27–28
Housing First 114–116, 117–118, 174
Housing Market Renewal (Pathfinder) schemes 25, 43, 98–102, 190, 191
housing needs, OAHN (Objectively Assessed Housing Need) figures 63, 68, 91–94, 171
housing quality 24–25, 42–43, 59, 60, 98
  conversions 47–48
  CPO (compulsory purchase order) powers 187–188
  decent homes standard 40, 43, 44
  existing stock and tenure types 43–46
  futureproofing of housing stock 195
  health costs of poor quality homes 43, 45, 190
  Housing Market Renewal (Pathfinder) schemes 25, 43, 98–102, 190, 191
  insulation grants removal 102–104
  new builds 46–47
  policies to remedy 190–195
  private rented sector (PRS) 104–108, 185, 186, 190
housing security 24–25
housing shortage 23–24
housing standards see housing quality
housing stock 30
Housing Subsidy Act 1956 17
Howard, Ebenezer 7–8
HuffPost UK 82
Hulme Crescents, Manchester 148

I

IL (Infrastructure Levy) 90–91
income stagnation 161–162
Income Support 112
Increase of Rent and Mortgage (War Restrictions) Act 1915 13, 107, 185
inflation 72
  see also house price inflation
Infrastructure Levy (IL) 90–91
Institute for Fiscal Studies 36, 126–127
Institute of Civil Engineers 75
insulation grants, removal of 102–104
interest rate rises 37, 38, 72, 127
Ishak, Awaab 25, 44, 45, 187

J

Jenrick, Robert 81
'Jerry-building' 19
Johnson, Boris 96, 103, 136
Joseph Rowntree Foundation 38, 99, 125
JSA (Jobseeker's Allowance) 112

K

Kemp, Peter 14–15
Key Cities 95, 159
Khan, Sadiq 53
King's College London 83
King's Fund 33
Kingspan 'K15' insulation 49

L

Labour governments 43, 61, 65, 68, 81, 98–99, 102–103, 105, 114, 122, 123, 170, 171, 173, 175, 181, 194
Labouring Classes Dwelling Houses Act 1866 15
land 79–87, 88, 180
  '5 year forward supply' requirement 64
  financialisation of 83–85
  land value uplift 84–86
  prices, inter-war years 69
  privatisation of public land 81–83
  public land privatisation 81–83
'land banking' 84
Land Commission Act 1967 181
Land Compensation Act 1961 187
land value capture 180–182
  regional iniquities in 90–91
Lawson, Nigel 147
Leeds 5
Leeds City Council 160
Leese, Richard 154, 156
Legal and General (L&G) 173
Letchworth Garden City 7–8
Letwin Review, 2018 65–66
'Liberator' building society 10
Lichfields 93–94
life expectancy, early industrial period 4
Lisbon, Portugal 141
Liverpool
  early industrial period 4, 5
  Housing First 115
  housing quality 192
  municipal housing 15–16
Living Wage Campaign 162
Lloyd George, D. 10, 16, 69–70
local authorities
  house building 69, 70–71, 87
  planning
    '5 year forward supply' land requirement 64
    lack of resource in 67
    OAHN (Objectively Assessed Housing Need) figures 63, 68, 91–94, 171
    Strategic Housing Market Assessments 92
  sale of public spaces 82
  temporary accommodation spending 40–41
  see also homelessness and rough sleeping; temporary accommodation

Local Government Association 40–41, 65, 84, 109, 129
Local Housing Allowance 110, 112, 113, 176
Local Plan (Town & Country Planning Act) 1990 62
Local Plans 62, 64, 68, 90
  affordable housing need assessment 92–93
  green belt land 63
London
  affordability of housing 143
  construction costs 71
  green belt 63
  municipal housing 16
  regional iniquities in policy-making 89, 95
  short-term rentals 141
  urban regeneration 143–147
  see also Greater London
London County Council 6–7, 8
London Docklands Development Corporation 144
London Labour Assembly 47
London School of Economics 97
London Stock Exchange, 1986 deregulation ('Big Bang') 84
Longshaw, Paul 131–132
'luxury flats' developments 56
  see also gentrification

M

Macfarlane, Laurie 138
Manchester
  construction costs 71
  early industrial period 4, 5
  gentrification 151–152
  Housing Market Renewal (Pathfinder) schemes 100
  IRA bombing, 1996 148
  population decline 147
  population increase, early industrial period 2–3
  regional iniquities in policy-making 93–94, 96–97
  temporary accommodation 41, 110
  urban regeneration 147–152, 158
    affordable housing 153–157
  see also Greater Manchester
Manchester Enterprises 149
Manchester Evening News 96–97, 110, 150
Manchester-led Independent Economic Review (MIER) 149, 158
Mangnall, Andrew 106
Manson, Fred 145
Martin, Joe 73
materials, construction costs 71–72
May, Theresa 90, 122, 129, 136
McDermott, Yvonne 153–155
Mearns, Andrew 6

Merry, John 51, 52, 53–54, 131, 132
MIDAS 72
Midlands
  Housing First 115
  Housing Market Renewal (Pathfinder) schemes 99
  regional iniquities in policy-making 95, 96
Midlothian Council 124
MIER (Manchester-led Independent Economic Review) 149, 158
migrant labour, in the construction industry 73, 74
migration 28
Mills, John 125
Milton Keynes 42, 63, 124
Ministry for Housing, Communities and Local Government 111
  'Land Release Fund' 82
Ministry of Health Act 1919 42
Ministry of Housing 8
Ministry of Housing, Communities and Local Government 140
MIPIM 149
'model villages' Victorian period 7
Montgomery, Adam 124
Morris, Neal 72
Morris, William 7
Morse, Anyas 103
mortgage finance 85, 179
  building societies 9–13
  buy-to-let properties 177–178, 182
  deregulation 83–84
Mortgage Guarantee Scheme 138
Mosscare St. Vincent 173, 197
mould/damp issues 43, 44, 45, 187, 190
  see also housing quality
'move-on' accommodation, shortage of 24, 30–32, 113, 122
Moynihan, Daniel 109–110
municipal housing *see* council housing
mutual aid organisations 9

N

National Audit Office 103, 138
National Health Service (NHS) Property Services 82
National House Building Council 46
National Housing Federation 33–34, 41, 67, 91, 111, 126, 172
National Model Design Guide 46–47
National Planning Policy Framework (NPPF), 2012 61–62, 63, 64–65, 68, 80, 90, 92, 181
Nationwide Foundation 178
Network Homes 71, 127
Network Rail 82
Nevin, Brendan 99–101
new builds, housing quality 46–47

New Economy 149, 158
New Local Government Network 111
new towns 8–9, 17, 19, 42, 63, 70
New Towns Act 1946 8–9, 17, 19, 70
New Towns Committee 70
New Zealand 142
Newcastle, Housing Market Renewal (Pathfinder) schemes 100, 101
Next Steps programme 119
Niemitz, Kristian 29
'No Department for Social Security (DSS) Discrimination' campaign 113–114
Norman, Charlotte 173–175, 197
North East of England
  Housing Market Renewal (Pathfinder) schemes 99
  regional iniquities in policy-making 96
North of England, regional iniquities in policy-making 95, 96
North West of England
  affordable housing 173
  regional iniquities in policy-making 96
'Northern Gateway' project, Manchester 149–150
Northern Housing Consortium 34
Northern Research Group ('Red Wall' MPs) 96
Nottingham 5
NPPF (National Planning Policy Framework), 2012 61–62, 63, 64–65, 68, 80, 90, 92, 181

O

OAHN (Objectively Assessed Housing Need) figures 63, 68, 91–94, 171
Octane Capital 44
Office for Budget Responsibility 126
Office for National Statistics (ONS) 35, 72, 92, 136, 161, 193
Old Nichol slum, East London 6–7, 16
Older Persons Shared Ownership 130
Olympia & York 144
'One Public Estate' programme 81–82
ONS (Office for National Statistics) 35, 72, 92, 136, 161, 193
Openshaw, Peter 131, 132–134, 135
Orr, David 126
Osborne, George 136
Our Towns and Cities White Paper, 2000 99
outsourced labour, in the construction industry 73, 75, 88
overcrowding 27–28
  houses of multiple occupancy 44
Overseas Entities 142, 182
owner occupation *see* homeownership/ owner occupation

Index

P

'party pads' 57
'Pathfinder' programme 25
pension funds, affordable housing funding 172–173
permitted development, and conversions 47–48
PFI (Private Finance Initiative), Salford 51–52, 53–54
Phillipson, C. 151–152
Pinsent Masons 72
Planning Act 2008 90
Planning and Infrastructure Bill 65
'planning gain' 181–182
  see also Section 106 agreements
Planning Practice Guidance 92
planning system 61–62, 65–67, 87, 164
  development of 18–20
  planning reform 64–65, 68–69, 80–81
  planning restrictions 69–70
  regional iniquities in 89–94
Planning White Paper 2020 64–65
Planning White Paper 2021 80–81
policy failures 59–60
polyisocyanurate 49
population projections see OAHN (Objectively Assessed Housing Need) figures
Port Sunlight (Lever Brothers) 7
post-war housing system 1, 20–21
  building societies 9–13
  Garden City movement 7–9, 16, 18
  municipal housing 15–18
  planning system development 18–20
  Victorian reformers 2–7
poverty
  child poverty, Greater Manchester 130
  private rented sector (PRS) 38
PricewaterhouseCoopers 143, 192–193
private rented sector (PRS) 1, 58, 122, 124
  adapted/accessible homes 32
  affordability of housing 35, 36, 37–39
  buy-to-let properties 177–178
  CPO (compulsory purchase order) powers 187–188
  fees and charges 39
  future for 188–189
  housing insecurity 25
  housing quality 44–46, 78–79, 104–108
  inter-war period 13
  landlord licensing and reform 104–106, 108, 186–187
  'move on' accommodation shortage 31
  overcrowding 29
  policies to remedy 185–189
  post-war period 14–15
  poverty in 38

quality, service and price comparisons 34
rent controls 10, 11, 13–15, 17, 21
tenancy cultures, international comparison 106–107
property tax reforms 180–182
Propertymark, Wales 105
Protection from Eviction Act 1964 185
Public Health Act 1848 5
Public Health Act 1875 5, 42
public health, and housing 43
public health measures, Victorian period 5–7, 15
public land, privatisation of 81–83
public sector wages 163

R

Raynor, Angela 68
Raynor, William 3
Raynsford Review of Planning 48
Recommended Rate System 11–12
Regeneration and Levelling Up Bill 2022 81, 91, 140, 188
Regeneration and Levelling Up White Paper 2022 65, 86, 90–91
regional iniquities in policy making 89
  funding 94–97
  planning 89–94
'regulated rents' 14
Regulation of Building Societies Act 1836 9
'Regulator of Social Housing' 126
Rent Act 1965 14, 107–108
Rent Act 1968 14
Rent Act 1977 14
rent controls 10, 11, 13–15, 17, 21, 107, 185
Rent to Buy 130
rental sector see private rented sector (PRS); social rented housing
Renters' Rights Bill 105–108, 186, 187
Renting Homes (Fees, etc.) Act (2019), Wales 105
Reserve Asset Ratios 12
Resolution Foundation 161–162
'ribbon developments' 18–19, 70
Richard, David 65
Right to Acquire 123, 127–128, 132
Right to Buy 42, 87, 122, 123–125, 129, 132–133, 146
  removal of 169–170, 175–176
Rochdale Borough Housing 44
Rogers, Charlotte 29
rookeries 3, 5, 16
Rose, Damaris 145
Rough Sleepers Initiative 118, 119, 179
rough sleeping see homelessness and rough sleeping
Royal Bridgewater Hall, Manchester 148

Royal Economic Society 39
Royal Town Planning Institute 91
RSW (Rent Smart Wales) 105
rural areas, gentrification 56, 57
Russia 142
  invasion of Ukraine 37, 71–72, 127, 182
Ryan-Collins, Josh 83, 84, 180

S

Sa, Filipa 140
Sage 172–173
Salford
  cladding and fire safety 50–55
  Derivé housing development company 131–135
  housing conditions, early industrial period 3
  PFI (Private Finance Initiative) 51–52, 53–54
  private rented sector affordability 39
  private rented sector housing quality issues 45
Scotland
  private rented sector (PRS) regulation 105
  Right to Buy abolition 124–125
  short-term let licensing 57
  short-term lets regulation 139, 140
Scott Committee, 1941 70
Scottish Cities Review, 2003 99
second homes 29, 30, 138–140, 180
Section 8 evictions 106
Section 21 'No Fault' evictions 40, 104, 105, 106, 118
Section 52 agreements 62
Section 106 agreements 62, 64, 86, 181–182
  Manchester 156–157
  regional iniquities in 90–91
self-employed labour in the construction industry 73, 75
self-help organisations 9
Seppala, James 172–173
Shapps, Grant 136
Shared Ownership 130, 171
Shelter 40, 46, 116, 124, 160, 172
short-term rentals 30, 138–140, 181–182
  gentrification 56, 57
  Lisbon, Portugal 141
Siderise cavity barriers 49
single-occupant households 23, 27, 28
Skelmersdale 63
skills shortage, construction industry 72–74
slum clearance 43
  interwar years 16, 17, 19, 42
  London 6–7, 16
  post-war period 43

slum conditions, early industrial period 3–7
SMEs (Small and Medium Enterprises), in the construction industry 75, 78
Social Impact Bonds 118
social rented housing 10, 15–18, 25, 58, 59, 69, 119, 122–123, 164–165
  access to 33–34
  Affordable Homes Programme 122, 129–131
  Derivé, Salford 131–135
  energy efficiency 44
  government investment and funding 170–173
  and homeless people 31
  housing association building 125–128
  Housing Revenue Account 122, 123, 128–129
  interwar years 19
  overcrowding 29
  policies to remedy house price inflation 177–178
  policy remedies 169–176
  post-war period 2, 21
  quality of housing stock 43–44
  quality, service and price comparisons 34
  replacement of homes 129
  Right to Buy 42, 87, 122, 123–125, 129, 132–133, 146
  removal of 169–170, 175–176
  shortage of 24
  waiting lists 31, 111, 169
Social Security Act 102
social unrest. early industrial period 4
Soha Housing 172
Soper, Donald 2
South East of England, regional iniquities in policy-making 89, 95, 97
South West of England, short-term lets and second homes 139–140
Southern Housing 127
Southwark Council 145
spare room subsidy ('bedroom tax') 110, 112–113
  Manchester 153–154
Stamp Duty Land Tax 86, 99
  surcharge 142
Starmer, Kier 65
Stewart, Alasdair 112–113
Stockport 3
Strategic Housing and Economic Land Availability Assessment 92
Strategic Housing Market Assessment 92
'strategic land banking' 84–85
street homelessness *see* homelessness and rough sleeping
Sunak, Rishi 136
Supplementary Special Deposits Scheme, 1973 12

Index

Surrey Council 97
'sustainable development, presumption in favour of' 64, 80, 90

T

temporary accommodation 2, 40–41, 109–110, 118, 122, 164–165
  expenditure on 160, 179
  Manchester 158
  and organised crime 31
Tenant Services Authority 126
Terminus House, Harlow, Essex 48
Thames, David 150
Thatcher, Margaret 1, 123, 133
Tocqueville, Alexis de 4
tourism
  gentrification 56, 57
  second homes and short-term rentals 138–140
Town and Country Planning Act 1932 19
Town and Country Planning Act 1947 18
Town and Country Planning Act 1947 8, 20, 62, 63, 69, 70, 180, 196, 197
  'beauty standards' in design 46–47
Town and Country Planning Act 1953 181
Town and Country Planning Act 1954 181
Town and Country Planning Act 1971 181
Town Planning Act 1925 19
Towns Fund 96–97
traffic issues 19, 70
'Transitional Grant' funding 97
Treasury 159–160
  80:20 ratio 95–96
  'Green Book' appraisals 89, 171
Trudeau, Justin 142
Tudor Walters Report, 1918 16
Turning Point, Glasgow 114

U

UK Collaborative Centre for Housing Evidence 137
UK, population growth 23, 27, 28
UK Women's Budget Group 36
Ukraine, Russian invasion of 37, 71–72, 127, 142, 182
UN General Assembly 167
under-occupancy 27, 28
Unitary Development Plans 62
Universal Credit 112, 113
Universities Superannuation Scheme 172
University College London, Institute for Innovation and Public Purpose 180
University of York 178

urban regeneration 43, 99, 143, 164
  affordable housing 153–157, 162–163
  gentrification 56, 57, 144–147
  impact of government policies 159–161
  London 143–147
  Manchester/Greater Manchester 147–158
  new approach to 183–184
  wage stagnation 161–162
Urban Regeneration Companies 99
Urban Splash 102
Urban Task Force 99

V

vertical integration, lack of in construction industry 73–74, 78
Victorian period, housing reform 2–7, 15–16

W

wage stagnation 161–162
Wales
  empty homes 29
  holiday homes 30
  private rented sector (PRS) regulation 105
  Right to Buy abolition 124, 125
  short-term lets regulation 139, 140
Wareing, Kate 172
Warm Front grant scheme 102–103, 104, 190, 191
Warm Homes 103
Warmisham, John 131–132
Welfare Reform Act 2012 112
welfare reform, impact on homelessness and rough sleeping 110, 112–114, 118
Welwyn Garden City 8
West Yorkshire, housing quality 192
Whitworth Art Gallery, Manchester 148
Williams, Jennifer 41, 96–97, 110, 150
Woodman, Tim 140
Working Tax Credit 112
Wright, Sharon 112–113
Wythenshawe 63

Y

Yorkshire and Humberside, regional iniquities in policy-making 96

Z

'Zillow' 38
zoning 62, 63, 65

www.ingramcontent.com/pod-product-compliance
Lightning Source LLC
Chambersburg PA
CBHW051537020426
42333CB00016B/1979